The Influence of Angus Snead Macdonald and the Snead Bookstack on Library Architecture

by
CHARLES H. BAUMANN

The Scarecrow Press, Inc.
Metuchen, N.J.   1972

Copyright 1972 by Charles H. Baumann

ISBN 0-8108-0390-9

Library of Congress Catalog Card No. 74-171928

ACKNOWLEDGMENTS

The author wishes to express his appreciation to the following individuals for their assistance: to Dean Robert B. Downs, of the University of Illinois, without whose encouragement this study would not have been undertaken; to Dean Guy Garrison, of Drexel Institute, who, as advisor, made many useful suggestions; to Herbert Goldhor, Winton Solberg, Walter Allen and Lucien White, all members of the faculty of the University of Illinois, for critical reading and comments; to Mrs. Angus S. Macdonald for providing access to her husband's papers; to Mrs. Harold Cherry and others at the University of Wyoming Library who made it possible to maintain a steady work schedule; and to the administration of that University for granting two leaves of absence. Finally, thanks are due to a very tolerant and helpful wife.

CONTENTS

Chapter		Page
I.	Introduction	9
II.	The Development of the American Library Building to 1941	18
III.	Macdonald's Youth and the Snead Family's Introduction to the Bookstack	56
IV.	Macdonald as President of Snead and Company	89
V.	Macdonald Develops a Theory of Library Planning and Construction	118
VI.	The Module is the Message: Macdonald as Consultant and Publicist	143
VII.	Other Forces Responsible for Change	185
VIII.	Summary and Conclusions	217

Appendices

I.	Supplementary Material	233
II.	Library Building Survey, 1930-1960	255
III.	Snead and Company Bookstack Installations	266

Selected Bibliography 285

Index 305

LIST OF FIGURES

Figure		Page
1.	The Mediceo-Laurenziana in Florence	20
2.	Arts End, Bodleian Library, Oxford University, 1610-1612	21
3.	Cincinnati, Ohio, Public Library, 1874	22
4.	Winn Memorial Library, Woburn, Massachusetts, 1878	30
5.	Washington, D.C., Public Library, 1902	35
6.	Evanston, Ill., Public Library, 1908	36
7.	First floor plan, Springfield, Massachusetts, Public Library, 1912	39
8.	Basement floor plan, Springfield, Massachusetts, Public Library, 1912	40
9.	Sections through open plan libraries	42 & 43
10.	Bookstack section, Snead bookstack, State, War and Navy Department Building, 1888	66
11.	Shelf detail, Snead bookstack, State, War and Navy Department Building, 1888	67
12.	Perspective view, Library of Congress bookstack, 1897	71
13.	Ornate iron work between decks, Library of Congress, 1897	72
14.	Longitudinal section, north stack, Library of Congress, 1897	73
15.	Snead cast-iron, multi-tier construction	79
16.	Snead bracket stack designed in 1895	80
17.	Standard stack, Type A	91

18.	Bracket stack	93
19.	Compact storage, rolling type	94
20.	Stack aisle reflector	97
21.	Light distribution pattern	98
22.	Convertible stack, Joint University Libraries, 1941, with only every third column bearing the structure's load	108
23.	Reading area, Colorado College of Education Library, 1938-39. Note heavy structural columns	109
24.	Modular construction, detail	145
25.	Modular construction, later version	146
26.	Interior of Snead model, first floor	159
27.	Compact storage	164
28.	Column and beam design, University of Iowa as designed in 1946	170
29.	A. T. Stewart store (1863)	187

Unless otherwise noted, all figures were obtained from Snead and Company files.

Chapter I

Introduction

This work was originally prepared as a dissertation for the Graduate School of Library Science at the University of Illinois. With only minor revision, and with some new illustrative matter, it is offered now in book form.

The Problem

Some years ago A. F. Kuhlman, then Director of the Joint University Libraries, saw the need for a book which would "faithfully and interestingly describe the contribution that Snead and Company has made to the library world over the years...."[1] Mr. Kuhlman's proposal was not discovered until long after this dissertation was begun. Only in small part does this work meet his requirements. For the most part, Snead and Company's contributions are used to demonstrate, in this paper, the evolution of the bookstack (their chief product) into the modern modular library. Through the presentation of information about this evolutionary process, a proposition is tested.

This proposition might be stated as follows: Angus Snead Macdonald, President of Snead and Company for almost 40 years, was one of the principal forces responsible for the radical changes in library architecture after World War II. These changes focused on a far more flexible interior design, a design which Macdonald named "modular". While it may seem unnecessary to some, documentation is offered to demonstrate that a fundamental change in library planning did indeed occur. Alterations in bookstack design by Snead and Company, which contributed to the realization of the new library architecture, are examined in some detail, and other forces, unrelated to Snead and Company, are considered briefly in

Chapter VII. Obviously, the paper is partly biography, partly library history, and partly a history of Snead and Company.

Taking a broad view, we find a number of influences on library architecture that can be detected and a number of individuals who have been given credit for modifying it. In their writings Ellsworth and Githens have given Macdonald considerable credit. Other writers give credit to Wheeler and Githens, and to the development of the open plan. Still others have credited Keyes D. Metcalf, or the architects of certain European libraries, such as those who designed the Public Library at Viipuri, Finland (now U.S.S.R.), or the Swiss National Library. While concentrating on Macdonald, some brief attention will be given to these other forces.

Sources

Vital to any study of this kind are the sources. The published literature on library buildings, their planning, construction, and equipment, is almost endless. Hundreds of books, pamphlets, and articles were examined in the course of this study. These represent only a fraction, although, it is believed, the most important fraction, of the literature.

More important, perhaps, than the published sources are those that remain unpublished or that appeared in near-print formats only. Through the generosity of Mrs. Macdonald, the subject's widow, the author was given unlimited access to Macdonald's correspondence and those business papers of Snead and Company that remain. Fortunately, for the purposes of this paper, the most important period of Macdonald's correspondence, that of the 1940's and 1950's, appears to have been carefully preserved. It, along with company records for the same period, occupies four four-drawer filing cases. The papers also include, on a haphazard basis, portions of earlier correspondence and documents. There is, for example, a fascinating but somewhat irrelevant glimpse of Macdonald in Europe in 1931, arranging franchise agreements for Snead with various foreign corporations. There is also some material on the planning of the great book tower for the Sterling Library at Yale, dating from the mid-1920's, and, most fortunately, correspondence concerning the early drafts of his im-

Introduction

portant article of 1933, "A Library of the Future."

By far the best photograph of Macdonald that remains is in a newspaper clipping, probably from the New York World-Telegram of September 30, 1931. It shows a dapper business man on the boat deck of the Ile de France. A high forehead, steel-rimmed glasses, and a neat business suit with vest and watch chain stand out against the blurred background of the ocean liner. His face is young, full, self-assured, and broken by a confident smile. Unfortunately, this photograph could not be reproduced, and efforts to locate the original have failed.

Most of the papers of the earlier period of Macdonald's life and of Snead and Company were either destroyed years ago or lost in the transfer of the Snead plant to what was to become the Virginia Metal Products Corporation. The latter company was visited in August of 1966 in an unsuccessful attempt to locate the missing documents.

The Macdonald papers include four broad types of materials. There is, as might be expected, correspondence concerning specific jobs or with friends in the library world which, for the purposes of this study, make up the most important segment of the papers. There is more than one file drawer of installation photographs, some covering the early period of Snead and Company. Financial reports, statements, and other records about various jobs of the post-war period remain, but are impossible to organize into a coherent financial picture. The few annual reports to stockholders and the two reports by the company's auditors are more useful, although they provide only a limited view. Finally, there are 15 annual cumulations of "Memindex" cards extending from 1938 to 1960. These predated cards were carried by Macdonald and served as a traveling appointment calendar. Since these cards frequently included notes, such as "In Peoria with Robert H. Muller, President Owen... ." (March 1, 1948), or measurements of the ceiling heights and column spacing of the Kitty Hawk Room of Dayton's Biltmore Hotel (February 28, 1948), or lists of dinner guests in his home, they form a partial diary. The Macdonald papers also include a miscellany of architectural and shop drawings, publications of Snead and Company, and a prospect file for a brief period covering the last years of the company. Unless otherwise stated, references to correspondence or other unpublished material are to the Macdonald papers, which may be found in the Special Collections Department of the University of Virginia Library.

To discover or confirm details on certain important library buildings, field visits were made. Files of documents were examined in the libraries at Colorado State College, University of Iowa, Princeton University, Skidmore College, and the Library of Congress. A number of other library buildings were also inspected, including those of St. Louis University and Washington University in St. Louis, University of Wisconsin at Milwaukee, Western Michigan University, Massachusetts Institute of Technology, and Wayne State University. These strengthened impressions gained from numerous other library visits made for other purposes during the past decade. Documents were also examined in the offices of the American Library Association and the law firm of Dixon, Todhunter, Knouff and Holmes, both in Chicago.

Examination of the card catalog of the Library of Congress revealed an extensive scrapbook concerning Bernard Richardson Green. Green's patents formed the basis of the Snead stack business and the scrapbook, made available on microfilm, formed an important resource for Chapter III.

Personal interviews were conducted with two of the leading figures in library planning in recent years, Keyes D. Metcalf and Ralph E. Ellsworth. Ellsworth was chosen because of his long association with Macdonald and his frequently expressed admiration of the man.[2] Metcalf knew Macdonald longer, but remained more detached. When asked what he believed to be Macdonald's greatest contribution, Metcalf replied, "He made us think." This could be interpreted as a gracious evasion, but after reading several references to Macdonald in Metcalf's writings, it is fair to conclude that he was sincere.

Donald Bean also granted a personal interview. Bean might be considered as an arch rival of Macdonald in the library equipment field during the years just before and after World War II. Mac-

Introduction   13

donald, in fact, attempted to hire Bean away from the Library Bureau of Remington Rand in 1945. Bean did much to corroborate some of the innovative claims of Snead and Company. He also offered valuable criticism, being quick to see some of Macdonald's shortcomings.

Telephone interviews were also conducted with a number of people associated with library planning. These included Larry Phillips of the Library Bureau's Chicago office and long familiar, as a competitor, with Snead's reputation, and Thelma Andrews, planner of the modular library building at Hardin-Simmons University.

Correspondence was conducted with many of Macdonald's former associates, including Alfred Morton Githens and Joseph L. Wheeler, the principal library planners of a slightly earlier period, and of considerable importance in their own right. Githens was probably Macdonald's closest friend in his later years. Unfortunately, some of Macdonald's more intimate friends in the library world, such as Theodore Koch, James Thayer Gerould, and Milton J. Ferguson, are no longer living.

Appendices

There are three appendices. The first simply consists of some illustrative material that was too cumbersome to include in the text. The second is a list of libraries showing the shift to the modular plan. It has certain inherent weaknesses because not all libraries published articles on their new buildings, and, of those that did report, many were difficult to classify because of the skimpy information available. The minimum requirements for a library's inclusion in this survey are stated at the head of the appendix. Appendix III is a list of all Snead and Company bookstack installations of which record remains.

Limitations

It will become apparent to the reader that, in spite of attempts to take a broader view, this work concentrates on the larger libraries, particularly the large academic libraries. This appears to be a natural result of Snead and Company's marketing interests.

Also, it was usually the bigger jobs that seemed to challenge the company and its president to develop variations in their products. The innovative installations have received the greatest attention, undoubtedly distorting, to some extent, a true picture of the company's activities.

Although the word "architecture" appears in the title, emphasis has been placed on those aspects of building design which affect the operation of libraries. Relatively little attention is paid to the aesthetic implications of the new modular plans.

Another important limitation can be found in depicting Macdonald as a whole person. Emphasis here is placed on his contributions (and those of his company) to the library world. His personal life, full of associations with the near-greats and, occasionally, the greats of his time, has been largely ignored. His associations with the princes of the Catholic church, with Margaret Sanger, a very close friend, have been omitted, as have his acquaintances with Ernest Hemingway, Buckminster Fuller, and others. Macdonald obviously enjoyed such relationships. He had great pride, also, in himself and his company. He clung to the title "President, Snead and Company" after it had lost much of its meaning. Fearful that his contributions would be forgotten he must, too, have been aware that a great tradition stretching over a century was ending with him. The story of Angus Macdonald is a bitter-sweet one, reaching pinnacles of greatness as well as depths of despair. He was tested far more than most men, and, in spite of great personal courage, the closing years of his life were pitched in a minor rather than a major key.

Yet, if on occasion he failed, he seems to have possessed an agile mind and a willingness to tackle the unknown that belied his years. In his middle sixties, when most men are thinking of retiring, he was rebuilding the company, setting the library world agog with yet another major new product, winning a half-dozen law suits and, in his spare time, learning to fly an airplane. His last letters, written just before his death on February 21, 1961, reveal a mind still alert, a spirit still unwilling to accept defeat. Much of this color and vitality, which makes Macdonald the man so fascinating,

Introduction

has been lost or deliberately suppressed, making it possible to concentrate on the chief problem of the study.

Although incomplete, the sources available for this study were numerous. In spite of this fact, Angus Snead Macdonald remains something of an enigma that cannot be resolved by his correspondence or the reminiscences of his family, friends, and business associates. That he was colorful, imaginative, and the possessor of great personal charm, there can be no doubt, but the final authority is always denied to the biographer of someone he has not known and can never know.

Methodology

The research procedures employed in this study are generally referred to as the historical method. After the major sources were gathered, the documents were examined critically. Whenever possible, two or more independent sources were located to corroborate the evidence found in the Macdonald papers. For this reason, on critical issues, additional sources were located. In most cases these sources strengthened the interpretation, but in some, as in the case of Macdonald's role at Princeton's Firestone Library, they clearly weakened it. On only one important issue were the Snead and Company records actually misleading: the official Company story would have the investigator believe that its association with the bookstack business began with the Library of Congress. Critical investigation, however, revealed it had entered the field almost a decade before with a less appealing product.

Finally, in the difficult matter of establishing causality, an attempt was made to gather as much evidence as possible to clearly establish Macdonald's role. In an effort to avoid overstating the case, as might be done in the purely biographical, or "Great Man" approach, multiple causes for the change in library architecture are documented.

Related Research

The author was unable to locate any comparable study on Macdonald or Snead and Company. The lengthiest biographical material on Macdonald was obituaries of not more than a page or two. The treatment of Snead and Company, even in its own publications, was no more complete. Probably the fullest discussion of the development in post-World War II library architecture appeared in a 10-page article by Ralph Ellsworth in the Library Quarterly.[3] The arrangement of Chapter VI was suggested, in part, by this article.

Suggestions for Further Study

This study has suggested a number of others which might be undertaken:

1. An examination and evaluation of the influence of other individuals involved in the development of the modular plan should be conducted while sources are still available. The activities of such architectural firms as Tilton and Githens, and O'Connor and Kilham seem particularly worthy of greater investigation.

2. A review of the stack industry, particularly during the great multi-tier era, appears to be in order. To what extent did the various manufacturers limit library design and their own competition, or stimulate product and architectural improvements? Library Bureau, with its unique origins, is particularly worthy of such study.

3. Still another study might look at a much broader question concerning the relationship between technological advances and practices of library administration and architecture. What conclusions can be drawn about the influence of technological advances on libraries of the future?

Notes

1. Letter of A. Frederick Kuhlman to William Randall, April 7, 1952. Kuhlman suggested that Randall would be the "ideal person" to undertake the project. The author would confirm Kuhlman's judgment, but, unfortunately, Randall became too busy with other tasks, which included the presidency of a southern college.

2. For example, see the dedication in Ellsworth's Planning the College and University Library. . . (Boulder, Colorado: The Author, 1960) which reads, "To Angus Snead Macdonald,

Introduction

originator of most of the new ideas in library planning."

3. Ralph Ellsworth, "Library Architecture and Buildings," Library Quarterly, XXV (January, 1955), pp. 66-75.

Chapter II

The Development of the American Library Building to 1941

Among the better-known names in library circles for approximately two generations were those of Snead and Company and its colorful president, Angus Snead Macdonald. Snead and Company was active as a manufacturer of bookstacks from the closing years of the nineteenth century to the middle of the twentieth century. Macdonald joined the firm in 1905 and served as its president from 1915 to 1952. The company specialized in the manufacture of a product that is now seldom seen in new American libraries: the multi-tier, self-supporting bookstack.

In the period prior to World War II, numerous library buildings were built with a multi-tier stack which featured very low ceilings, narrow aisles and closely spaced book shelves. In effect, the bookstack was a solid block of books with just enough room for people to pass among them. Typically, in a time of less stringent fire codes, the exposed steel or cast-iron columns that supported the shelves also bore the weight of the tiers above.

Snead and Company was one of several companies that built the graceful metal framework, installed the marble (or glass, or slate) slabs that served as both floor and ceiling, contracted for the lighting, and supplied the miles of shelves. Throughout the "bookstack era," a number of business firms, such as Art Metal, General Fireproofing and Library Bureau (later a division of the Remington Rand Corporation), were available to provide keen competition for Snead. Each, of course, claimed advantages for its product. Before examining the Snead bookstack in detail, and delineating its influence on library architecture, it will be necessary to provide a glimpse of library buildings as they existed before the bookstack era.

In the long history of library development, Angus Snead Macdonald and Snead and Company occupy an exceedingly brief period.

The American Library Building to 1941 19

Even if one omits consideration of libraries before the development of the codex, or modern book form, if he ignores the time taken to build and destroy the libraries of the Hellenistic world, the great libraries at Pergamon and Alexandria, and the "public" libraries of Rome, he finds that Snead and Company, active in the library field from roughly 1890 to 1950, occupies only a minute portion of the nearly 2,000 years since libraries cared for the codex, and the many centuries before, when they sheltered the scroll and clay tablet.

The Great Hall

In broad, general terms the libraries that were fortunate enough to occupy their own buildings prior to the nineteenth century can be classified as the "hall" type. Actually, with considerable modification, this basic plan persisted in America almost to the end of the nineteenth century. Essentially, the plan consisted of one large oblong room with the bookcases arranged along the walls. Windows either pierced walls and bookcases or, in later hall-type libraries, were placed above the bookcases at regular intervals. (See Figures 1 to 3.)

Always the library's plan appears to have been influenced by at least three factors: the rate of book production and philosophies of book preservation, the level of education and changing attitudes towards readers, and the modifications made possible by technological improvements in the buildings. As books became cheaper and more plentiful, as more and more readers, with varying cultural backgrounds, sought library service, and as techniques for building, heating, and illuminating libraries improved, the plan of the library reflected these changes and improvements.

Chained Books

While it is easy to overemphasize the story of the "chained" books, they do illustrate a modifying factor in library planning. In the Middle Ages books were exceedingly scarce. Book production depended upon hand operations of the scriptoria or, in the early Renaissance, the first, relatively slow efforts of the hand-powered printing

Figure 1. The Mediceo-Laurenziana in Florence. After an engraving by Francesco Bartolozzi (1727-1815). Constructed under Pope Clement VII from designs of Michelangelo.

The Bettmann Archives, New York

Figure 2. View of the Bodleian Library, Oxford University, 1610-1612, from the Arts End. (Courtesy, Gale Research Corp.)

Figure 3. Cincinnati, Ohio, Public Library, 1874.
(Courtesy, Gale Research Corp.)

presses. Books were few in number, and libraries very small. Most libraries counted only a few hundred volumes in their collections.[1] The readers were a highly select group of monks, churchmen and scholars. The method of storing books in locked cupboards proved unsatisfactory. Books and readers were separated by cupboards, but undoubtedly more important was the problem of lost books.

The chain, a "technological improvement," was introduced and was popular from about the thirteenth through the mid-seventeenth century[2] in European libraries. The chain forced certain fundamental changes in the operation and equipment of libraries. Obviously, a surface within the chain's length was needed to support the book while it was being read. For small collections, a series of desks with sloping tops, perhaps a shelf below and a bench nearby, was sufficient. For larger collections variations on the lectern, or "stall," were used. These devices were, essentially, double-faced bookcases, several feet long with a sloping shelf for reading, book shelves below, and often additional shelves above. The chains were of sufficient length to allow the books to be read on the sloping shelves. In some cases the reader was required to stand; in others, benches or stools were provided.[3] Generally, these cases or lecterns were placed at right angles to the wall with regularly spaced windows between them.

Wall Shelving

As book production increased and libraries grew larger throughout the early Renaissance period, the system of chaining books gradually was discontinued. A new system of accommodating the collections, wall shelving, appears to have been introduced on a larger scale at the library of the Escorial in Spain (1563-1584).[4] As libraries continued to grow, it became necessary to reduce the size and number of windows in the walls (and find other means of introducing daylight), and to add a gallery for convenient access to the shelves as they climbed toward the ceiling. The Bibliotheca Ambrosiana in Milan (1603-1609) packed the walls with books and provided a gallery, or narrow walkway, to gain access to the topmost shelves. The purpose of this system was not entirely practical. The reader or visitor to such a library was expected to respond to the "magical effect" of so many handsomely bound volumes, all coordinated with the room's decor.[5] In addition, the wall shelving left the central part of the room free for the display of curiosities and rarities. According to one authority, Alfred Hessel, "in this way the library took on more and more the character of a baroque exhibition room."[6]

Library Growth

It should be remembered too that, nationally, library growth has always been uneven, dependent upon the attitudes toward learning, the general wealth and well-being of the country, and the vicissitudes of war. In the late sixteenth century, Germany, as the center of the international book trade, forged ahead only to receive a severe check from the Thirty Years' War (1618-1648).[7] The Bayerische Staatsbibliothek in Munich already held 17,000 volumes and the Österreichische Nationalbibliothek, 9,000 volumes by 1600. France appears to have gradually taken the lead in the eighteenth century, Great Britain in the nineteenth, and the United States (and perhaps the Soviet Union), in the twentieth. The weakness of such a generalization, however, should always be kept in mind since almost all libraries have been growing more rapidly in each succeeding century. Leyh reports that, up to 1800, there were but five libraries in France with more than 100,000 volumes, and that the Universitätsbibliothek at Tübingen (later to become one of the world's great libraries) was adding but 45 volumes per year as late as 1777.[8]

To illustrate the lowly state of library development in the United States, the following comparison is offered. In 1825, Harvard, the largest library in the country, possessed only 25,000 volumes, but libraries at the Vatican, Munich, Petersburgh, Vienna, Göttingen, Copenhagen, Berlin, and Wolfenbüttel held collections exceeding 200,000 volumes; at the head of the list was the Royal Library at Paris with 800,000 volumes and 70,000 manuscripts.[9] The British Museum had not yet exceeded 200,000 volumes, al-

The American Library Building to 1941   25

though it would soon do so.

The sheer number of books in libraries made the chained books less and less practical. The gallery too made chaining impractical, for there was no place in the gallery for the reader to work comfortably. The Bodleian Library (1610-1612), and others built at Oxford in the seventeenth century, favored wall shelving with galleries, but the books in the galleries were not chained. [10]

The Alcove System

Where ceilings were high enough, adding a second tier of shelving with a gallery was not always the best method of accommodating the expanding collections. In 1700, for example, Sir Christopher Wren designed buttresses for one library, the walls of which were sagging dangerously due to the increased weight of a recently added gallery. [11] Sir Christopher is better known in the history of library architecture for the building he designed for Trinity College, Cambridge (1676-1695). In this building the windows were placed high in the walls, making it possible to shelve books along the walls, as well as in cases standing at right angles to the walls. This arrangement created a series of alcoves along the walls which were separated by a center aisle. Special reading tables with stools occupied the alcoves. [12] The Long Room at Trinity College, Dublin (1712-1732) followed Wren's design, but on a much larger scale. [13]

It was inevitable, of course, as the pressure for more shelf space continued, that wall shelving, the gallery and the alcove should merge. The university libraries of Edinburgh (1825-1827) and Copenhagen (1857-1861) employed two levels of alcoves on either side of a central aisle. [14] In 1860 the Long Room of Trinity College, Dublin, was also enlarged and the gallery arrangement that was to serve for 100 years was added. [15] The form crossed the ocean and first appeared in Boston in the mid-nineteenth century. The Boston Athenaeum (1855) employed two tiers of alcoves with a cast iron gallery. The Boylston Street building of the Boston Public Library (1858) extended the alcoves to three tiers. The same general plan was followed in the Peabody Institute at Baltimore (1861) and the Public Library of Detroit (1865), and culminated in the Cincinnati

Public Library (1874) in which alcoves and galleries were piled up to five levels. In these buildings, the chief source of light in the center of the great hall was from one or more skylights in the ceiling. The center was devoted to reading tables and exhibits. As Boll and others have pointed out, these libraries tended to place books, readers and staff together in one great room, although toward the end of the period separate quarters for staff in the basement were being provided. [16]

The decline of the alcove library is also related to the sudden increase in book production in the early nineteenth century. Printing technology, in part responding to demand and in part spurring still greater demand, is an important factor in the spread of reading and library growth. The first efficient paper-making machines were set up in 1803 at Frogmore, England, by the Fourdrinier brothers. In 1800 annual paper production in England was approximately 11,000 tons, all hand-made, but by 1860 about 100,000 tons were being produced, almost all of it by machine. [17] The application of steam power to the printing press by Friedrich König in 1811 and the invention of a successful rotary press by Richard Hoe in 1847 increased the output of the printing press from 300 impressions per hour to 8,000. [18] Bishop and others have pointed out that these advances "sounded the doom of the one-hall library,"[19] but for a time the form persisted.

Rise of the Public Library

But even if book production had not created storage problems, was the same basic plan that was used in the elegant libraries of Europe, with their restricted clientele, appropriate for the masses using the libraries of the United States? Authorities in the latter part of the nineteenth century expressed doubts. The public library movement had its roots in the social, mechanics', Sunday school, and other privately supported and quasi-public libraries of the eighteenth and early nineteenth centuries. These libraries, generally small, were related to the spread of education, the extension of suffrage, and other reforms which gained acceptance in the early nineteenth century. The movement rests, too, on the Protestant

religious heritage which stressed man's infinite perfectability. As
Ditzion has said, "... the main currents of nineteenth-century
American thought, no matter what their origin or direction, sup-
ported the foundations and growth of the free library movement."[20]

America's growing industrial power which concentrated
wealth and a heterogeneous population in large urban centers was
also a fundamental prerequisite. This growing industrialism was
also dependent upon new machines made possible by a better under-
standing of science, which in turn demanded a better-educated public, and reinforced the optimistic view that people and the times
were capable of unlimited improvement. The clientele of libraries
changed radically: the masses, not just the select, were being
served.

The public library, as we know it today in the United States,
began in Boston at almost exactly the same time that Hoe was developing the rotary press. To be sure there were "public libraries"
in America before the mid-nineteenth century. It is known, for
example, that a small library, established in 1656 by the will of
Captain Robert Keayne, received support from the Town of Boston.
Peterborough, New Hampshire, supported a library as early as
1833, but it was Boston in 1852 that set the pattern for other cities
to follow in terms of legal organization, service and buildings. In
the long view, it is men like Ticknor, Everett, and Bates who exer-
cised a permanent influence on the public library movement. The
collections of the Boston Public Library grew rapidly in the early
period, reaching 100,000 volumes within the first decade of its
existence. Gratifyingly, the library was popular, circulating over
180,000 volumes in 1861, or slightly more than one volume for
every resident in Boston. Most of the circulation "pressure" was
borne by the 20,000 volumes in the "lower hall."[21]

Under the twin demands of growing collections and heavy
public use, the library building dedicated by the City of Boston
in 1858 quickly became crowded and difficult to manage. As
Whitehill has pointed out, "it was a noble experiment, but built
in years when nobody knew what a popular public library might

become.... "[22] By 1868 it was showing signs of its inadequacy, and by 1878 the Examining Committee recognized that a new building would soon be needed. It was crowded, noisy, difficult to heat and ventilate, and impossible to fire-proof.[23] Further, with the shelves scattered around the perimeter of the building, it was inefficient to manage as a "closed stack" system.

Justin Winsor, the librarian, recognized the shortcomings of his galleried alcoves of the "Upper Hall." He observed that this system, popular in most large libraries, had "come down to us with other monastic ideas, when the monks were the only users of the books, when the seclusion of the alcoves comported with their literary habits...."[24] Instead he advocated a separation of books and readers, and pointed out that operating an alcove library on the closed stack system was inefficient because the page was required to travel too far to obtain the requested item. He concluded, "the main idea of the modern public library building is, then, compact storage to save space and short distances to save time."[25] He saw this idea put into practice first in the Roxbury Branch (1872-1873), and later at Harvard University (discussed in Chapter III).

Winsor, of course, was not the first to advocate a separation of books and readers, nor was he the last. Leopoldo della Santa expressed the theory as early as 1816,[26] but it was not until the closing years of the nineteenth century that the idea was reflected in the way American library buildings looked and functioned. In 1887, J. N. Larned observed in his "Report on Library Architecture":

> The old type of library building [i.e., the "hall" or "alcove"] with its wall-scaffolding of book-shelves in galleries of alcoves, with its profligate waste of inner space, and with its many zones of temperature from floor to ceiling had nearly disappeared [except] ... as it appears in the building which the Library Association of Newark, N.J., has now under way [and] ... two or three smaller edifices.[27]

Larned went on to document his statement with references to over a dozen buildings then under construction. He expressed his own personal preference for the stack system, provided it did not exceed three tiers, and hailed the demise of the alcove system as a "departure from the medieval to modern conditions." Two years later, another report supported Larned's observations and noted that the stack system was becoming "the rule rather than the exception."28

Writing some years later, the architect and historian A. D. F. Hamlin states, "The alcove system has been generally abandoned since about 1890, because projecting stacks or cases ... cast wide shadows and cut off a large part of the room from the view of the attendant in charge."29 The spaciousness, the "magical effect" of books displayed for all to see, was giving way to another system that cared for books more economically, afforded them better protection from theft, dust, fire and heat, but also hid them away from the view of the borrower.

The Contribution of H. H. Richardson

During the 1880's, the influence of Henry Hobson Richardson on America's architecture was profound and it is natural that his style should affect library buildings as well. Wheeler and Githens have not treated Richardson's work with enthusiasm, describing the height of his influence as a "period of retrogression," and his libraries as "heavy, forbidding, poorly lighted, inconvenient... ."30 It is true that the heavy masonry, of which Richardson was especially fond, excluded daylight, and one writer referred to his libraries as "rabbit warrens of many small rooms,"31 but in some ways his buildings represent a transition from the alcove to the later type which employed separate stack and reading rooms. In the Winn Memorial Library, Woburn, Massachusetts (1878), for example, the basic arrangement of the "T" plan, which was to be so popular in the early twentieth century, is suggested (Figure 4). There are two reading areas vaguely separated by, and under the supervision of, the main desk. This desk also controlled access to the book room. The book room, however, instead of being a compact, multi-tier stack, contained a dozen sprawling alcoves.32 His Ames Memorial Library, North Easton, Massachusetts (1879), used a similar plan.

Richardson designed a total of six libraries, including one

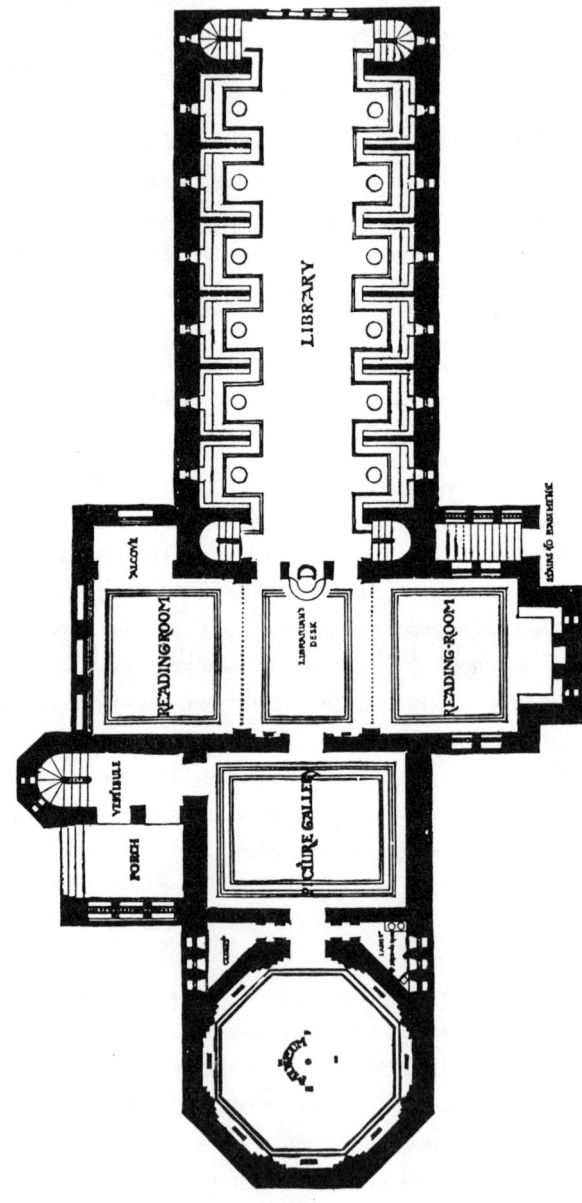

Figure 4. Winn Memorial Library, Woburn, Massachusetts, 1878.

at the University of Vermont (1886), and the Howard Memorial Library in New Orleans (1889), executed after his death. [33] All show the same restricted use of glass and the characteristic Romanesque style. According to Wheeler and Githens, Richardson's influence was further enhanced by confusion among librarians concerning the proper form for a library building. [34] There were those, obviously, who still favored the great hall; there were others who strongly preferred the bookstack with separate reading rooms; and there were still others who supported the plan put forth by William F. Poole in 1881, of separate fire-proof rooms. [35] This confusion is borne out in the "Reports on Library Architecture" of 1887 and 1889 referred to above.

Boston Public Library

Charles Follen McKim was an architect destined to have an even greater influence than Richardson. McKim had worked under Richardson for a time in the 1870's and had even assisted with drawings for Richardson's Trinity Church on Copley Square in Boston (1872-1877). In 1887 it became McKim's task to design a building for the Boston Public Library. It would complement Richardson's work, since the new library was also to be located on the square. However, McKim drew inspiration from an Italian Renaissance palace for the library, rather than from Richardson's favored period. Although artistically the Trinity Church is in the Romanesque tradition, one of Richardson's biographers has desribed the Boston Public Library as the "best and in all fundamentals the most Richardsonian of their [McKim, Mead and White] works ... The substitution of Renaissance for Romanesque forms .... hardly diminishes the essential similarity."[36]

But if there is an artistic relationship between the work of these two great architects, their library floor plans show little similarity. Drawing also upon the Bibliothèque Ste. Geneviève in Paris (1843-1850), McKim placed the great reading room, Bates Hall, on the second floor, as Henri Labrouste had been forced to do by the restrictions of a narrow site in Paris. Labrouste also took the opportunity to place the heavily loaded book room under the reading room and made daring use of new materials. McKim, working more than 40 years later, was more conservative in his use of materials and failed to relate the book collection, separated from the reading rooms, as well as Labrouste had. However, the basic plan, bookstacks in the rear, one great reading room across the front on the second floor with a grand interior staircase leading to it from the lobby below, swept the country. For almost 50 years the plan was copied and modified in large public and academic libraries, often repeating the number (13) of great arched windows of the reading room and the centered triple portal below. The architectural decoration of these buildings might be Georgian or Greek, but the fundamental arrangement and fenestration of the Boston Public Library are still evident in many parts of the country. The building represented the pride of the city and its respect for learning. It was a major work of art, one which, as Burchard maintains, pleased most Americans, particularly the wealthy men who found themselves on the boards of trustees of libraries and museums across the land. [37]

In spite of the enduring popularity of the basic arrangement, not everyone was satisfied with McKim's work. Librarians were unhappy because no librarian had been consulted during the planning; the Boston Evening Record objected to the statues of nude boys; and Mayor Matthews complained about the cost. [38] Some criticisms of the building were more fundamental. Dana objected, as early as 1897, because, "the borrower cannot see the books; he cannot even see the person who sees the books...." He observed that, "the power of a library lies first in its books," and that the building should be "plain and manifestly adapted to the purpose for which it was designed."[39] Manifestly adapted to its purpose it was not. It has been described as a lovely Italian palace with a library fitted into it. [40]

Stack of the Boston Public Library

If the front half of the building, with its majestic reading room, grand staircase and great arched windows, proved popular, the rear half, devoted largely to the bookstack, did not. Instead

The American Library Building to 1941   33

of a solid block of stacks, such as Winsor and others advocated, McKim forced the six floors of closed stacks around a Mediterranean courtyard. Originally he planned to devote the entire "U"-shaped rear of the building to stacks, but the need for additional space for the bindery and newspaper room altered this plan somewhat. The arrangement of moving books around the courtyard proved unnecessarily slow and complicated.

The stacks themselves were divided into six fireproof stories with a capacity of about 1,000,000 volumes. When compared to the front portion of the building, they were of extremely plain finish and the low ceilings reminded one visitor of the catacombs. The ceilings and rows of pine book shelves were painted white. Unshielded electric light bulbs dangled from long cords to be moved by the stack attendant to the exact spot he desired. Natural light was provided, but the window arrangement ignored the spacing of the wooden book cases. The delivery desk was connected to the stacks by pneumatic tubes, for requesting books, and by a "railway," similar to that used in large retail stores at the time, for delivering the books. [41]

In virtually all respects the stacks of the Boston Public Library represent the road not taken by American libraries: the arrangement, the material of which the shelves were constructed, the lighting, the fenestration, and the delivery system were all rejected. Only the pneumatic tube system won a lasting popularity. At this time, in Washington, D.C., the Library of Congress was also nearing completion. Its stack, based on entirely different principles, developed by Bernard R. Green, was to have a far more important influence. A detailed treatment of this stack will be presented in the following chapter.

Rise of the Bookstack: Stack at the Rear

America's larger libraries, built in the first third of the twentieth century, drew their inspiration from these two primary sources: from the Boston Public Library and the artistic genius of Charles Follen McKim, and from the Library of Congress and the Yankee ingenuity of Bernard Richardson Green. The general plan of the Library of Congress, incidentally, was not very influential. It focused on a circular reading room related to a similar design developed for the British Museum by its librarian, Sir Anthony Panizzi, 40 years earlier. The round plan found favor with a number of national libraries but, with the exception of a few early collegiate library buildings, never attained popularity in the United States.

After 1890 another scheme, sometimes referred to as the "T" plan, gained widespread approval. This plan invariably placed the bookstack at the rear, forming the stem or vertical portion of the "T", and the reading rooms at the front. Actually, few public libraries were large enough to justify a great reading room comparable to Boston's Bates Hall, and few placed their reading rooms on the second floor. Usually, in the early twentieth century, the reading rooms were placed at the front, but on either side of the lobby and delivery room, with the stacks, naturally, behind the delivery room. The public libraries of Washington, D. C. (1902), and Louisville, Kentucky (1907) are good examples of this plan. More often the reading rooms or work rooms extended to the rear of the building, enveloping the stacks on three sides, forming a more rectangular outline and obliterating any obvious resemblance to the "T". Evanston, Illinois (1908), and St. Louis, Missouri (1911), demonstrate this development of the plan. Figures 5 and 6 illustrate these two versions of the "T" plan.

A survey conducted by the American Library Association in 1927 revealed that about three-fourths of the public library buildings, both in large and smaller cities, had a rectangular outline and that most of the remainder were T-shaped. Rarely were they over three stories high. This survey also revealed that during the first two decades of the century there was a tremendous building boom in public libraries, with over 450 buildings being erected in the period 1901-1910 and 180 between 1911 and 1920.[42] These figures are, however, very misleading and are useful, perhaps, only as a relative measure. The amount of building stimulated by the Carnegie Corporation alone in the period 1897 to 1907 was far greater.

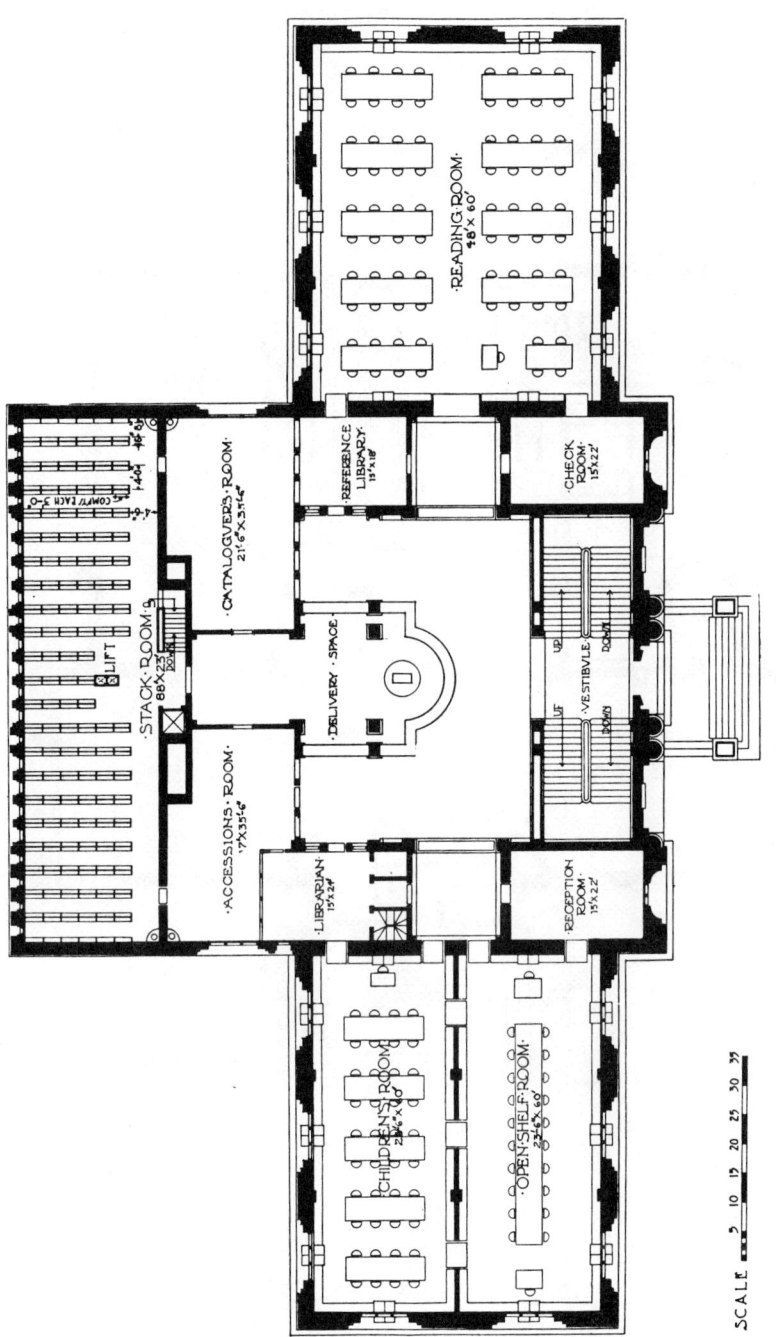

Figure 5. Washington, D.C., Public Library, 1902.

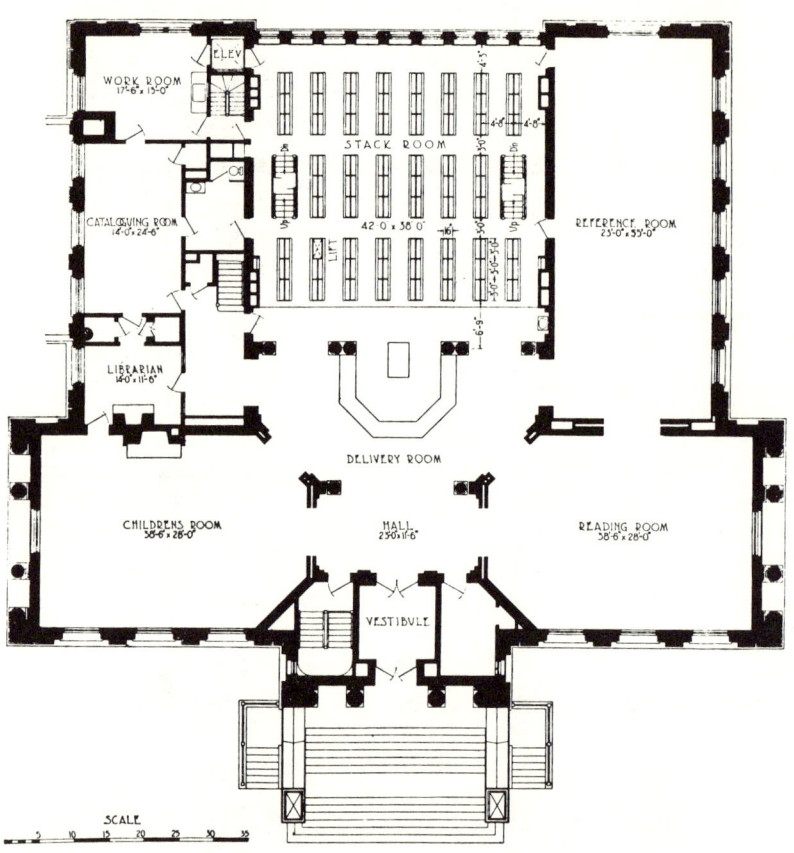

Figure 6. Evanston, Ill., Public Library, 1908.

The American Library Building to 1941   37

Money grants from the Corporation and Andrew Carnegie resulted in the erection of slightly over 1,000 buildings in the United States in the first decade of the program and, by the time the grants were halted in 1917, over 2,000 libraries had benefited.

At this time the architectural style of the World's Columbian Exposition, held in Chicago in 1893, was having a sweeping influence on American taste. The Romanesque of H. H. Richardson was replaced by the Classic style, popular with the École des Beaux-Arts in Paris. This new style was influential with the architects who designed the buildings for the Chicago Exposition. Since the Classic style became so popular, and because there was a tendency on the part of architects to force libraries, and other institutions, into a preconceived picture of the building, the efforts to bring about a change were slow to bear fruit. The judgment of Louis S. Sullivan, famous for his "form follows function" dictum is harsh:

> The damage wrought by the World's Fair will last for half a century.... It has penetrated deep into the American mind.... Thus we have now the abounding freedom of eclecticism, the winning smile of taste, but no architecture. [43]

John Cotton Dana, the librarian, was equally severe when he referred to the "lying exteriors of the Chicago World's Fair buildings," and looked forward to the day when "it may be possible to erect a thoroughly useful and entirely workable building which shall be in every part a library and also an artistic monument."[44] Alfred M. Githens, who began practicing architecture at the turn of the century, has a more tempered view:

> Some of the handsomest of the great libraries belong to this era [1890-1915]. The majesty of great monumental architecture, exquisite finish, precious materials, a broad flight of steps ... one great reading room and a series of carefully proportioned smaller rooms--these are characteristic. [But] ... grandeur was carried to extremes. Massive walls and heavy vaulting contradicted the underlying trend of the time toward lighter construction and the frank use of steel. Aesthetics and architectural precedent overrode functional usefulness. [45]

It was natural for the Carnegie officers, who had such a heavy responsibility for the building boom before World War I, to issue a set of guidelines. They published a small pamphlet, "Notes on the Erection of Library Buildings," in 1911; it was later revised, and was reprinted many times. It was the work of James Bertram, later secretary of the Corporation, and contained suggested floor plans by Edward L. Tilton. The pamphlet expressed concern over wasted space in entry areas, halls and delivery rooms, and it pointed out that "a frequent cause of waste is the attempt to get a Greek temple ... with a $40,000 appropriation."[46] The "Notes," aimed at the small library, stressed simplicity and suggested the substitution of movable bookcases for permanent partitions. Although its use was not mandatory, Yust maintains that "probably no four-page pamphlet on the subject has had a wider standardizing influence."[47] At least in smaller buildings, there was a counter-trend to the inflexible arrangements of the larger, stack-at-the-rear buildings.

The Open Plan: Stacks Below

Tilton, at the time he drew the floor plans for the Carnegie pamphlet, must have been at work on the Springfield, Massachusetts, Public Library (1912). Springfield appears to be the first expression of what was later known as the "open plan." This building, the thoughtful work of Tilton and Hiller C. Wellman, the librarian, placed its main floor on a high basement. In the basement there was a two-tier stack capable of holding 300,000 volumes. The reading and reference room on half of the main floor had a gallery which suggests the mezzanine of a modern public library. With its gallery, the room had a capacity of an additional "100,000 of the library's best books on all subjects."[48] The main floor avoided permanent partitions, and some subject specialization is evident in the provision of space for an Art Department. On the floor above were housed special collections for medicine, artisans and mechanics, and certain offices. Skylights poured natural light into the central delivery hall and main floor reading rooms; the second floor obtained light from the open space under the skylights and the exterior; and the newspaper and children's rooms received adequate daylight through the high basement windows. The book

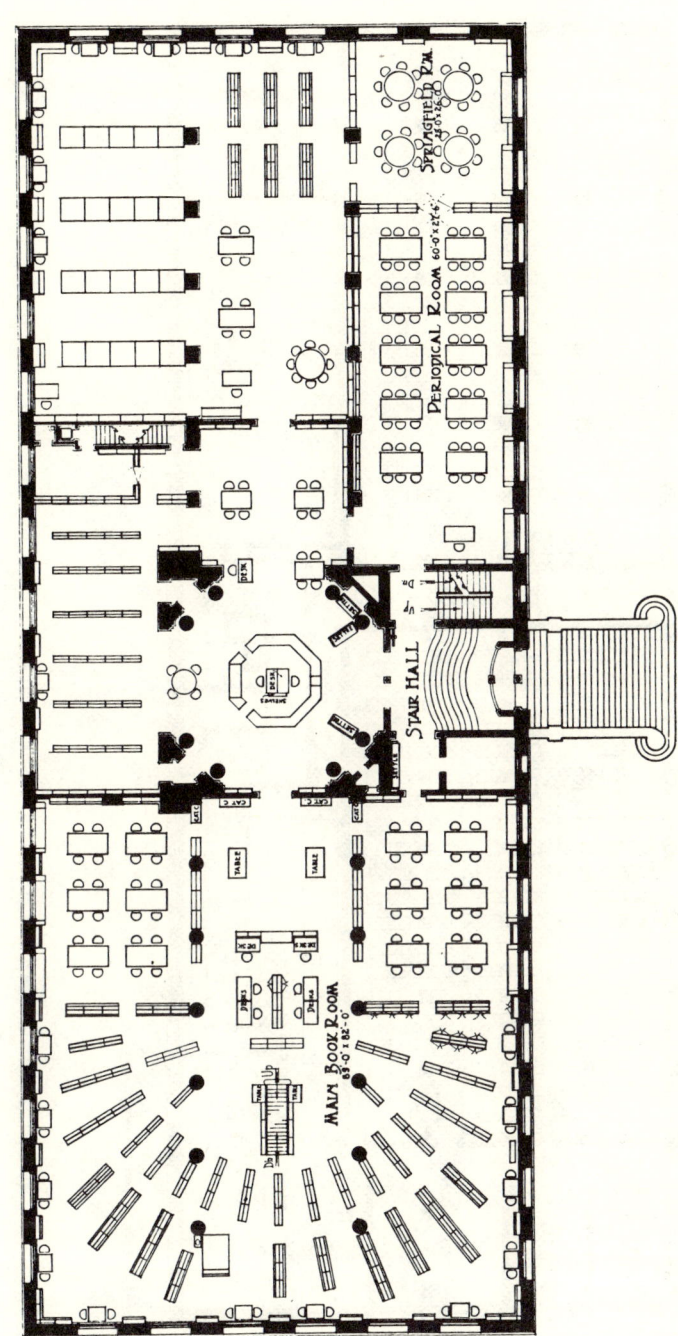

Figure 7. Springfield, Mass., Public Library, 1912. First Floor Plan.

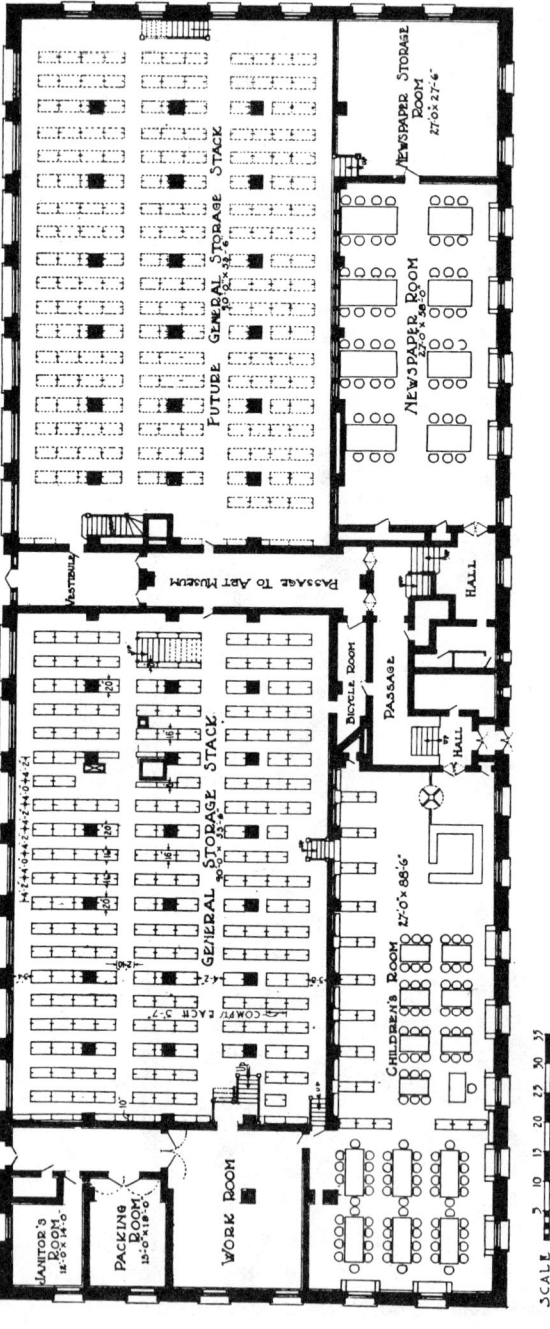

Figure 8. Springfield, Mass., Public Library, 1912. Basement Floor Plan.

stacks were lighted by large basement windows at the rear. (See
Figures 7-8).

Tilton quickly followed this success at Springfield with a
similar plan for the smaller Somerville, Massachusetts, Public
Library (1913). In this building, however, he placed the two-tier
stack in the center of the basement, surrounded by offices and
reading rooms. Although the stacks were completely cut off from
the outside, natural light filtered into them through glass walls on
the interior sides of the surrounding rooms. Tilton's Manchester,
New Hampshire, Public Library (also 1913) is another example of
open planning, but the bookstack is placed at the rear of the rectangular building instead of in the basement, thereby somewhat in-
hibiting the flexibility of the main floor.

It was not until 10 years later that the Wilmington Institute
Free Library, in Delaware, erected another relatively large open-
plan building. Again Tilton (with his partner since 1917, Alfred
Morton Githens) was the architect. Wilmington all but eliminated
the high basement and the long flight of stairs it required. It was
set in a small park, presenting a handsome, classic Roman facade
to the public, and won for the architects the coveted Medal of Excellence from the American Institute of Architects.[49] The plan
resembled the earlier buildings, as Githens's sections, Figure 9,
illustrate. The main floor avoided permanent partitions and focused
on the high-ceilinged central hall, with natural light coming from
the skylight two floors above. The main reading and reference
room, to the east of the central hall, contained 50,000 volumes
on open shelves. As at Springfield, the periodical reading room
was on the opposite side of the central hall. A two-tier stack,
below the main floor, provided a capacity for an additional 300,000
volumes. The children's room was also located in the basement,
but received natural light due to the sloping lot.[50] The Wilmington
plan was adapted to the smaller Highland Park, Michigan, library
in 1926.

With the Enoch Pratt Free Library, in Baltimore (1933),
the open plan received the attention it deserved. The story of

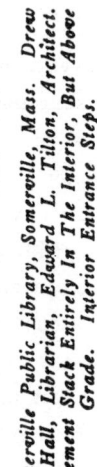

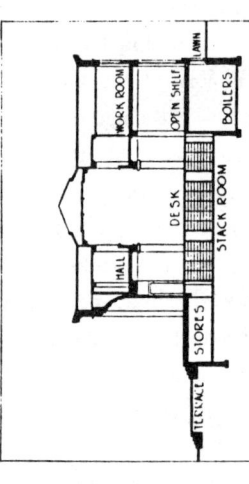

Somerville Public Library, Somerville, Mass. Drew B. Hall, Librarian, Edward L. Tilton, Architect. Basement Stack Entirely In The Interior, But Above Grade. Interior Entrance Steps.

McGregor Memorial Library, Highland Park, Mich. Miss Sleneau, Librarian, E. L. Tilton and A. M. Githens, Associated Architects. Main Floor Near Grade Level With Stacks Below Resembling Arrangement Of Wilmington Library.

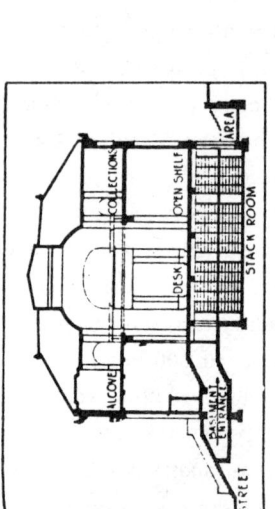

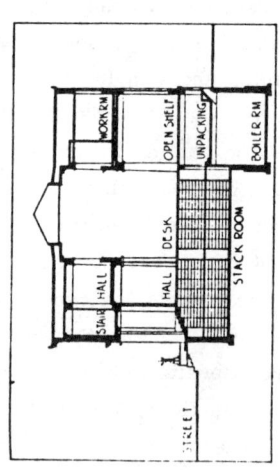

Springfield City Library, Springfield, Mass. Hiller C. Wellman, Librarian; Edward L. Tilton, Architect. Constructed On Hillside Sloping Up Toward The Back; Stack Carried To Rear Wall, With Outside Windows Opening On Artificial Areaway.

Wilmington Public Library, Wilmington, Delaware. Arthur L. Bailey, Librarian, E. L. Tilton And A. M. Githens, Associated Architects. Main Floor Near Grade. Stack Partly Below Grade.

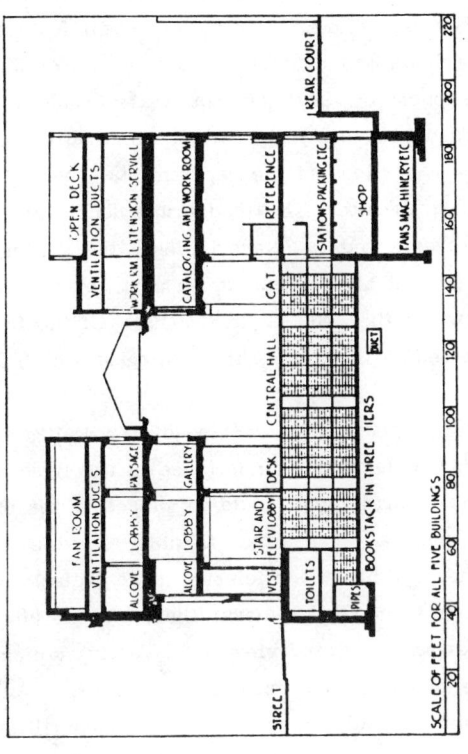

Enoch Pratt Library, Baltimore, Md. Joseph L. Wheeler, Librarian, Clyde and Nelson Friz, Architects, E. L. Tilton and A. M. Githens, Associate and Consulting Architects. Main Floor Directly At Sidewalk Level, And Sloping Sharply Down Toward The Rear, Large Stack In Three Tiers.

Figure 9. Sections through open plan libraries.

this building is well known. Its innovations in the development of the open plan are not so important as the choice of site, the application of the open plan to a truly large library building, and the influence it had on later buildings. Instead of in a park, as at Wilmington, Joseph Wheeler placed his library on a busy downtown street, with attractive display windows at the sidewalk and an entrance without any steps. In this respect it adapted some characteristics of the department store. The building still featured the great central hall with its grand columns soaring almost 50 feet above the floor to support the skylight, but it also made a first tentative step toward dependence on artificial illumination for readers in certain interior portions of the departmental reading areas. Githens, the consulting architect, had had grave doubts about this feature, but finally acquiesced. [51] Nevertheless, the ceiling of the main floor is over 20 feet high, dictated, in part, by the desire to provide large windows at the ends of the rooms. Of the five open-plan libraries discussed to this point, the ceiling at Enoch Pratt was the highest.

The open plan, especially as developed at Wilmington and Enoch Pratt, recognized the prime importance of the first floor. Stacks, not requiring natural light, could be placed in the basement. The first floor was made as accessible, flexible, serviceable and attractive as possible. Although sufficiently large collections were held on the main floor to attract readers, there was no attempt to overwhelm the reader with a grand view of the entire collection.

The influence of the Enoch Pratt Library has been profound and enduring. If Dana had advocated a minimum of partitions at least as early as 1900, [52] and Wellman and Tilton had shown that it could be done in 1912, it was not until after Enoch Pratt that the flexibility of the open plan became popular in public libraries. Open-plan libraries were built in Rochester, New York (1936); Toledo, Ohio (1940); and, as far as conditions permitted, Brooklyn, New York (1941). There were, of course, other open-plan libraries both before and after Enoch Pratt, but most of those erected before were small (possibly under Carnegie influence) or were the work of

Edward Tilton. Tilton has been credited as the one architect who, until the 1930's, appreciated the virtues of the plan.[53]

The Stack in the Center

While the open-plan was gaining popularity, the various arrangements that placed the bookstack at the rear of the building were generally dominant; however, one other plan, that which placed the stack in the center of the building, might be mentioned. This plan was first developed in a public library at Portland, Oregon, for the Multnomah County Public Library (1913). Like the Somerville, Massachusetts, library referred to above and completed the same year, it supported the theory (first tested at the Library of Congress) that a bookstack could be built in the dark. The Portland library relied entirely on artificial light in the stack and surrounded it with reading rooms and offices. Its facade, incidentally, still showed the strong influence of the Boston Public Library, although differing in architectural style: a row of great arched windows (nine instead of thirteen) marched across the second floor over the smaller windows and centered triple portal of the floor below. The center stack appears to have gained popularity along with subject specialization. The arrangement of the public service units of the library along subject lines, rather than by type of material, placed a premium on the need for a number of smaller reading rooms, instead of fewer large rooms.[54] The smaller reading rooms could be grouped around the stack, giving each subject reading room an abundance of daylight and immediate access to an appropriate section of the book stack.

The public libraries of Cleveland (1925), Los Angeles (1926), Richmond, Virginia (1930), and Fort Worth (1939) are examples of the center stack plan. Actually it is somewhat misleading to consider Cleveland and Los Angeles in this group since their stacks, although placed near the center of the building, are not solid blocks. Both divided the stack into quarters surrounding a great hall and developed the subject plan, while Richmond did not. The main defect of the Cleveland plan consisted of its scattering of subject divisions over too many floors. Enoch Pratt neatly solved the problem eight years later, [55] by placing most divisions on the main floor.

Open Access

The Cleveland plan illustrates another factor influencing the relationship of books to readers: open access. It will be recalled that with the rise of the bookstack in the latter part of the nineteenth century and, even before, in the larger gallery libraries, the reader had generally been separated from the books. An attendant acted as the intermediary, except for the relatively small popular or open-shelf collections. As early as 1897, William Howard Brett had suggested that librarians base their service on "the nobler assumption that the users of libraries are honest," and only place restrictions on public access to rare or little-used materials. [56] Brett claimed that the Cleveland Public Library was the first large public library to grant general public access when it opened the library's collections in 1890. By 1897, two other large American libraries had adopted the practice, according to Brett.

The philosophy of free access to the collections is clearly reflected in the Cleveland building of 1925. The typical divisional reading room has its own two-tier stack along the inner wall with most of the ranges readily available to the public. Indeed, the stack is so scattered that it is not a "stack" at all, in the general usage of that word, at the time. Cleveland's plan was modified and its divisional arrangement widely emulated, but few adopted its philosophy of nearly total access to the collections. The economies of the large block stack, and the related supervisory problems, generally favored a closing off of the larger portions of the libraries' materials. Enoch Pratt, which merged the divisional and the open-plans, retained a large closed stack area immediately below the main floor. Also an important influence at Enoch Pratt, according to Wheeler and Githens, was the philosophy of L. Stanley Jast, an English librarian. He, and others, argued that the collection should be divided for public convenience, keeping only the most active materials in public view. [57]

The American Library Building to 1941

Academic Libraries

The influence of the Boston Public Library can be seen in college and university library buildings as well as in the public libraries. Indeed, the larger academic buildings appear to have clung to the grand staircase, enormous reading room on the second floor, and closed bookstack at the rear, longer than did their public counterparts. Prior to the adoption of this plan, college libraries were generally of the great hall or alcove type. Boll has pointed out that, in New England at least, as the library outgrew its room in the multipurpose college building, it was frequently placed in a two-story structure, which it shared with the chapel. The library, with its heavy load of books, was placed on the main floor with the chapel above. Both could make use of an identical fenestration which also tended to reinforce the trend toward the alcove system in the library. [58]

Growth of Higher Education

One might suppose that the placing of the library on the main floor was also necessary to simplify service to hordes of young readers. Up to around 1900, however, this was not the case. First of all, enrollments were small. The typical college had an enrollment of a few hundred, and some schools, such as the University of Pennsylvania, did not consistently enroll more than 100 students until well into the nineteenth century. [59] The following list of the size of graduating classes of 1836 supports this view: Yale, 81; Union, 71; Princeton, 66; Dartmouth, 44; Harvard, 39; Brown, 22; Columbia, 20. [60] Even had there been large numbers of students, they most likely would have found the library closed. Relying on the sun for heat and light, the library was an uncomfortable place much of the year. It was regarded as a storehouse and the domain of the faculty. As late as 1853 Amherst built a library building without central heat, and kept it open less than five hours per week. [61]

During the latter part of the nineteenth century, however, college enrollment rose rapidly in the United States, and the trend continued into this century. The total number of undergraduates

increased from 52,000 in 1870, to 232,000 in 1900, to over
1,000,000 by 1930. The number of institutions rose from 563 to
977 to 1409 during the same period. [62] More important for the library than the size of the undergraduate student body was the development of professional schools and, particularly, of graduate instruction and research. It has been estimated that in the nineteenth
century 10,000 Americans sought advanced study in Germany. They
brought back the desire for genuine graduate study in America modeled on the German system. [63]

By 1900, according to Brubacher, the American university
"had come of age."[64] It is of interest to compare the situation 30
years before and after the turn of the century. Although Yale
granted the first earned Doctor of Philosophy degree in 1861, the
founding of Johns Hopkins University in 1876 is generally credited
with the beginning of graduate education in the United States.[65] In
1870, then, there was no graduate enrollment in the modern sense.
Between 1890 and 1900, however, the enrollment of the graduate
schools rose from 2,000 to 6,000 students, and by 1930 there were
47,000 persons at work on advanced degrees. [66]

According to Wilson and Tauber, "the American university
library has shared in this growth. In fact, the increase in its
resources and its services to scholars has been one of the most
pronounced aspects of university development."[67] The book stock
of many academic libraries grew at impressive rates. In 1870 only
Harvard, with 184,000 volumes, could boast of a library exceeding
100,000. Yale was in second place with 90,000 volumes. Some of
the leaders of the future, such as California and Illinois, had fewer
than 5,000 volumes; Michigan had 22,000; Amherst, Brown, Cornell,
Dartmouth, Princeton, and Virginia ranged in size from 28,000 to
38,000 volumes. [68] By 1900 there were 11 academic libraries with
a volume count in excess of 100,000. Harvard and Yale were still
the leaders, Harvard having recently passed the half-million mark.
Chicago, Columbia, Cornell and Yale all had 300,000 volumes or
more. [69] The expansion that occurred during the first 30 years of
the twentieth century is even more pronounced. There were almost

The American Library Building to 1941 49

90 institutions with libraries of over 100,000 volumes in 1929/30. Harvard, Yale, Columbia, and California all reported libraries with more than 1,000,000 volumes. Chicago, Illinois, Cornell, Wisconsin, Michigan, Pennsylvania, and Stanford held between 500,000 and 1,000,000 volumes.[70]

Effect of Growth on Libraries

To accommodate this growth, beginning in the late nineteenth century, the bookstack and the large reading room provided the solution. First at Harvard in 1876, but more especially after 1895, the bookstack, usually at the rear of the building, won out over the book room. It maintained its popularity to the beginning of World War II, which clearly marks the end of an era in library design. According to Reynolds, the bookstack became the dominant form after 1902 among libraries built by members of the American Association of Universities.[71] Reynolds has also observed that the increasing popularity of the bookstack made it desirable to have the main reading room on the second floor, near the main circulation desk, which would align with the middle tier of the stacks. This obviously resulted in quicker service to the library users. Several large libraries, such as Rochester, Yale, Columbia, and Texas, attempted "tower" stacks, particularly after 1930. However, the stack at the rear, of limited height, was popular with both college and university libraries because, wherever enough land was available, it permitted indefinite extension to accommodate an ever growing book collection. The bookstack also provided, in its later development, convenient, quiet quarters for the growing numbers of graduate students. If Jast saw the stack-at-the-rear as "a sort of warehouse clapped on to a library,"[72] and others bemoaned the lack of imagination on the part of architects in dealing with it, its location at the rear, or in the center, doomed it to being a "plain Jane," a solid, efficient worker, but rarely rising above the work-a-day world, except in the impractical tower form.

If the stack was plain and functional, the large reading room that was equally characteristic of the plan, often was not. Noisy and difficult to ventilate properly, it nevertheless presented a

classic challenge to the architect that he often met with skill and
sensitivity. The large rooms also made efficient use of floor
space (if not cubic space), and were easy to supervise. Although
the room itself might be a work of art, Munthe complained, in
1939:

> By far the greater number of reading rooms still provide nothing but big flat tables with chairs on both sides and no partitions between the individual places. They remind one of long mangers for wholesale feeding--at any rate they are not conducive to concentrated mental work. [73]

A few academic libraries built at the end of the era, such
as Colorado (1939) and Nebraska (1940), dispensed with the grand
reading room in favor of a number of smaller subject (divisional)
reading rooms. There was growing pressure, too, for open access
to the stacks for all students. (More will be said about this in
Chapter VII.)

In 1938, Offor, who had made a survey of American libraries
for the (British) Library Association, observed that Michigan (1919)
and Minnesota (1923-1924) "grapple more effectively with the essentials of planning" and have inspired a more or less "standardized
plan" which placed the stack at the rear, reserve book room and
other smaller rooms on the main floor, and the catalog room and
great reading room on the second floor. Nevertheless, he concluded that university libraries "have not received the careful consideration they demand."[74]

Among academic libraries, through 1941, the stack form
was dominant; and there was little to indicate to the casual observer
that it would not remain so.

Notes

1. Although some of the ancient libraries, such as the Alexandriana, were probably larger, and certain monastic libraries of the twelfth century were approaching 1,000 volumes, Clark shows that the typical English College library in the fifteenth century ranged from under 100 volumes to about 400 volumes. See John Willis Clark, The Care of Books (Cambridge, England: The University Press, 1901), pp. 144-8, and Chapter III passim.

2. John Jorg Boll, "Library Architecture, 1800-1875" (unpublished Ph. D. dissertation, Graduate School of Library Science, University of Illinois, 1961), p. 41.

3. The reader is referred to Clark, op. cit., for a thorough description of this equipment.

4. John Jorg Boll, op. cit., p. 43.

5. Ibid., pp. 62-3.

6. Alfred Hessel, A History of Libraries, trans. Reuben Peiss (Washington, D. C.: Scarecrow Press, 1950), p. 55.

7. Ibid.

8. Georg Leyh, Das Büchermagazin in seiner Entwicklung (Berlin: Elsendruk, 1929), p. 1.

9. William Woodbridge, Universal Geography, cited by William Warner Bishop, "University Libraries: Some Reflections on the Dedication of the Sterling Memorial Library of Yale University," Library Quarterly, I (July, 1931), p. 244.

10. J. N. L. Myres, "Oxford Libraries in the Seventeenth and Eighteenth Centuries," The English Library Before 1700, ed. Francis Wormald, and C. E. Wright (London: Athlone Press, 1958), p. 245.

11. Ibid., p. 237.

12. J. C. T. Oates, "The Libraries of Cambridge," The English Library Before 1700, p. 230.

13. R. B. D. French, "The Great Library of Trinity College, Dublin," Library Journal, LXXXIV (November 15, 1959), p. 3534.

14. John Jorg Boll, op. cit., p. 45.

15. R. B. D. French, loc. cit.

16. John Jorg Boll, op. cit., p. 97.

17. S. H. Steinberg, Five Hundred Years of Printing, (Baltimore: Penguin Books, 1961), p. 278.

18. "Printing Press," Encyclopaedia Britannica, 1966, XVIII, pp. 548, 543.

19. William Warner Bishop, "The Historical Development of Li-

brary Buildings," Library Buildings for Library Service, ed. Herman H. Fussler (Chicago: American Library Association, 1947), p. 2.

20. Sidney Ditzion, Arsenals of a Democratic Culture, (Chicago: American Library Association, 1947), p. 51.

21. Walter Muir Whitehill, Boston Public Library, A Centennial History (Cambridge, Mass.: Harvard University Press, 1956), p. 65.

22. Ibid., p. 131.

23. Ibid.

24. Justin Winsor, "Library Buildings," U.S. Bureau of Education, Public Libraries in the United States of America, Special Report, Part 1. (Washington: U.S. Government Printing Office, 1876), pp. 465-6.

25. Ibid., p. 467.

26. Leopoldo Della Santa, Della Costruzione e del Regolamento di una Pubblica Universale Biblioteca (Firenza: Gaspero Ricci, 1816), p. 35.

27. J. N. Larned, "Report on Library Architecture," Library Journal, XII (September-October, 1887), p. 379.

28. Addison Van Name, "Report on Library Architecture," Library Journal XIV (May-June, 1889), p. 162.

29. A. D. F. Hamlin, "Some Essentials of Library Design," Snead and Company Iron Works, Library Planning, Bookstacks and Shelving (Jersey City, N. J.: Snead and Co. 1915), p. 103.

30. Joseph L. Wheeler and Alfred M. Githens, The American Public Library ... (New York: Charles Scribner's Sons, 1941), p. 4.

31. Helen G. Montgomery, "Blueprints and Books: American Library Architecture, 1860-1960," Library Journal LXXXVI (December 1, 1961), p. 4077.

32. In fairness to Richardson, the compact, metal bookstack was not yet readily available. See the following chapter for details concerning its development.

33. Mariana G. VanRensselear, Henry Hobson Richardson and His Works (Boston: Houghton, Mifflin, 1887), pp. 67-69, 78-82 and Gertrude G. Drury, ed., The Library and Its Home (New York: H. W. Wilson Co., 1933), p. 17.

The American Library Building to 1941   53

34. Joseph L. Wheeler and Alfred M. Githens, op. cit., p. 5

35. Poole's plan called for a series of rooms, each with ceilings 15 feet high and shelving only seven or eight feet high. Each compartment would contain the books on a particular subject and be staffed by a subject specialist. See William Frederick Poole, "The Construction of Library Buildings," Library Journal, VI (April, 1881), p. 70.

36. Henry-Russell Hitchcock, The Architecture of H. H. Richardson and His Times, (New York: The Museum of Modern Art, 1936), p. 298.

37. John Burchard, The Architecture of America, A Social and Cultural History (Boston: Little, Brown, 1961), pp. 230, 243.

38. Walter Muir Whitehill, op. cit., pp. 154-160.

39. John Cotton Dana, "The Public and Its Public Library," Popular Science Monthly, LI (June, 1897), pp. 246-8.

40. Joseph L. Wheeler and Alfred M. Githens, op. cit., p. 6.

41. "The Boston Public Library," Scientific American, LXXIII (November 9, 1895), pp. 289, 297-298; and Louis F. Gray, "The New Public Library of the City of Boston," Library Journal, XIX (November, 1894), pp. 365-70.

42. American Library Association, A Survey of Libraries in the United States (Chicago: The Association, 1927), IV, pp. 188-190.

43. Louis H. Sullivan, The Autobiography of an Idea (New York: American Institute of Architects, 1924), p. 325.

44. John Cotton Dana, op. cit., p. 25.

45. Alfred Morton Githens, "Libraries," Forms and Functions of 20th Century Architecture, ed. T. Hamlin (New York: Columbia University Press, 1952), III, pp. 683-4.

46. "Notes on the Erection of Library Buildings," Library Journal, XL (April, 1915), pp. 243-7.

47. William F. Yust, "Recent Tendencies in the Planning and Architecture of Central Library Buildings," Library Journal, LV (November 15, 1930), p. 904.

48. Hiller C. Wellman, "Report of the Librarian," Fifty-third Annual Report of the City Library Association of Springfield, Massachusetts, for the Year Ending April Thirtieth, 1910, p. 21.

49. Alfred Morton Githens, "The Complete Development of the Open Plan in the Enoch Pratt Library at Baltimore," Library Journal, LVIII (May 1, 1933), p. 382.

50. Arthur L. Bailey, "Wilmington's New Library Building," Library Journal, XLVIII (September 15, 1923), p. 752.

51. Alfred Morton Githens, "The Architect and the Librarian," Library Buildings for Library Service, ed. Herman H. Fussler (Chicago: American Library Association, 1947), p. 98.

52. John Cotton Dana, A Library Primer (2d ed.; Chicago: Library Bureau, 1900), p. 27.

53. Joseph L. Wheeler and Alfred M. Githens, op. cit., p. 320.

54. H. S. Hirshberg, "Four Library Buildings," American Library Association Bulletin, XXVII (December 15, 1933), p. 732.

55. Ibid., p. 737.

56. William Howard Brett, "Freedom in Libraries," The Library Without Walls, comp. Laura M. Janzow (New York: H. W. Wilson Co., 1927), p. 179, reprinted from International Conference of Librarians, 2nd, London, 1897, Proceedings and Transactions.

57. Joseph L. Wheeler and Alfred M. Githens, op. cit., p. 326.

58. John Jorg Boll, op. cit., pp. 51-4.

59. Edward Potts Cheyney, History of the University of Pennsylvania, 1740-1940 (Philadelphia: University of Pennsylvania Press, 1940), pp. 225, 245.

60. Samuel Eliot Morison, Three Centuries of Harvard, 1639-1936, (Cambridge, Mass.: Harvard University Press, 1963), p. 253. This was an off-year for Harvard, which usually had larger graduating classes.

61. John Jorg Boll, op. cit., pp. 12, 412.

62. U. S. Bureau of the Census, Historical Statistics of the United States, Colonial Times to 1957 (Washington, D. C.: Government Printing Office, 1961), pp. 210-11.

63. Bernard Berelson, Graduate Education in the United States (New York: McGraw-Hill, 1960), p. 11.

The American Library Building to 1941   55

64. John S. Brubacher, <u>A History of the Problems of Education</u> (2d. ed. ; New York: McGraw-Hill, 1966), p. 463.

65. Ibid.

66. U. S. Bureau of the Census, <u>Historical Statistics... loc, cit.</u>

67. Louis Round Wilson and Maurice F. Tauber, <u>The University Library</u> ... (2d. ed. ; New York: Columbia University Press, 1956), p. 6.

68. U. S. Commissioner of Education, <u>Annual Report, 1870,</u> 41st Cong., 3d. Sess., House Ex. Doc. 1, pt. 4, pp. 506-517.

69. U. S. Commissioner of Education, <u>Annual Report, 1900-1901,</u> 57th Cong., 1st Sess., House Doc. no. 5, pp. 1688-1707.

70. U. S. Office of Education, <u>Biennial Survey of Education, 1928-1930,</u> Bulletin, 1931, no. 20 (Washington, D. C.: Government Printing Office, 1932), II, Tables 8, 11, 32, pp. 414-663.

71. Helen Margaret Reynolds, "University Library Buildings in the United States, 1890-1939", (unpublished Master's thesis, Library School, University of Illinois, 1946), p. 61.

72. L. Stanley Jast, "Horizontal vs. Vertical Book Stacks," <u>Library Journal,</u> LII (June 15, 1927), p. 666.

73. Wilhelm Munthe, <u>American Librarianship from a European Angle</u> (Chicago: American Library Association, 1939), p. 32.

74. R. Offor, "United States and Canada: Buildings," Library Association, <u>A Survey of Libraries</u> (London: The Association, 1938), pp. 357-358.

Chapter III

Macdonald's Youth and The Snead Family's
Introduction to the Bookstack

In the previous chapter it was concluded that on the eve of America's entry into World War II, the architecture of large libraries was still generally dominated by two more or less complementary problems: the need to store books economically and the necessity to supply an abundance of natural light for the reader. The bookstack and the high-ceilinged reading room were the solutions favored by architects and librarians. These next two chapters will be concerned with the bookstack, and particularly its development in the hands of Snead and Company. Snead is important for two reasons: first, it was one of the great bookstack manufacturers, specializing in service to the very large research library, and second, it provided the link between the library world and Angus Macdonald. It was the gradual evolution of the bookstack that stimulated Macdonald's concept of the modular library. Because Macdonald was associated with Snead and Company for over 40 years, and was its president for more than 30 years, it is necessary to look with some care at the company and its product. The man, the company, and the product were so closely related that it is impossible to tell the story of one with referring to the other two.

Angus Snead Macdonald

Angus Snead Macdonald was born in Louisville, Kentucky on November 7, 1883. His father, Allan Macdonald, had married Fannie Burnley Snead in 1878. Fannie was the daughter of Charles Snead, the founder of Snead and Company. Allan appears to have had some difficulty in deciding upon a career. He taught for a while at Austin College in Texas, then moved to Louisville where, with his brother, he established the Louisville Rugby School, financially an unsuccessful venture. He had a brief career in manufacturing in Louisville, but this also failed, and finally he moved to San Francisco (in the middle or late 1890's) where he held positions on the San Francisco Call and the State Board of Development. Allan, according to the records that remain, never saw his family again. [1]

With the father gone, Angus' mother apparently turned to her family, especially her brothers, for assistance. In his late childhood, Angus lived with his uncle Udolpho Snead and Aunt Emerin in their large, comfortable house in Louisville, In spite of the fact that he was born with the name of Macdonald, his associations with the Snead side of the family were undoubtedly more important in shaping his career.

Macdonald was educated at the Louisville Male High School, graduating in 1901, [2] in his seventeenth year. The diploma he received was later converted to a bachelor's degree when the school became known as the University of Louisville. Apparently, the training Louisville offered was of good quality, for he was able to pass the entrance examinations at the Columbia University School of Architecture, in the fall, without difficulty. [3]

Education at Columbia

In October, 1901, Seth Low resigned as President of Columbia University to enter the mayoral contest in New York. Dr. Nicholas Murray Butler was appointed acting President, and then, in January, 1902, installed as President. Such changes in administration were far removed, however, from the young Angus Macdonald, who had entered Columbia's School of Architecture that October to begin a rigorous four-year course.

The head of the school was William Robert Ware. He had come to Columbia in 1881 from the Massachusetts Institute of Technology, and was nearing the end of his teaching career. He is generally credited with founding collegiate architectural education in America, having established the first school at M. I. T. in 1866. [4]

It is especially appropriate that Macdonald should have come to Columbia, since it was Ware, with the collaboration of Justin

Winsor, who adapted "for the first time, Henri Labrouste's ideas of stack construction" in America.[5] These stacks, using a self-supporting, cast-iron framework, helped to spark a new industry that was to occupy most of Macdonald's career.

Ware had built an excellent school at Columbia. If, as Burchard maintains, Ware and others missed an opportunity to build a new architecture grounded in engineering and science rather than the methods of the École des Beaux-Arts,[6] it is perhaps expecting too much of a new educational system. It was natural for Ware to adapt to American conditions the best that Europe had to offer.

And Ware built well: he attracted a faculty which, for a time, placed Columbia "in the front rank of American schools of architecture."[7] In 1882, William Ware obtained from the office of McKim, Mead and White the erudite Alfred D. F. Hamlin, still fresh from three years of study at the École des Beaux-Arts in Paris. Hamlin was soon to establish himself as an authority in architectural history and ornament, and wrote the standard <u>Text-Book of the History of Architecture</u>,[8] a book Macdonald almost certainly used. In 1891 Frank Dempster Sherman joined the school's faculty. Sherman has been described as a born teacher and a developer of the shorthand method of casting shadows.[9] He "completed the splendid trio, Ware, Hamlin and Sherman, which guided Columbia through those early years of leadership in the building of a broad and scholarly professional education."[10]

The School of Architecture then, as Macdonald found it, was a good school, and moreover, a relatively popular one. However, although the "splendid trio" were there, and six other capable men had been added to the faculty over the years, the School had definitely lost much of its earlier momentum. Ware had placed heavy emphasis on scholarly, historical research at the expense of more intensive instruction in design. It took only Ware's retirement in 1903, during a period of strong Beaux-Arts influence, to set in motion a special board of architects, appointed by the University's Trustees, to review the curriculum and methods of instruction.

This review resulted in a "swing to the opposite extreme"[11] in 1905-1906, the year after Macdonald graduated. From 1901 to 1905 Macdonald might have sensed the anticipation of one era closing and a new one about to begin.[12]

The course offered to the freshman architectural student in 1901 had a strong historical approach. He listened to lectures on Ancient Architectural History by the versatile Maximillian Kress, and on the History of Ancient Ornament by Hamlin. There were various courses in drawing, both freehand and architectural, including a course in Historical Drawing that accompanied Kress's course in Ancient Architectural History. Kress also gave a course in Archaeology in French, Hamlin and Ware taught Beginning Architectural Design, and English language skills were developed in Architectural Essays. To complete the first year program Sherman offered a three-hour course in Analytical Geometry and Differential Calculus.[13]

The second year followed much the same pattern, but with the emphasis on the medieval rather than the ancient period and with Kress switching to German in the archaeology course.[14] The Architectural Design course carried "special drill" on the orders of classical architecture. This portion of the course was undoubtedly a favorite of Professor Ware, who had published, in 1902, an elementary book on the subject.[15]

The third year covered the Renaissance and, briefly, the modern period, while the fourth picked up the loose ends on Specifications, and the Theory of Professional Practice. In addition to a thesis, the fourth year student was offered a choice: "[he] may elect a specialized course in Advanced Architectural Engineering and Practice in place of the usual course in Advanced Design."[16] Had Macdonald known that soon he would be entering Snead and Company, which had greater need for engineering than designing skills, he might have chosen the advanced engineering course. However, an examination of his transcript establishes that he took the Design course instead,[17] indicating, perhaps, that his plans did change.

While at Columbia, Macdonald won the honor of being an officer (Secretary) in the Architectural Society of Columbia University. Even assuming that this was a thankless honor, when it is added to his varsity track team activities, we have a picture of one who participated fully in the life of the academic community. However, the Architectural Society is important for another reason; it published a Yearbook which preserves for us some (presumably the best) of Macdonald's efforts as a student designer and draftsman. The 1904 Yearbook contains three of his studies as a third year student. These architectural drawings tend to be "flat," lacking the stronger contrast of light and shadow used by his classmates in identical problems.[18] Unfortunately, no Yearbook was issued in 1905, his senior year.

One other fact about Macdonald, the student, might be mentioned. Of the 28 students who were enrolled in his first year class, only seven received their degrees in June, 1905.

A precise record of the books that Macdonald himself used while at Columbia is lost. However, the records that remain of the textbooks employed by the school are useful in gaining a general picture of the instructors' thinking. There were Ware's American Vignola and Hamlin's A Text-Book of the History of Architecture, both of which have already been mentioned. Hamlin's work was a brief, but solid, job of recording the architectural monuments and movements of the Near East and Europe. It disposed of "modern" architecture in Europe and the United States in a few pages. No mention was made of Horatio Greenough, or of Sir Joseph Paxton's Crystal Palace. It deplored, in 1896, the skyscraper as "rarely pleasing to the eye," but saw merit in the works of a "Chicago firm of architects" (undoubtedly Sullivan) in their "complete suppression of classic mouldings or details."[19] The first year student also encountered Franz Reber's History of Ancient Art,[20] Eduoard Corroyer's L'Architecture Gothique,[21] and Palustre's L'Architecture de la Rennaissance.[22] The latter two stress, as might be expected, the ecclesiastical architecture of France.

Precisely what effect the School's training had on Macdonald is impossible to determine. There seems to be little cause to doubt that he was at least a competent student and that he received a sound education, but it seems unlikely that one can find here the source of his later pioneering ideas on library architecture. If anything, the training Macdonald received at Columbia was more likely to result in his advocating libraries with monumental stairs and richly panelled interiors, as exemplified by the two third-year student exercises. Columbia at this time was part of, indeed a founder of, that conservative tradition which distinguished the architectural education of the time. It was hardly a Bauhaus.

In June, 1905, as Macdonald left Columbia, Snead and Company, having recently transferred its plant from Louisville to Jersey City, was busy manufacturing stacks for the New York Public Library.

Macdonald as Architect

Whatever one is to make of the fact that Macdonald elected advanced design rather than architectural engineering in his senior year, it is doubtful that he had even a brief architectural career. He has written, "[I] never practiced architecture except on myself ... ."[23] and that he joined Snead and Company in 1905.[24] However, his widow believes that he did serve with an architectural firm in New York for about a year after graduation.[25] Whether or not he actually had this experience is beside the point. He undoubtedly had hoped to be an architect, but had little or no opportunity to put his training to practice except on his own homes and in the limited situations presented by Snead and Company as it installed its equipment in libraries, office buildings and the like. Although he seems to have preferred to be known as an architect, the circumstances and obligations of his career would more nearly earn him the title of business man.

The architecture that he practiced on himself is of some interest. He experimented with a rammed earth house in the late 1930's which still stands on his farm near Orange, Virginia. Two other buildings are known to remain. These buildings are homes which he designed for his family, and were done long after 1905.

The first is a substantial stone and timbered country house in Connecticut, near Hadlyme. It had a hill-top, rural setting, and inspired a painting by Guy Wiggins, an artist and friend of Macdonald. Apparently it served as a weekend retreat, and fits into the picture one might have of a successful Eastern business man. One can easily picture it as an appropriate setting for the wedding reception of his daughter in 1932. From the correspondence that remains, it is clear that Macdonald lavished a great deal of care on the planning of the home at Hadlyme, and watched with anguish as it passed into the hands of strangers in the mid-1930's.

The second house, on the slopes of Clark's Mountain, Virginia, shows more originality. Designed in the early 1940's, but not built until 1947, it rambles up the hillside in a complex but effectively related series of levels. In addition to its pleasant natural setting, the most unusual feature of the house is its flat roof. Over adequately protected timbers, a six-inch layer of sod was applied. The sod was intended to protect the house from the hot Virginia sun, and since there are several tall trees beside the house, the sod roof, complete with its own willow tree, shrubs and fish pond, provides a pleasant roof garden. [26] Although the house is very comfortable, many of the interior details have been simplified. This was necessitated by Macdonald's use of local materials and relatively unskilled local labor. The house includes several fireplaces, a "conversation pit" capable of seating 20 people, and a fine view of the Blue Ridge Mountains. Macdonald drew inspiration from a house he had seen in Norway. This house, too, had a sod roof and was made entirely of local materials.

Snead and Company

In 1905, when Macdonald joined Snead and Company, his uncle, Udolpho Snead, was president. It will be recalled that it was in Udolpho's house in Louisville that Angus Macdonald was reared. It is quite probable that the uncle, whom Macdonald admired, persuaded him to abandon his plans to become an architect. Macdonald's older brother, Harry Peake Macdonald, was already with the company. Harry had graduated from the Massachusetts

Macdonald's Youth

Institute of Technology, in 1901, having majored in civil engineering.[27] Apparently it was upon his sister's two bright young sons that Udolpho planned to build the company's future. Udolpho's own marriage appears to have been childless.[28]

The advertising of Snead and Company proudly proclaimed its history as beginning in 1849, and a mid-nineteenth century history of Louisville, Kentucky, supports this claim. Apparently Charles Scott Snead early recognized the possibilities of iron as the servant of architecture. The volume credits Snead with being a "pioneer of this business in Louisville, and his is the only establishment in the West where ornamental iron is the chief business of the foundry." Among the products listed are cast iron side walls, store fronts, columns in any classic style, window and door frames, girders ("a novel article"), and a miscellany including spittoons and tea kettles.[29]

Snead, however, had made a number of false starts before finding his success and fortune in iron. When only 17 he saw his hopes for a career in banking dashed by the panic of 1837. In the next decade his adventures in a grocery business and a flower milling enterprise both ended in failure.[30] Only when he turned to iron was his future assured.

Throughout the latter half of the nineteenth century the company continued this tradition in Louisville under the founder. By 1895 it had expanded its list of materials and services to include, in addition to the basic structural elements of a building, stairways, elevator cabs, gates, towers, sidewalk lights, and offered "fine casting in iron, brass, bronze and aluminum ... wrought iron work [and] electroplating in all metals." The company also offered to take contracts "for the entire iron work of buildings, large or small, in any part of the country."[31]

Early Bookstacks

It will be recalled that toward the end of the nineteenth century the preferred physical arrangement of the large American library was still being debated. Whether the devices for shelving books should be arranged in compact tiers or spread out over several floors, and whether the material should be metal or wood, was by no means agreed upon. Snead and Company believed that the bookstack orginated as follows:

> The prototype of the modern bookstack was designed in 1876 by Professor William R. Ware of Ware and Van Brunt, and Mr. Justin Winsor ... for the extension of Gore Hall, the library of Harvard College. A shell was built of masonry walls pierced by rows of small windows. ... Into this were packed book ranges, row on row, tier on tier. ... The aisles between the ranges were 28 inches wide and the tiers seven feet high. ... The stack was six tiers high, self-supporting throughout, and depended on the building only for protection. The vertical supports were of cast iron, the deck flooring of perforated cast iron slabs, and the shelves of wood, supported at the ends by light zinc Z bars fitting into the uprights. [32]

In spite of the company's view, it is doubtful that the idea originated with Ware. Ware had been to Paris and London in 1866[33] and, as indicated earlier in this chapter, probably drew inspiration from Labrouste's iron shelving at the Bibliothèque Nationale or from the space-consuming arrangement at the British Museum. Henry Van Brunt, Ware's partner, acknowledged the debt to these two mid-nineteenth century libraries in a speech before the American Library Association.[34] Another writer, Georg Lehy, believes that the bookstack received its first practical expression in the slightly earlier Bibliothèque Ste. Geneviève (1843), another Labrouste masterpiece.[35] In any event, it should be remembered that the use of iron in bookstack construction in Europe anticipated its introduction in America by at least a quarter-century.

There were those, such as William Frederick Poole, who considered the stack a prison for books, in part because the early bookstacks were "uncomfortable" places for books and people, "with the inevitable accumulation of heat at the top and the constant need for stair climbing."[36] Poole argued that the constant climbing of stairs "becomes wearisome and positively injurious to health." He reported the case of one healthy attendant who, in less than a year, became lame and exhibited "the same symptoms as the treadmill prisoners in England."[37]

In a sampling, taken in 1893, of librarians who had had experience with bookstacks and with other methods of storing books, four favored the stack method and four were opposed.[38] Nevertheless, "with Winsor's backing, the bookstack became the leading alternative to the buildings of old ... and was followed in most of the large libraries built after 1876."[39] The Ware-Winsor design was copied by a number of libraries built in the latter part of the nineteenth century, including the Boston Athenaeum and the Army Medical Museum and Library in Washington.[40]

Bernard Richardson Green

The bookstack idea and Snead and Company were brought together by Bernard Richardson Green. Green had worked on a number of government buildings in Washington. Like Ware, he was a New Englander and a graduate of Harvard's Lawrence Scientific School (1863,)[41] and by 1890 had achieved a considerable reputation in Washington as a civil and architectural engineer. He was an active member of Washington's All Souls (Unitarian) Church, and a fine example of those who carried on the New England intellectual and cultural traditions that stressed reason and civic responsibility. At this time the Army's Corps of Engineers was frequently in charge of government projects in Washington. Under Colonel (later General) Thomas Casey, Green worked on the Army Medical Museum and Library (1887)[42] and the State, War and Navy Department building (1888). The latter also housed the War Department's 45,000-volume library in the center pavilion, arranged "in the 'stack system,' or iron nettings, that extend from floor to ceiling on every side... ." (Figures 10-11) This design originated in the office of the Corps of Engineers,[43] but resembled the Gore Hall stack. The shelves, of open-bar construction, were of cast-iron as were many of the supporting members and the extremely ornate railings. The shelf support retained the familiar "z" notches of Gore Hall. These stacks were manufactured by Snead and Company, and were installed by them after a "long delay."[44] The entire arrangement appears to have been very heavy and awkward to use, and Snead and Company avoided any reference to this installation in its promotional literature after 1890. If Green was the designer (the

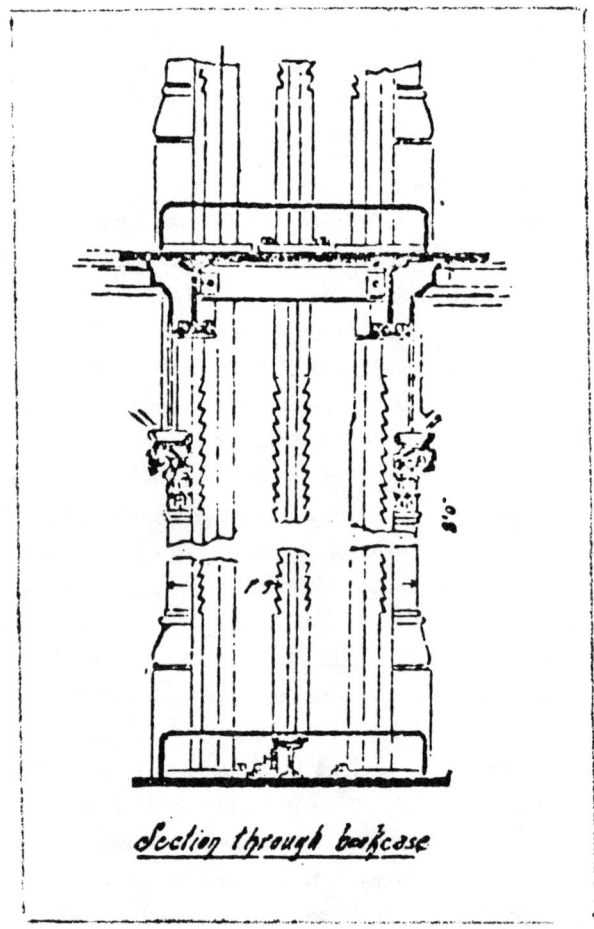

Figure 10. Snead Bookstack; State, War and Navy Department Building, 1888. Bookstack section.

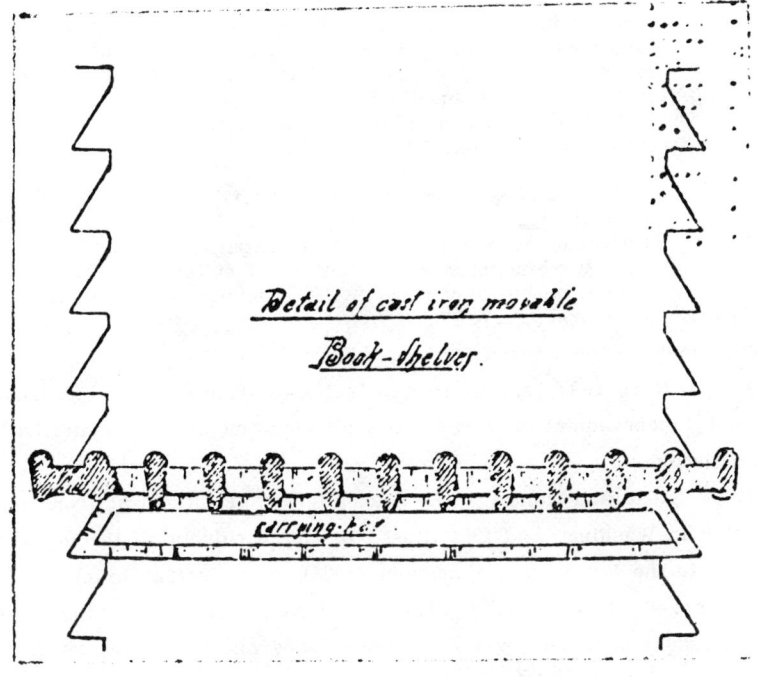

Figure 11. Snead Bookstack; State, War and Navy Department Building, 1888. Shelf detail.

open-bar shelf and his office's involvement indicates he might have been) he does not seem to have left any published record admitting it.

That these early stacks, by their various manufacturers, were not entirely satisfactory is made clear by the following statement by the surveyors of the Army Medical Library in 1944:

> A structure to house research collections ordinarily has at its heart a bookstack. Modern bookstacks began with the Library of Congress building that was finished ten years after [i.e., in 1897] the Army Medical Library, and thus definitely placed the latter in an outmoded era even in its early years... [The stack of the Army Medical Library] is unsatisfactory from the point of view of providing proper physical accommodations, particularly for valuable books. [45]
>
> Shelves and sections are full to overflowing... If one adds to this the dry heat in winter, the dust and humidity to which the books are exposed through wide open windows in a Washington summer, and the fact that the shelves cannot be adjusted properly, the picture becomes very unfavorable... . [46]

The stacks manufactured in the pre-Library of Congress period, or from 1876 to 1897, appear to have suffered from a relatively crude finish, inconvenient or unreliable shelf adjustments, and primitive ventilation.

Snead and Company, as a supplier of architectural iron, was active in Washington at this time. It had manufactured the 908 iron steps in the Washington Monument (1885), a project on which Green had served as engineer.[47] When the construction of the Library of Congress was turned over to Colonel Casey and his engineers in October of 1888,[48] the formal situation was created that brought Green, Snead, and an improved bookstack design together. Casey immediately appointed Green the Superintendent of Construction and it was in this capacity that he took up the problem of shelving the 700,000 volumes in the Library's collections. The plan for the new building called for an ultimate storage capacity of 4,500,000 volumes, by far the largest library to be built in the United States up to that time.

Speaking before the Washington, D.C., Library Association

some years later, Green stated that he designed the stacks for the new library in 1890, after giving the problem considerable thought and study:[49]

> When the building was begun eight years ago, bookstacks, properly so called, were few in number and small in extent, and probably the best existing example was that of Gore Hall extension at Harvard University. Its fundamental principles were excellent, and in its day ... it was a greatly advanced design.... With this exception, there was little to pattern after in designing the best possible stack--one which would provide the greatest security, convenience of access ... as well as the maximum storage capacity--and it was necessary to investigate the needs of the librarian, the readers and the books themselves. [50]

Green went on to list the 18 requisites which expanded on this statement and included particular attention to the care of the books. The ideal stack should be free from fire, dust, weather, pests and vermin, be well-lighted, and well-ventilated, not only throughout the stack, but through the individual shelf.

The Ware-Winsor design, with its wooden shelves, relatively crude foundry work, and open, iron grid floor, failed to meet many of these criteria. In addition, it presented another fundamental problem: in carrying the stack to six tiers the Harvard design had probably pushed cast-iron to its practical load limit. [51] The design that Green devised to accommodate the rapidly growing collections of the Library of Congress called for nine tiers and employed steel columns as the basic supporting element.

Although later modified and expanded, Green's basic design was patented by him between June, 1890, and October, 1893. [52] With the exception of the stone floors, the design employed metal exclusively. It might be called the complete design because it considered the framework, the shelf and its support, special materials such as newspapers, as well as ventilation and lighting, and even the book end. Further, in providing the first efficient pneumatic tube and conveyor system, Green took a big step in reducing some of the objections to the very large stack. [53] It was possible to retrieve a book from any part of the stack within a few minutes.

Green built a model of the stack and then advertised for bids. Snead and Company was awarded the contract to manufacture

and build the three original bookstacks with a capacity of almost
2,000,000 volumes.[54] The initial contract for $106,000 appears
to have been awarded in 1891.[55] The patents which Green held
were turned over to Snead and Company, and Snead paid royalties
to the owner. From the beginning, Green believed that it would
be "a simple thing to make a stack twenty or more stories or tiers
in height and of almost any ... dimensions."[56] Snead and Company
were destined, eventually, to fulfill this prediction.

By 1893, Snead and Company was able to display its new
product among the many modern wonders at the World's Columbian
Exposition in Chicago. The two-story mock-up displayed the American Library Association's selected library and won a medal.[57] The
Company published a little announcement, apparently indended for
distribution at the Fair.[58] The Library Journal also carried a
descriptive article in 1893 and indicated that a "handsom illustrated
twenty-three page pamphlet" was available from the manufacturer.[59]

Green's Design

The stack as built in the Library of Congress, and in several other early installations (see Figures 12-14), consisted of a
framework of steel vertical and horizontal supports. The steel
columns generally consisted of two "T"-shaped pieces placed face-to-face, and to which were fastened the cast-iron shelf supports.
These supports were cast with a series of indentions at the front
on which a peg, projecting from the shelf, rested. The rear of
the shelf was supported by a hook or lug attached to the support.
At the Library of Congress these columns and supports were placed
approximately 38 inches apart. Horizontal supports of rolled steel
were riveted to the columns, supporting the white marbel deck.
The shelves consisted of a series of inverted "U"-shaped bars
made from light sheet steel, just under one inch wide, and held
together at the ends and the middle by light cross braces. A thin
steel diaphragm, at the deck level, provided a base shelf and protection for the books below. However:

> An open slit of five inches is left in the deck along the
> front of every range, protected by a slight curb, [the
> steel floor support] serving to admit light from the side

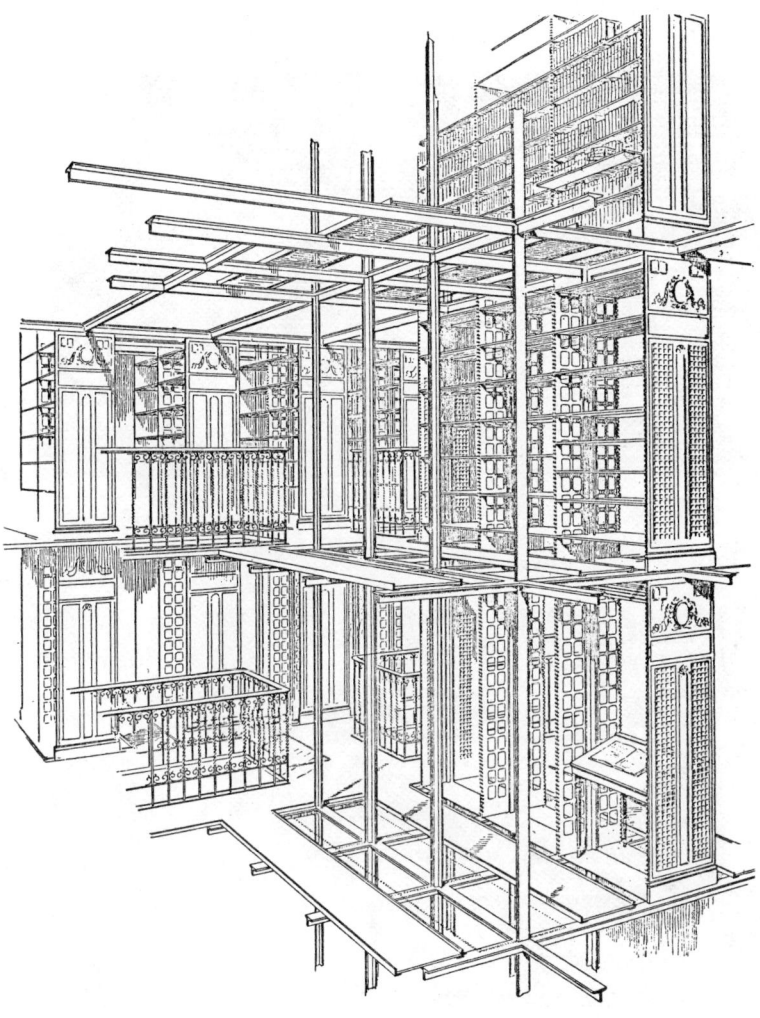

Figure 12.   Perspective view, Library of Congress bookstack, 1897.

Figure 13. Ornate iron work between decks, Library of Congress, 1897.

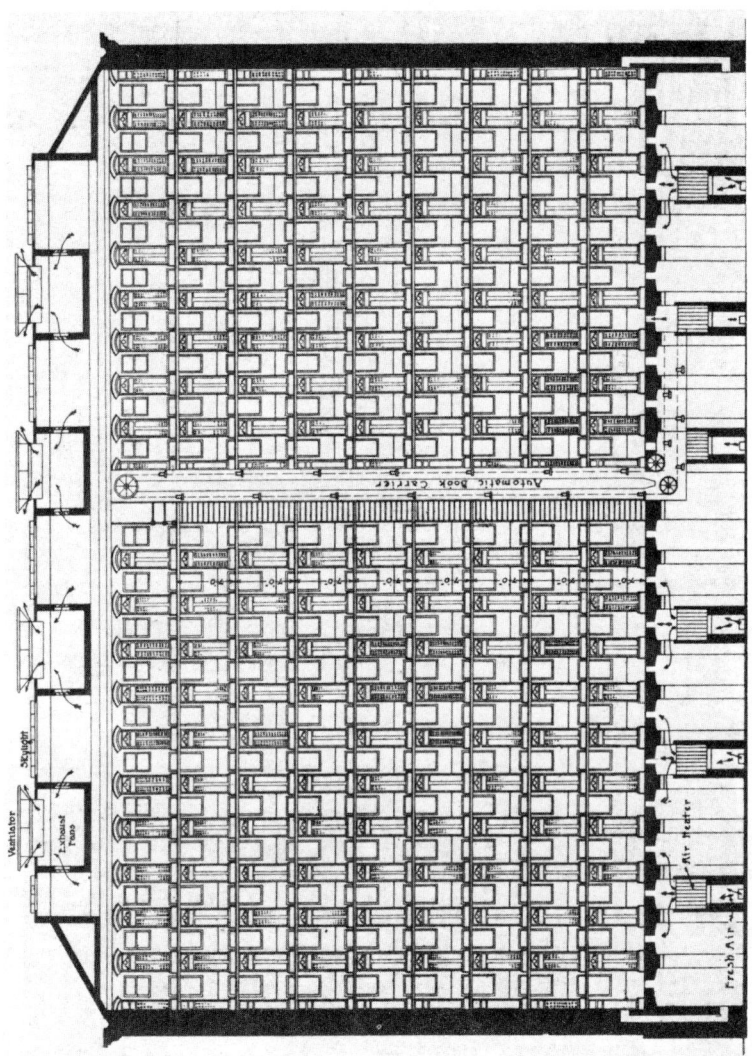

Figure 14. Longitudinal section, north stack, Library of Congress, 1897.

> windows, free circulation of air ..., and furnishing convenient communication between the stories. [60]

In a time when ventilation and control of dampness in buildings were not so well understood, Green's insistance on allowing air to circulate, not only between decks but through the shelf and the open cast-iron shelf support, is understandable.

The conveyor Green worked out for the new library consisted of a pair of endless chains driven by an electric motor. From the chains were supported a series of metal trays or baskets. The back and sides of the trays were solid, but the bottom was made of a number of brass bars whose ends turned upward. These bars or "teeth," by passing through a similar set of teeth on "stations" at the various decks of the stacks, could pick up the books left there by an attendant. Green could well boast that:

> A mechanical book carrier to accomplish more than the old, simple dumb-waiter is a novelty because never before was it called for, nor have the conditions for its satisfactory operation existed in libraries heretofore. In this building, accommodations for such apparatus were incorporated in the foundation plans. [61]

The route for each basket began on the first tier, up through the other eight tiers picking up books on the way, then down into the cellar, then horizontally through the cellar under the first deck and emerging upward at the central desk where the books were "combed" from the trays into a padded box. To return a book, a similar process was followed, with the exception that the attendant at the central or main desk operated a control which insured the book's being deposited at the proper deck. The trip from the farthest point in the system (lower deck) to the delivery desk took about three minutes. Communications between the desk and the attendants in the stacks were maintained by pneumatic message-carrying tubes, and by speaking tubes (later by telephone).

Although the conveyor system was eventually acquired by Snead and Company, the contract for the conveyor in the Library of Congress was awarded to George Miles for $14,500 and was one of the last items in the building to be completed. [62] Snead and Company later made considerable improvements in this conveyor, and installed it in many of the great bookstacks built by the company.

Green seems to have been more concerned about the quality of air that passed through his stacks than were any of his predecessors. Instead of allowing the dust-laden air and sudden rains to be blown through open windows, he sealed them. To a large extent, the stack relied on artificial ventilation. Air was drawn in from the relatively cool grass-covered courts by electrically-driven fans. The air was filtered, heated to the desired temperature, and then allowed to rise through the stacks. In the roof of the stack were additional fans to pull the air through if necessary. The sealed windows minimized any interruption of this process. Since the stacks were illuminated by electric lights, Green felt the roof need not be devoted to a skylight. Natural light was admitted by windows facing the light courts. However, as will be shown later, one of these courts was to disappear during Green's tenure as Superintendent of Buildings and Grounds. The reliance on artificial light and ventilation, while not total, was certainly another important contribution.

The major characteristics of Green's design, then, were carefully made, rust-free, easily adjusted shelves, an effective communication and book conveying system, adequate artificial light, and a modern ventilation system that included sealed windows. With minor modifications this system is still in operation. It is easy to overlook the revolutionary character of these features in the building, and it explains why Metcalf was able to say 50 years later, "Modern bookstacks began with the Library of Congress."[63]

Snead and Company and the Bookstack

Snead and Company, once involved in the bookstack business, soon found it a major item, and in time it came to dominate their production. The officers of the company, generally, were the owners and always included one or more members of the Snead family or close relatives such as Angus Snead Macdonald. This policy appears to have been followed throughout the life of the company and continued, with minor exceptions, until its remaining assets were sold to Globe Wernicke in 1952.[64] The last Snead, William S. Snead, left in the early part of 1942,[65] but Macdonald remained as President until the dissolution of the company.

The Company conducted its business from Louisville, Kentucky, until 1898 when a fire destroyed most of its plant on Market Street between Eighth and Ninth Streets. The framework of two of the buildings was shipped to Jersey City, New Jersey, for re-erection in 1900. By 1901 the Company issued a bound 36-page volume indicating it was doing business at the foot of Pine Street.[66] William R. Snead was listed as President, Charles S. Snead as Vice President. This plant in Jersey City, by 1942, occupied a site of four acres and was served by a siding from the Central Railroad of New Jersey.[67] The Company employed generally about 200 persons, except in 1931 when the payroll declined to 135, and during World Wars I and II when the number of employees rose to 500[68] and 600 respectively.[69] Charles Scott Snead, the founder of the Company, appears to have remained in Louisville where he died in 1903, leaving "a large fortune" and a good reputation. He was 83.[70] Actually, he outlived William R. Snead, his son, who had been made President at about the time the plant moved to Jersey City. W. R. Snead died in 1902, and was succeeded by Udolpho Snead, who was president when his nephew Angus Macdonald joined the company in 1905.

In addition to Green, the patent literature reveals that it was chiefly the Snead family (William R and Udolpho) who were obtaining the patents and presumably supplying the ideas in this early period.[71] Even the venerable Charles Scott Snead obtained a patent for a sand molding machine as late as 1892, and in 1907 Harry Peake Macdonald obtained the first of a long series of patents that resulted in improved molding devices called the "Macdonald Roller Ramming and Pattern Drawing Molding Machines."[72]

The move eastward was counter to the general movement of the center of manufacturing, but it undoubtedly was wise if the company had committed itself to concentrating on library business; for it was in the East that the large libraries were located at the time, and Jersey City's "Horseshoe" district was swarming with immigrants, a ready source of cheap labor.

Across the river in Manhattan, the old reservoir at 42nd Street had been filled in, in 1899, and by 1900 work had commenced on another great library building, the New York Public. The ubiquitous Bernard Richardson Green had been one of a panel of three judges in the preliminary competition of architects' plans.[73] Through an error, bids for the stacks were advertised in the fall of 1903. The specifications were incomplete and had not received proper approval. The situation was ripe for controversy. On October 29th, four recognized stack manufacturers of the time, Van Dorn Iron Works, Library Bureau, Snead and Company, and Art Metal submitted bids and erected full-scale models. Art Metal's bid of $1,378,000 was judged too high. Snead's, the next highest at $856,000 was approximately $100,000 over Library Bureau's, but was preferred by the architects and trustees. The two lower bidders protested vigorously and the Board of Estimate finally rejected all bids. A tighter set of specifications were written and a second call for bids was made in August, 1904. Six firms now bid, including the renowned Hecla Iron Works. This time Library Bureau was the highest bidder and Snead at $916,700 was second highest. Hecla Iron was second lowest bidder at $756,000. Nevertheless, Snead was again chosen.

> In some models the finish was poor in workmanship, in others, it was medium. The Snead model excelled all in finish... [and] came nearest to meeting the requirements.[74]

The Board of Estimate awarded the contract to Snead on November 18, 1904, but Hecla brought suit. Hecla claimed Snead had used unfair tactics in attempting to frighten other bidders by referring to the Green patents, and that a Parks Department foreman had offered to "swing" the bid for $75,000. Snead countered that Hecla had not submitted a model as required. The New York Daily News picked up the story and charged that "Learned and ingenious rogues" were at work,[75] that the specifications were written to favor Snead, and that the Snead bid included $220,000 "velvet" to be allocated to certain officials. However, Dr. John Shaw Billings, the Director of the Library and one of the most highly regarded figures in American librarianship, pointed out many inaccuracies in the paper's charges to the District Attorney. On April 18, 1905 the News printed a complete "Retraction and Apology."[76]

Meanwhile Snead and Company had begun work on the New York Public Library's contract number four, as the stack contract was designated. The first columns were set in July, 1905.

The stacks supplied to the New York Public Library were essentially the same as those of the Library of Congress. Steel columns supported the bookstacks and the cast-iron shelf supports were attached to these columns as in the latter. However, in the New York library, the columns also supported the floor of the main reading room on the third floor of the building. The main floors were made multiples of the stack tiers in height, and the tier height was increased from seven feet at the Library of Congress to seven feet six inches "in order that the first, third and fifth stack decks might line up with the main floors of the building."[77] While not as many tiers in height as the Washington library, the stack nevertheless was a huge block with a capacity of 3,000,000 volumes. Snead stacks installed in reading rooms and elsewhere in the building, brought its total capacity to 3,500,000 volumes.

In the early period of the company's involvement in the bookstack business, roughly to World War I, the Snead stack naturally was installed in a number of medium-sized and small libraries as well. In order to meet the needs of the smaller libraries and the prices and special features of its competitors, Snead modified and expanded its basic product. Almost immediately, the Green-designed book support was offered in a single, molded piece (similar to the one displayed at the Columbian Exposition in 1893) and the structural steel column was eliminated in the smaller stacks. The shelf supports became open-work partitions separating each compartment and serving as the structural support for the tier above (Figure 15). The system could also be modified to make attractive free-standing units. In addition, largely to meet the

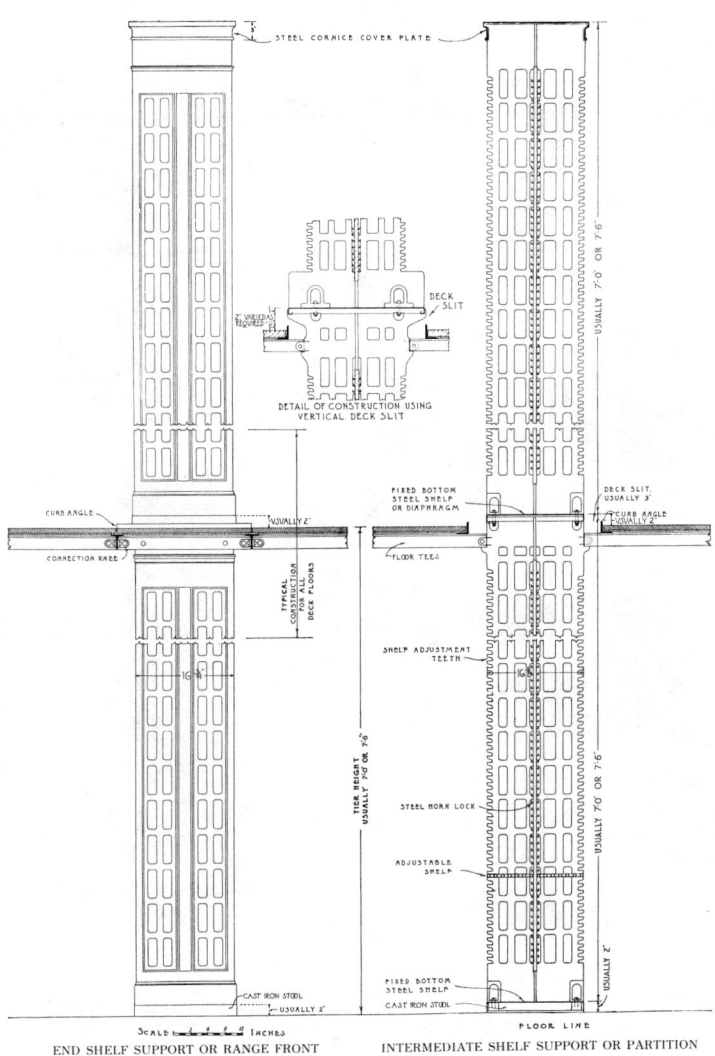

Figure 15. Snead cast-iron, multi-tier construction.

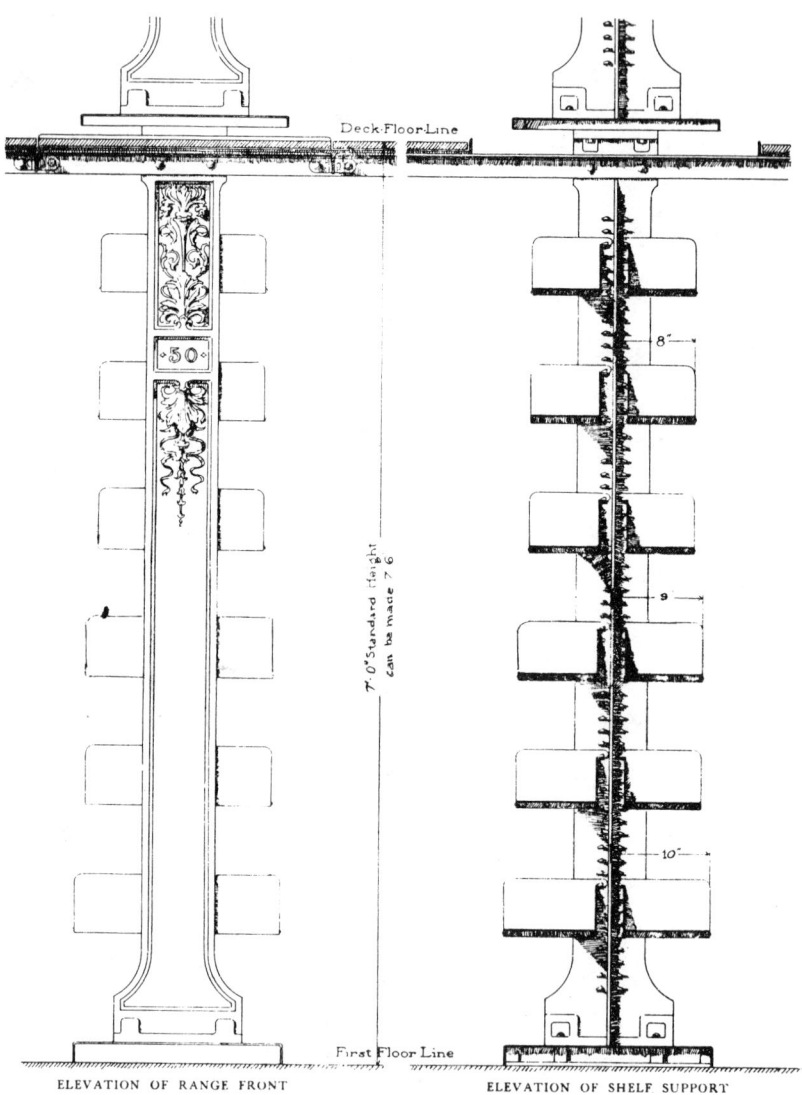

Figure 16. Snead bracket stack designed in 1895.

price of competitors, Snead offered a bracket stack. This stack at first employed cast-iron pilasters and brackets, and depended upon lugs on the brackets to engage hooks molded into the pilaster or column (Figure 16). The brackets supported a steel plate shelf. A patent on this stack, designed by Charles Trowbridge for Snead and Company, was filed in January, 1896.[78] The Snead bracket stack was modified, converted to steel and, by 1930, was at least as modern and light as others in the industry. However, in the early period, it is obvious that this type of stack was of secondary interest, and generally followed rather than led the industry. The chief emphasis in the catalogs up to 1915 was on the cast-iron partition, or as it came to be called in the industry, the "standard" stack.[79]

It is interesting to observe the multitude of competing designs, materials, and manufacturers in the early twentieth century. Wooden shelves, often made by the local carpenter or cabinetmaker, were preferred by many. William F. Poole, at least in the pre-Library of Congress period, preferred wood because it did not damage the bindings as iron had done at the British Museum,[80] and W. R. Eastman in 1901, while admitting that iron construction was best and a necessity "where three or more stories of cases are stacked," pointed out that metal was two to five times more expensive than wood.[81] Metal was also criticized by these writers as being less tasteful, less human and less homelike. Nevertheless, for the shelving problems of larger libraries, metal provided the answer, and for a long while cast-iron competed with steel, bracket stacks competed with standard stacks, and the various manufacturers, including Snead, Library Bureau, Art Metal, Van Dorn, and General Fireproofing, competed with each other.[82] In the long run, the cast-iron standard stack, as manufactured by Snead, was doomed, but in the period before 1930 it enjoyed considerable popularity.

In addition to the advantages enumerated above, cast-iron offered one other benefit that was impossible to duplicate in rolled steel:

> From one pattern, by mechanically operated moulding

machines an almost limitless number of identical shelf supports can be made, each having ... the same mouldings and panels for architectural design. [83]

In a time when public taste preferred a relatively high degree of ornamentation, this was a distinct advantage. Thus the shelf supports, particularly those that formed the exposed end panels of stack ranges, could be varied to give each library a unique ornamental design. Motifs used elsewhere in the decoration of the building could be repeated in the stacks. For example, the decoration on the end panels of the New York Public Library varied from that of the Library of Congress, and a theological seminary, such as the one at Mount Airy, Pennsylvania, could have a pattern suggesting cathedral windows.

By 1915, Snead could boast installations in over 200 libraries including such far away places as Manila; Wellington, New Zealand; and Dairen, Manchuria. [84] Many of these libraries, such as the Southboro, Massachusetts, Public Library, were quite small, but others, including the public libraries of Fall River and Springfield, Massachusetts; Washington, D. C.; Denver, Colorado; Louisville, Kentucky; and Evanston, Illinois, might be classed as medium-sized institutions with stack capacities ranging from 100,000 to 500,000 volumes.

As might be expected, certain architects seemed to recommend Snead stacks frequently. Although Snead and Company was not involved in the wooden book shelving for the Boston Public Library (1888), [85] McKim, Meade and White did witness the installation of Snead shelving in four libraries, including the Low Memorial Library (1897) at Columbia University. Snead stacks went into Horace Trumbauer's Widener Memorial Library (1915) at Harvard, but not his Philadelphia Public Library (1927). The most frequently noted architect on Shead and Company's 1915 list is Edward L. Tilton. [86] By this time Snead stacks had been installed in eight of his libraries, including the important Springfield, Massachusetts, Public Library (1912). There is a long professional association between Snead and Company and Tilton, and later his partner and successor, Alfred Morton Githens.

Macdonald's Youth

In 1933, Dr. Theodore Koch, Librarian at Northwestern University, wrote:

> The University was fortunate in having as its official architect James Gamble Rogers, Inc., who has had most valuable experience recently in the planning of the Sterling Memorial Library and the Sterling Law Library at Yale University, the Atlanta University Library, the Library of Colgate-Rochester Theological Seminary and are now doing the new Columbia University Library.[87]

Snead and Company too must have considered themselves fortunate, for all the libraries listed by Dr. Koch, including his own Deering Library at Northwestern, were furnished with Snead stacks. The inference to be drawn from this discussion is that, although generally more expensive, Snead stacks were apparently preferred by certain architects.

Notes

1. Cornelia Macdonald, A Diary with Reminiscenses of the War and Refugee Life in the Shenandoah Valley, 1860-1865..., annotated ... by Hunter Macdonald, (Nashville, Tenn.: Cullom and Ghertner, 1934), pp. 416-418.

2. Columbia University, Registrar, Transcript of Academic Record of Angus Snead McDonald [sic] April 18, 1967.

3. Ibid.

4. Talbot Faulkner Hamlin, "Ware, William Robert," Dictionary of American Biography, XIX (New York: Charles Scribner's Sons, 1936), pp. 452-453. The University of Illinois, however, claims the first graduate; see Winton U. Solberg, The University of Illinois, 1867-1894 (Urbana: University of Illinois Press, 1968), p. 147.

5. Ibid., p. 452. See also Fritz Milkau, ed., Handbuch der Bibliothekswissenschaft (Zweite Auflage Herausgegeben von Georg Leyh, II Wiesbaden: Otto Harrassowitz, 1961), 11, p. 332.

6. John Burchard, The Architecture of America; A Social and Cultural History (Boston: Little, Brown, 1961), p. 126.

7. Horace Coon, Columbia; Colossus on the Hudson (New York: E. P. Dutton, 1947), p. 274.

8. Alfred D. F. Hamlin, A Text-Book of the History of Architecture (New York: Longmans, Green, 1896).

9. Horace Coon, loc. cit.

10. Arthur Clason Weatherhead, The History of Collegiate Education in Architecture in the United States (Los Angeles: By the author, 1941), p. 45

11. Ibid., pp. 47, 98-99.

12. It was not until the fall of 1905 that Hamlin added the Ateliers under McKim and Hastings and introduced other changes. Macdonald had graduated the previous June. Compare Columbia University's Catalogue and General Announcement, 1904-05 and 1905-06.

13. Columbia University, Catalogue and General Announcement, 1901-1902 (New York: Columbia University, 1902), pp. 66-8, 294.

14. Ibid., 1902-1903, pp. 67-8, 305.

15. William Robert Ware, The American Vignola, Part I, The Five Orders (Boston: American Architect and Building News Co., 1902), 46p., 18 plates.

16. Columbia University, ... 1904-1905, p. 317.

17. Columbia University, Registrar, "Transcript of the Academic Record of Angus Snead McDonald." Photocopy dated April 18, 1967, in author's possession, 1 p.

18. Columbia University, Architectural Society Yearbook, 1904 (New York: Columbia University, 1904), pp. 42, 47-8. The studies are of a Library Interior, a Monumental Stair, and an elevation of the Petit Trianon in Versailles. (t. p. missing)

19. Alfred D. F. Hamlin, op. cit., pp. 396-7.

20. Franz von Reber, History of Ancient Art, trans. Joseph Thacker Clarke (New York: Harper and Bros., 1882), 482 p.

21. Eduoard Corroyer, L'Architecture Gothique (Paris: Société Française d'Editions D'Art, 1891), 382 p.

22. Léon Palustre, L'Architecture de la Rennaissance (Paris: Société Française d'Editions D'Art, 1892), 352 p.

23. "Angus Snead Macdonald," unpublished autobiographical notes dated April 19, 1955, photocopy in author's files, p. 2.

24. Ibid., p. 1.

25. Interview with Mrs. Angus S. Macdonald, September 1, 1966.

26. Betty P. Ashton, "Orange Couple Lives Under Garden," Richmond, Virginia Times-Dispatch, July 16, 1958, p. 18.

27. Massachusetts Institute of Technology, Register of Graduates (Boston: Geo. H. Ellis Co., 1904), p. 125.

28. "Snead, Udolpho," New York Times, April 21, 1921, p. 13:7, (obituary notice).

29. Ben Casseday, The History of Louisville from the Earliest Settlement till the Year 1852, (Louisville, Ky,: Hull and Brother, 1852), Supplement page 9.

30. William Scott Snead, An American Saga: the Story of the Snead Family of Accomac County, Virginia, and of Kentucky, ed. William E. Stokes... (North Garden, Va., 1952), pp. 18-19.

31. Snead and Company Iron Works, Book Stack and Shelving for Libraries (Louisville, Ky. and Chicago, Ill.: Snead and Co., 1895), on end paper, rear cover.

32. Snead and Company Iron Works, Library Planning, Bookstacks and Shelving (Jersey City, N. J.: Snead and Co., 1915), p. 11.

33. Talbot Faulkner Hamlin, op. cit., p. 452.

34. Henry Van Brunt, ["Speech on Library Architecture,"] Library Journal, IV (July-August, 1879), p. 296.

35. Georg Leyh. "Vom Büchersaal zum Magazin," Overbibliothekar Wilhelm Munthe på Femtiårsdagen, 20 Oktober 1933, (Oslo: Grøndahl, 1933), p. 166.

36. William L. Williamson, William Frederick Poole and the Modern Library Movement (New York: Columbia University Press, 1963), p. 156.

37. W. F. Poole, "Speech on Library Architecture," Library Journal, XVI (Conference number, 1891), p. 101.

38. "Fixtures and Fittings," American Library Association Conference Proceedings, Library Journal, XVII (Conference number, 1893), p. 31.

39. Williamson, op. cit., p. 156.

40. Snead and Company, loc. cit.

41. "Green, Bernard R.," National Cyclopedia of American Biography, XX, p. 355.

42. "Museum and Library," Undated clipping from the National Republican in Scrapbooks of Dr. Julia M. Green, (Scrapbook, p. [18]). Microfilm copy of original in the Library of Congress.

43. "The New Department Building," Washington Evening Star, February 4, 1888, in Scrapbooks, [p. 68].

44. Snead and Company Iron Works, Illustrations of Ornamental Iron Work (Louisville, Ky.: Snead and Company, 1890), plate 18; and Thomas Lincoln Casey, "Report on Building for State, War and Navy Departments," U.S. War Department, Annual Report of the Secretary of War, 1887 (Washington: Government Printing Office, 1887), I, pp. 869-870.

45. Keyes D. Metcalf and others, The National Medical Library; Report of a Survey of the Army Medical Library (Chicago: American Library Association, 1944), p. 5.

46. Ibid., p. 7.

47. "Completing the Monument," Washington Evening Star, August 1, 1885 in Scrapbooks, [p. 13].

48. Lucy Salamanca, Fortress of Freedom; the Story of the Library of Congress (New York: J. B. Lippincott, 1942), p. 225.

49. "Monument of Books...", Washington Evening Star, November 27, 1896 in Scrapbooks, [p. 395]. Note: Serious claim has been made that the real designer of the Library of Congress bookstack was Niels Poulson, a great iron master and founder of the American-Scandinavian Society. However, this intriguing problem in historiography is outside the scope of this study. For Snead and Company the affiliation is definitely with Green, not Poulson and his rival Hecla Iron Works.

50. Ibid., [p. 395].

51. It is difficult to be certain of this point. However, later, Snead and Company recommended a seven-tier limit on cast-iron. Undoubtedly, greater heights were possible, but not without a sacrifice in the uniformity and bulk of the lower supports. See Snead and Company, Library Planning..., p. 77.

52. U. S. Patent Office, Official Gazette, LII, (September 16, 1890), p. 1785; LVII (December 29, 1891), p. 1796; LXVI (March 20, 1894), also p. 1796.

53. Bernard R. Green, "The Building of the Library of Congress," Annual Report of the Board of Regents of the Smithsonian Institution ... to July 1897, (Washington, D. C.: Government Printing Office, 1898), p. 630. A "Book railway" was being developed for the Boston Public Library at this time, but its design was entirely different and proved far less popular in libraries.

54. Snead and Company, Library Planning..., p. 12.

55. Thomas Lincoln Casey, ... Report Upon the Construction of the Building for the Library of Congress... Year Ending December 1, 1891, (U. S. 52nd Congress, First Session, Senate Miscellaneous Document no. 15), p. 3.

56. Bernard R. Green, "The Building of the Library of Congress," p. 631.

57. Snead and Company Iron Works, Book Stack ... (1895), p. 26.

58. Snead and Company Iron Works, Green's Patent Book Stack and Shelving for Large and Small Libraries, (Louisville, Ky.: Snead and Co., n. d.), two leaves.

59. "Green's Book-Stack and Shelving for Libraries," Library Journal, XVIII (May, 1893), pp. 154-155.

60. "Monument of Books," op. cit., [p. 395].

61. Ibid., [pp. 395-396].

62. Bernard Richardson Green, "Report of the Construction of the Building for the Year Ending December 1, 1896," U. S. 54th Congress, 2nd Session, House Document no. 20 (Washington, D. C., Government Printing Office, 1900?), p. 3.

63. Keyes D. Metcalf and others, op. cit., p. 5.

64. Snead and Company, Library Planning ..., p. 3, and examination of lists of officers.

65. Angus S. Macdonald, "To the Stockholders of Snead and Company," Report for the Heirs of the Estate of Udolpho Snead, unpublished report, Snead and Company, April, 1943, p. 2.

66. Snead and Company Iron Works, Bookstacks and Shelving for Libraries, (Jersey City, N. J.: Snead and Co., 1901).

67. [Application for Government Glider Contract, A. S. Macdonald supposed author], typewritten, 1942?

68. New Jersey Industrial Directory, selected years 1906-1943/44 quoted in letter from Mrs. M. K. Comes, Reference Librarian, Jersey City Public Library.

69. Letter from A. S. Macdonald to Ralph Ellsworth, dated August 21, 1945.

70. "Charles Scott Snead Dies," Louisville Herald, February 26, 1903 in Scrapbooks, [p. 468].

71. It seems to have been Snead policy to allow the patent to be listed in the inventor's name. Other workers, besides the family did hold some patents. See U. S. Patent Office, Official Gazette, and Indexes 1880-1952.

72. Snead and Company, Library Planning ..., [p. 257].

73. The other judges were John Shaw Billings, the Librarian, and William R. Ware of the Columbia University School of Architecture, "Plans for the Library," New York Times, May 24, 1897, p. 10.

74. Harry Miller Lydenberg, History of the New York Public Library... (New York: The Library, 1923), p. 489. I am indebted to this volume for many of the details concerning this episode in the history of Snead and Company.

75. New York Daily News, March 22, 1905, quoted in Ibid., p. 492.

76. Ibid., p. 492.

77. Snead and Company, Library Planning ..., p. 139.

78. U. S. Patent Office, Official Gazette, LXXVI, (Aug. 4, 1896), p. 700.

79. "Standard" here refers to support, not a level of excellence. Standard stacks were also made by Snead and others of sheet steel.

80. William F. Poole, "Why Wood Shelving is Better Than Iron," Library Notes, (U. S.) II (September, 1887), p. 95.

81. W. R. Eastman, "Library Buildings," Library Journal, XXVI (Conference Number, 1901), p. 42.

82. For a description of the bookstack industry in 1916 see "Bookstacks as Described by Their Manufacturers," Library Journal, XLI (April, 1916), pp. 252-258.

83. Snead and Company, Library Planning ..., p. 18.

84. Ibid., pp. 121-125.

85. Snead provided the ornamental gates and lamps at the entrance and other iron for this great library.

86. Snead and Company, Library Planning ..., pp. 121-125.

87. Theodore Wesley Koch, "The Charles Deering Library at Northwestern University," Library Journal, LVIII (March 1, 1933), p. 189.

Chapter IV

Macdonald as President of Snead and Company

In 1916, Angus Macdonald succeeded his uncle Udolpho as president of the firm.[1] Since joining the company in 1905, he had served an apprenticeship which included work in the foundry, in sales, and some experience in design. In 1913, for example, he and his brother Harry made some modifications in Green's shelf support. Exactly why Angus was chosen as president instead of his older brother Harry is not certain. Both he and his brother were well-educated and both seem to have been close to the uncle's family. Harry apparently had some history of illness before succumbing to cancer in 1921. Perhaps illness had troubled him as early as 1905, and may account for the uncle's persuading Angus to abandon plans for an architectural career.[2] Both brothers were named executors of Udolpho's estate when the uncle died in 1921, but it was Angus who accompanied the widow on the interment journey back to Louisville. Unfortunately for Snead and Company, the inventive Harry was to outlive his uncle by only four months.[3]

Meanwhile, in 1911, Angus had married the former Elizabeth Prentiss Avery who bore him a daughter, Frances Avery, in 1914, and in 1918, a son, Angus Avery.[4]

After the successful installation of the 2,000,000-volume bookstack at Harvard's Widener Library (1915), Snead and Company gradually shifted to war production. Initially, they produced cavalry lances, bayonets and shells for the Russian Army, then parts for mines used in the North Sea, and finally, 75-millimeter shells for the United States armed forces, attaining a production rate of 8,000 per day.[5]

Macdonald Modifies Green's Designs

Beginning with Widener, the Snead stack began a long

modification away from Green's design that eventually terminated in a modern steel bracket stack. In addition to an extensive use of carrels, the major stack modification for Widener involved a redesign of the lower portion of the shelf support to permit a wider base shelf (the "cover" of the stack tier below) and raising this shelf a few inches above the deck to allow a vertical ventilation slit. [6] This ventilation slit eliminated the troublesome opening in the stack floor and permitted shelving oversize volumes in each compartment. Harry and Angus Macdonald applied for a patent on this modification in April, 1913. [7]

Standard "Type A"

In 1922 Angus Macdonald redesigned the Green stack, along much more modern, lighter and simpler lines. This stack, while retaining the same principles of shelf support and using the same shelves as Green's design, consisted of three simple vertical supports, joined by steel horizontal supports. [8] It was designated as standard stack type A (Figure 17), and the older version was now referred to as type B. Type A could not be used as a single-tier, freestanding unit. For all practical purposes this new stack displaced the older model and was used on most jobs after it was introduced, including the Universities of Illinois (1925) and North Carolina (1929), the 16-tier tower at Yale's Sterling Library (1930), the Vatican Library (1929 and 1931), and Northwestern University's Deering Library (1932).

Bracket Stack

With the building of Columbia's South Hall (later Butler Library) (1934), cast-iron was abandoned in favor of the all-steel bracket stack designed by Macdonald and others in the company. In 1937 Columbia's Librarian, C. C. Williamson, stated "It is unusual to use the bracket type in so large a stack equipment... ."[9] Unconsciously, perhaps, he was paying tribute to the position of Snead and Company in the large bookstack field, [10] and also intimating that previously it was believed that bracket stacks had not been substantial enough for truly large, permanent installations. Snead had offered the bracket stack with condescension in 1915, and boasted

Figure 17. Standard Stack, Type A.

that 95 percent of its business was in cast-iron standard stacks. However, by 1940 they recognized substantial improvements in the manufacture of steel bracket stacks and admitted that cast-iron could not "compete in cost with prefabricated steel shelving, and are seldom supplied except to extend existing installations."[11] The bracket stack, as supplied to Columbia and other customers, frequently combined the familiar open bar shelf with a hinged bracket that could be folded for compact storage.

This stack could more readily accommodate shelves of varying widths, an old problem with the standard stack that was never completely solved. It could be adapted to free-standing, top-braced, or multi-tier installations with open bar or plate shelves (Figure 18). Too, the new stack seemed to lend itself more readily to special applications. At Columbia, the basic bracket shelf was modified easily to provide special sorting shelves. In January of 1932, Macdonald applied for a patent on an early version of compact storage.[12] Basically, a section of bracket stack was placed on large rollers or wheels (Figure 19). The units were parked in rows and could be moved without tracks or other guides. To gain access to the shelves, one pulled out the desired unit. These rolling cases were developed initially for the Toronto Public Reference Library, and were supplied also to the U.S. Department of Agriculture Library. They are still offered by Luxfer, Ltd., Snead and Company's former English franchise. For the Sterling Library, which elsewhere used cast-iron shelf supports, the bracket stack formed the basic support for the study carrel desk top and shelves.

A Standard Shelf Length

As might be expected, Macdonald gave a great deal of thought to shelf lengths before standardizing on three feet.[13] According to Metcalf, probably no one had studied the problem so intensively before.[14] The advantages of standardization from the standpoint of economy of production and interchangeability of parts was obvious, but what size should be the standard? Three feet had been a popular length with Snead and other manufacturers for some time, but a definite standard had never been set; and in 1915

Figure 18. Bracket stack.

Figure 19. Compact storage, rolling type.

Snead specified the length simply, "as required, ... about three feet... ."[15]

The Snead "Open Bar" shelf could, and occasionally did, span greater distances (as much as six additional inches) without noticeable deflection under a load. The original shelves in the Library of Congress were 38 inches long. To make maximum use of space for his layout of the stack in Harvard's Widener Library, Macdonald himself had chosen a shelf of about 40 inches. Economy in production operations, material and upright supports favored a longer shelf, but such a shelf was not so easy to handle, particularly in the close quarters of the bookstack, and Macdonald found the arrangement of books on the longer shelf to be confusing to the mind and eye. Three feet, he decided, was the best compromise length after all.

The Conveyor

The shelf supports and shelves were not the only parts of the "Snead System" to undergo modification. Metcalf credits Macdonald with developing the very simple and durable conveyor for the New York Public Library. At this same time, in the mid-1920's, both the University of Rochester and Yale University were planning new library buildings, and both hoped to install in their tower stacks a conveyor which was better suited to bookstack operation than those generally available at the time. Macdonald wrote to Donald B. Gilchrist, Librarian at Rochester:

> ... one of Mr. Rogers' men [James Gamble Rogers, architect for Yale's Sterling Library] stated that they were going to try to get someone to duplicate for them the Library of Congress conveyor which has been in constant and satisfactory use for about thirty years. I thought the matter over and then volunteered that we would build a similar conveyor... [16]

In 1928 Macdonald was able to report that a model conveyor was in operation in the plant in Jersey City.[17] The Green conveyor had been entirely redesigned by Charles C. Waite, an officer of Snead and Company, probably under Macdonald's direction.[18] Green's double chain drive, which tended to wear unevenly, was replaced by a single, heavier chain, and the conveyor was generally made more dependable. This mechanism, with minor modifications, can be found in the libraries of the universities of Illinois, North Carolina, Yale, Columbia, Oregon, Northwestern, and many others.

Lighting

Library lighting generally, and stack lighting in particular, concerned Macdonald in the 1920's, 1930's, and later. In 1931, he contributed an article to <u>Library Journal</u> on the subject.[19] In this article he described some of the problems of stack lighting and how Snead and Company had provided a special fixture for Yale's Sterling Library. He pointed out that the work plane of the bookstack was vertical, that some books were only 15 inches from the light source while others were as much as nine feet away. The ceiling was the logical place to mount any light source, yet such a fixture was limited in shape and size by the low ceilings of the stack room. Any fixture should shed dust, be easy to clean and not hinder, unduly, the replacement of bulbs.[20] Macdonald designed a shade (patent filed June, 1930)[21] which through a series of carefully placed perforations distributed the light more evenly and yet kept the most intense portion of the light from the stack attendant's eyes (Figures 20-21). Approximately 4,500 of these shades were installed in the Sterling Library.[22] After a series of tests, Joseph Wheeler succeeded in convincing the city authorities in Baltimore that this lighting fixture should be used in the stacks of the new Enoch Pratt Library (1933) even though Snead and Company had not won the stack contract for this landmark public library.[23] Dean M. Warren, an engineer employed by the General Electric Company, endorsed the design and stated, "The Snead Reflector is based on a new principle of light control by means of a perforated reflecting surface."[24]

An examination of photographs of many stack installations at the time will frequently show exposed or poorly protected light bulbs. These inadequate fixtures probably account for the popularity of Macdonald's economical design.

Figure 20. Stack aisle reflector.

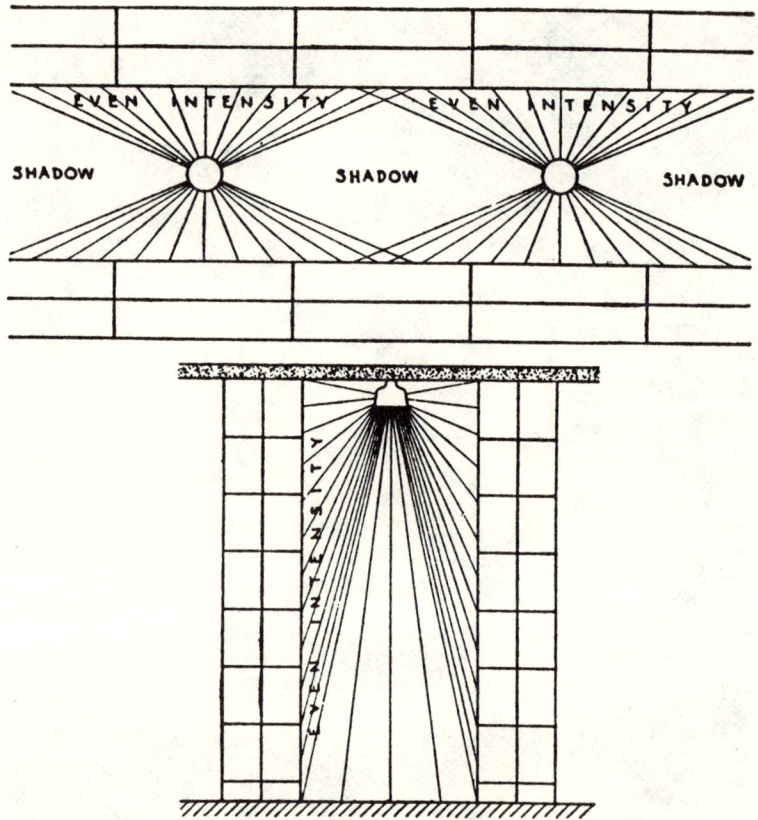

Figure 21. Light distribution pattern.

Floor Construction

As techniques for making and pouring concrete improved, this material gradually found its way into the stack room. It was the first in a series of steps that transformed the "traditional" stack room into the modular library form. Under somewhat different circumstances, concrete floors had been used in the John Crerar Library, Chicago (1912), which was essentially an office building. This construction appears to have been introduced into bookstack areas in the mid-1920's.[25] Librarians generally distrusted concrete's "tendency to dust,"[26] and as late as 1931 Art Metal recommended against its use.[27] Snead's first use of concrete on a large stack appears to have been at the University of Illinois Library (1926) where it was regarded as an "experiment."[28] The reasons for the change to concrete floors are undoubtedly manifold. Baber attributes it to a need to distribute "evenly heat and ventilation, of giving added fire protection and for housing special collections."[29] In 1940 Snead's catalog listed the following advantages:

> Tiers are insulated from each other against noise, dust and fire, and air conditioning is facilitated... [also] a continuous deck floor results in greater flexibility in the arrangement of the library interior. Shelving can be rearranged readily to provide new aisles or... space for study rooms... .[30]

At Illinois, every other deck was of solid concrete, but the conventional horizontal stack braces were still relied upon for support; and the alternate decks were of the familiar marble construction with vertical ventilation slits under the base shelf. The Illinois innovation was probably specified by the architect due to a special need for wind bracing.[31] The Snead stacks for the great Sterling tower at Yale, built after the Illinois library, relied on the older construction method. However, after the introduction of the continuous slab floor in the stacks of the Engineering Societies Library (stacks, 1930),[32] a more modern and attractive construction than that used at Illinois, the old marble decks were doomed. Snead reported:

> Within one year of [this] first installation... the Snead Continuous Deck Floor Construction was ordered for installation... for thirty-one of the most important

libraries in the country.[33]
The deck, only two and one-half inches thick, was described as "the most radical improvement in bookstack construction in the last thirty years... and... permits extreme flexibility in arrangement and use... ."[34]

Working with James Gamble Rogers, Snead supplied slab construction for the libraries of Northwestern (1932) and Columbia (1934) universities. These reinforced concrete slab floors extended continuously from wall to wall. All steel supporting elements, and electrical conduit and junction boxes were imbedded in the thin concrete deck.[35] This provided a smooth, flush ceiling which, when painted white, reflected light better and gave a neater appearance than the usual stack area ceiling. The floors were covered with asphalt tile. Some of the details of this construction probably were of Macdonald's inspiration since he filed patents on stack construction and flooring in July, 1930, and March, 1932, which employ concrete decks.[36]

In 1935 Macdonald applied for a patent on a steel floor similar to that used by Snead at the Library of Congress Annex (1937).[37] The Company maintained that the continuous deck was "pioneered" by them, and in 1940 they offered it in concrete, steel or a combination of both.[38]

Ventilation

This fundamental innovation in bookstack construction caused important changes in ventilation. Obviously, it was no longer possible to force air (or allow it to rise naturally) up through the many deck slits. One complicated solution was worked out by engineers for the Library of Congress Annex. It utilized duct work corresponding to the stack range spacing. Another, used earlier at Columbia's Butler Library, relied on hollow double walls on opposite sides of the stack room. One side served as plenum, the other as return. In each floor air escaped from controlled openings in the plenum wall and moved across the room to similar openings in the opposite wall. Still another means of ventilating the stacks was devised by Macdonald, and was known as the "zig-zag" method. It is one of the simplest schemes, and was employed in the stacks of the Sterling Law Library at Yale University (1931), Myron Taylor Hall at Cornell University (1932), and elsewhere.[39] In Macdonald's words:

> With this system the air is forced into the stack room all along the inner wall of the lowest tier and then allowed to find its way along the range aisles to the opposite wall. Here it impinges before passing up through a series of long openings or continuous slits in the first deck floor adjacent to the wall. The air flow is then reversed in direction and passes back through another series of openings along the wall... . This process is continued, the air zig-zagging back and forth until it reaches the top tier where it is exhausted and partly recirculated... .[40]

This system avoided expensive duct work, but open doors or windows could hinder its efficiency.

However, even before the advent of the concrete deck in stack rooms, Macdonald had taken an interest in ventilation. In a letter to Donald B. Gilchrist, Librarian of the University of Rochester, he observed that many library buildings had been equipped with elaborate ventilating systems, but frequently they proved inefficient or too costly to operate and were abandoned soon after the buildings were opened. He made certain general recommendations to Gilchrist, stressing the need for simplicity and economy, and warning against the damage to books and the discomfort to readers that could result from a poor system.[41] Like a number of others at the time, Macdonald recognized the need for a truly scientific study of the heating and ventilating of bookstacks and the relationship to book preservation. In the spring of 1928, in a series of letters to William C. Bond, Herbert Putnam and others, he urged that an investigation be made by the National Bureau of Standards, using the Library of Congress stacks as a laboratory.[42] By September, 1928, a committee consisting of Macdonald, personnel from the Library of Congress, the New York Public Library, the National Bureau of Standards and the American Society of Heating and Ventilating Engineers was formed. In February, 1929, the first draft of a report[43] by the National Bureau of Standards was circulated to committee members. The accompanying letter, from George K. Burgess,

Acting Director of the Bureau, proposed "to offer this report to Snead and Company for publication as a chapter in a revised edition of their textbook."[44] The "textbook," undoubtedly a revision of Snead's <u>Library Planning</u>... of 1915, was never published. However, the investigations of the Bureau of Standards were expanded and resulted in a number of reports published in the 1930's.[45] Harry Miller Lydenberg of the New York Public Library is credited with securing support from the Carnegie Corporation of New York which made these later studies possible.[46]

Additional Modifications

During the 1930's, there was a steady stream of modifications in Snead's various products. In addition to changes already noted, Charles C. Waite obtained a patent on the folding bracket shelf that was used in a number of Snead installations.[47] Macdonald designed a very handsome metal carrel in 1934,[48] and a year later, the metal deck already noted. In a burst of ingenuity that now seems to border on whimsy, Snead and Company took its fine bracket stack, turned it upside down, and hung it from the ceiling! This stack was installed at Colorado State College of Education (1939) and will be discussed later in this chapter. Undoubtedly this constant "tinkering" with the product involved certain developmental costs and disruption in the production department. On the other hand, for a company that did not have a wide variety of other popular products to add diversity and flexibility, as did Snead's major competitors, this tinkering may have been a necessity.

Business Problems

The decade of the 1930's also presented some unusual problems from the standpoint of business management. As Robert Muller has pointed out, the depression of 1929-1933 was slow to affect the library building industry. The building rate declined slowly until 1933, but "dropped considerably during the recovery period 1933-37 and rose sharply from 1938 until Pearl Harbor."[49] A further examination of Muller's list of 146 libraries reveals that an average of four were built in each year from 1932 through 1937.

The most active year was 1939 when 23 libraries were built.[50] With Columbia's Butler Library nearing completion and relatively little new business in sight, Macdonald wrote with a note of despair in the winter of 1934:

> Washington is not only a center of world interest on account of the social and economic experiments being carried on but it is also the almost exclusive source of any possible new business for Snead and Company. Consequently I go down there practically every week.[51]

In addition to the business problems of this period, Macdonald seems to have suffered from one of his few illnesses. The winter of 1933-34 apparently had been a severe one for him. He complained of a serious arthritic condition in his legs which caused him to be absent from the office for more than a month. This condition troubled him well over a year, but in late March, 1934, he was able to discard the crutches he had been using in favor of two canes.[52] And, typical of the man, his troubles seemed to collect and descend all at once. His 24-year marriage to his first wife, the former Elizabeth Prentiss Avery, was heading toward divorce.

However, in the summer of 1936, he was able to write:

> This summer I am going to be entirely too busy to take a vacation as on top of our regular run of work, our new big National Archives contract involving new designs, production equipment and tooling, and also a new branch plant in Maryland, keep my time more than full.[53]

And toward the end of 1936 he expressed hope of making up losses of the depression: "1936 will probably show us the best profit we have had for many years and in addition we will carry on our books a full year's business for 1937."[54]

Beginning with the National Archives (1936-37), for which Snead supplied much of the stack equipment, the Library of Congress Annex (1937), the libraries of Howard University (1938), Drew University and the University of Alabama (both 1939), Southern Methodist, Washington and Lee, and others (1940), with bookstacks ranging from 200,000 volumes at Southern Methodist to 10,000,000 at the Library of Congress Annex, the company seems to have shaken the grip of the depression. When one adds to this the large contract for "mobile walls" for the Bell Telephone laboratories and $1,700,000 in developmental contracts for Army and Navy gliders, it seems fair to conclude that Macdonald had placed Snead and Company on a sound financial basis on the eve of World War II.

In this later period, Snead and Company seems to have begun to specialize in college and university library work. An examination of a partial list of the company's installations made to 1940 reveals a ratio of almost two to one in favor of the academic library over the public library,[55] although, at this time, public libraries outnumbered academic libraries by almost five to one.[56] Of libraries built by members of the American Association of Universities between 1896 and 1939, almost two-thirds were equipped with Snead stacks.[57] An examination of Muller's list of academic libraries built between 1929 and 1940[58] shows that Snead installed its stacks in slightly over half of the larger libraries (16 of the 29 libraries with book capacities in excess of 200,000 volumes), and somewhat fewer of the smaller ones (stack capacities of 100,000 to 200,000 volumes). Of the very small bookstacks on the list, Snead equipment went into only a few. In the large public library market, however, Snead and Company obtained only a little better than their "fair share." Of the 37 cities with populations exceeding 250,000 in 1940,[59] 13 had large central libraries equipped by Snead.

Donald Bean, a long-time staff member of Remington Rand's Library Bureau (now retired), stated that the quality of Snead products was excellent, and in the large bookstack field the company was "tops." However, he criticized Macdonald and the company for permitting themselves to be ensnared by their own excellence and for not having made a greater effort to invade the small library market.[60]

That such a specialization had developed by 1930 and that it was probably troubling the officers of the company is supported by statements in their advertising literature, such as "It has sometimes erroneously been thought that Snead and Company was not interested in the small library. Quite the contrary is true... ."[61]

How well Snead did financially, how large a portion of the

market they captured in terms of dollars, exactly what constitutes a "fair share,"[62] what was the market and how many libraries of the time were so small as to rely on a local cabinet maker, all this is outside the scope of this study. Also intriguing would be a comparison of the Snead share of the market with that of such competitors as Art Metal, General Fireproofing, Library Bureau, and others. This too must remain for another study, since any comparison of job lists is extremely difficult. The purpose of this entire section is to establish that Snead and Company has developed a certain degree of prominence in equipping the large research library. Indeed, in the period prior to World War II, the company came close to dominating this segment of the library market. (For a list of Snead installations see Appendix III.)

Eroding the Stack Form

At Sterling Library (16 tiers), Columbia's South Hall and the University of Rochester Library (both planned for 19 tiers), and the University of Texas (planned for 27 tiers), Snead and Company carried the stack to its greatest heights. At the same time, forces were at work that were undermining the stack form. Not the least of these forces was Angus Macdonald and his company, and when the final underpinning of the bookstack's popularity was removed, the collapse was as sudden and complete as the collapse of Snead and Company itself.

Apart from the expense of providing an adequate staff in the very tall stack, American librarians seem never to have been completely satisfied with the stack form. In public libraries they were continually attempting to enlarge the collections in the reading rooms; and in the academic libraries, serving growing numbers of graduate students, there seems to have been a steady trend to enlarge the number of reader spaces in the stacks. In the very beginning, in Harvard's Gore Hall stack, a few tables and chairs were provided.[63] and Bernard Green was quick to point out the flexibility of his design for the Library of Congress:

> The shelves may all be removed from any bay or series of bays on a deck to make a passageway or insert any

convenient piece of furniture, such as a card catalog, desk, or cabinet... .[64]

Harvard's Widener Library (1915) made extensive provisions for student carrels and faculty offices, and Johns Hopkins' Gilman Hall (1914) provided for 300 graduate students at the edge of the stack.[65] Green further proposed before the Narragansett Conference of the American Library Association in 1906:

> Under present circumstances we are obliged to thoroughly equip book stacks with artificial illumination and to use it frequently.... . Why not, therefore, disregard the daylight altogether... in its place we may secure absolute uniformity and any desired brilliancy at every point of every possible stack with the incandescent light.[66]

Three years later, before the American Association for the Advancement of Science, Green had the opportunity to describe his "Book Stack in the Dark."[67] The entire South-East Court of the Library of Congress had been filled with Snead stacks, which added over 1,000,000 volumes in shelving capacity. The demand for carrel windows in the stacks temporarily checked the popularity of Green's solution, at least among academic libraries. The variations possible on the relationship of the bookstack to the reading and administrative areas of the building are numerous. At about the time Green was first proposing the idea, the Louisville Free Public Library (1907) placed its relatively small Snead stack in the center of a wing and, on some floors, surrounded the stack by work rooms. Clerestory windows were used in the upper two decks, however.[68] The Somerville, Massachusetts, Public Library (1912) placed its two-tier stack in the basement and surrounded it with work and reading rooms.[69] Multnomah County (Portland), Oregon, Public Library (1913) used a central stack and many public libraries in the succeeding decades did not hesitate to build their stacks "in the dark."

To reverse the argument, Wheeler and Githens wrote in 1940:

> The increasing tendency to place large storage stack areas [in public libraries] either under the main floor or in the center of a large building directly discourages the use of carrels, because daylight is not available.[70]

Yale's stack tower in the Sterling Library (1930) was windowless until it emerged above the surrounding roofs at the eighth tier; Columbia's Butler Library (1934) appears to be the first to combine the concrete slab construction, refrigerated air conditioning and a flexible bracket stack to provide reader or work spaces anywhere in the central stack tower. The shelves could be removed from any of the columns to provide an aisle, work space, or support a carrel. [71] The flush concrete floors and air conditioning are especially important factors in the gradual modification of the stack.

Convertible Stack

For the Library of Congress Annex (1937), Snead and Company revived its old "type B" cast iron stacks. Supporting columns were spaced every 10 feet, the decks were of prefabricated steel sections and the entire building, including the stacks, was supplied with refrigerated, conditioned air. Green's "type B" design was modified to permit its being suspended from the ceiling. The patent on these modifications and some of the ventilation details was granted to W. C. Bond, the Superintendent of the Buildings and Grounds, and apparently was not assigned to Snead and Company. [72]

Again, emphasis was placed on flexibility through a stack design:

> ...that would provide as far as possible for every contingency of use... The shelf supports... may be removed quickly and a work space left free. When so desired, partitions and doors which snap into place convert a bay of shelves into a locked enclosure. [73]

A more usual pattern was to combine the "convertible stack" with bracket shelves, as was done at the Rockford College Library (1940), in Illinois, and the Joint University Libraries (1941, Figure 22). Here the load-bearing columns were set on nine by nine foot centers, and parts of the stacks were devoted to offices, typing rooms and the like.

All of these buildings used the standard tier height of seven feet, six inches. However, to meet the special curriculum requirements of Colorado State College of Education, which required reading areas or "rooms" in the stacks, the tier height

Figure 22. Convertible stack, Joint University Libraries, 1941, with only every third column bearing the structure's load.

Figure 23. Reading area, Colorado College of Education Library, 1938-39. Note heavy structural columns.

was increased one foot (Figure 23). The spacing of the load-bearing columns was nine feet, six inches, on center in both directions. A principle of column-spacing for future American libraries was clearly beginning to emerge. The spacing must accommodate multiples of the three-foot shelf and the stack range placed four feet six inches on center. For this library the bracket stack was modified. It was hung from steel channels in the ceiling. The shelf-supporting columns actually contacted the floor through small adjustable feet that distributed the weight and prevented lateral movement when the shelves were loaded.

Macdonald, apparently, still had doubts about the desirability of using free-standing stacks in this kind of an installation. By suspending the stacks from the ceiling, the floor was kept free of all anchor plates, thus contributing to flexibility. The decks were of steel, and appear to be a variation on a design patented by Macdonald in April, 1935.[74] His influence generally on this building was graciously (but belatedly) acknowledged by the librarian, Earle Rugg, when he wrote in 1950:

> ...we acknowledge especially the great technical assistance of Mr. Angus Macdonald, President of Snead and Company. We are indebted to him for many of the pioneer conceptions of the structure of our building.[75]

A footnote following this tribute referred to Macdonald's article "A Library of the Future," to be discussed in the next chapter.

Rugg had wanted a particularly flexible building to fit his theories of how the library might relate more closely to the teachers college curriculum. He believed that colleges generally, and teachers colleges in particular,

> rarely [make] any conscious attempt to correlate course and library activity, notwithstanding the fact that the great majority of courses designed to prepare teachers are largely based upon and assume various mature reading, study and research abilities.[76]

Rugg's plan required a well-trained staff of "reading counselors" that advised and worked with students not only in the reading rooms, but in the stacks too, if necessary. The typical carrel arrangement in the stacks was displaced by reading areas with tables and chairs.

In this stack, with only a 200,000-volume capacity, space was provided for 300 readers. Rugg further believed that flexibility to convert spaces from one function to another was very important.[77] Staff work space was also included in the stacks.

While structurally the building might be characterized as "conglomerate," having an old renovated unit, a new high-ceilinged reading room and lobby, and the stack area in between with its spartan finish and relatively low ceilings, it nevertheless is very important from the standpoint of Macdonald's influence on the future library architecture and his plans for Snead and Company. In this building, the stacks were open to all readers, and the provision for about one-third of its reader spaces in the stacks shows a clear breakdown in the segregation of the stack and reader functions, and is a further expression of the librarian's desire for flexibility. Structurally too, the stack was beginning to lose its identity. In addition to the higher ceilings, only one-third of the columns were used to support the structure and book shelves. Unlike other Snead convertible stack columns, Colorado State College employed heavy "I" beams with perforated channels attached to accommodate the lugs of the shelf brackets. The intermediate columns, hung from the ceiling, supported shelves only, and not the structure above.

However, the building lacked the courage of its convictions. Less than a half of the addition was of this new flexible construction. Furthermore, the lack of provision for neatly finishing the stack area gave it a cold, all-steel appearance that looked more like a passageway in a New York subway than a series of inviting reading areas. At the request of Macdonald, Rugg listed other disadvantages: the stairs were a little cramped due to the nine foot (clear) column spacing, and the steel decks were noisy in spite of the asphalt tile covering.[78] However, in another letter, requested by Macdonald for use in planning the Joint University Libraries' stack (also of convertible construction), Rugg stressed the stack's flexibility and the new teaching opportunities made possible by the mixing of books, students, staff and faculty.[79] The true significance of this experiment lies in the influence it had on Ralph Ellsworth and other library planners, particularly those in the college and university field.

It is clear then, that during Macdonald's tenure as president of Snead and Company, Green's design underwent extensive revision. Indeed, with the development of the continuous concrete (or steel) deck and the bracket stack, Green's influence had all but disappeared. Only the tell-tale open- or U-bar shelf, now fitted with a bracket, remained in some installations.

More important, with the convertible stack, Macdonald had achieved a partial fulfillment of the dream he had described in the library literature and before professional audiences five or six years before. A development can be seen, beginning around 1930 with the continuous concrete floor; to his theoretical designs of "A Library of the Future" in 1933; to the convertible stack, illustrated in the highly flexible arrangements of 1939 and 1940; and culminating in his writings and the modular libraries of the post-World War II era. In its more complex form, the convertible stack is the "library of the future" and, with a few modifications, the modular library. It is here that Macdonald made his most important contribution.

Notes

1. Cornelia Macdonald, op. cit., p. 417.

2. Letter from Amy B. Macdonald (Mrs. Angus S. Macdonald) to the author dated May 7, 1967. (In author's files).

3. "Harry Peake Macdonald," New York Times (August 26, 1921), p. 13.

4. Cornelia Macdonald, op. cit., p. 418. Married Amy Barker, October 6, 1935.

5. Angus Snead Macdonald, [Application for Government Glider Contract,...,] p. 1, 1942?

6. Snead and Company, Library Planning..., p. 68.

7. U. S. Patent Office, Official Gazette ... CCVL (December 25, 1917), pp. 892-893.

8. Ibid., CCCXXV (August 18, 1924), p. 521.

9. C. C. Williamson, "Some Unusual Features of South Hall...," A. L. A. Bulletin, XXXI (October 15, 1937), pp. 798-9.

10. Other manufacturers offered a sheet metal standard stack.

11. Snead and Company, Snead Bookstacks, 1940, p. 15.

12. U. S. Patent Office, Official Gazette, CDLV (June 18, 1935), pp. 667-8.

13. Snead and Company, Snead Bookstacks..., (1931), pp. 5-6.

14. Interview with Keyes D. Metcalf, June 16, 1967.

15. Snead and Company, Library Planning..., p. 72.

16. Letter of Macdonald to Donald B. Gilchrist, May 25, 1926.

17. Macdonald to W. C. Bond, Superintendent of the Library of Congress, September 19, 1928.

18. U. S. Patent Office, op. cit., CDLI (February 12, 1935), p. 447.

19. Angus S. Macdonald, "Library Lighting," Library Journal, LVI (March 1, 1931), pp. 203-10.

20. Ibid., p. 208.

21. U. S. Patent Office, op. cit., CDXVI (March 29, 1932), p. 1280.

22. William S. Snead, "The Bookstack Tower of the Sterling Memorial Library," Yale University Library Gazette, V (July, 1931), pp. 77-80.

23. Joseph Wheeler, Letter to the author, dated July 30, 1966.

24. Dean M. Warren, "Library Lighting--A Scientific Problem," Library Journal, LIX (March 15, 1934), p. 249.

25. Carrol Preston Baber, "A Study of Four University Library Buildings," (unpublished Master of Arts thesis in Library Science, University of Illinois, 1927), pp. 50, 66.

26. Frank K. Walter, "Random Notes on Metal Book Stacks," Library Journal, LII (April 1, 1928), p. 299.

27. Art Metal Construction Company, "Catalogue" Sweet's Catalogue File (Architectural) ..., (1931), p. C4214.

28. Frank K. Walter, op. cit., p. 297.

29. Baber, op. cit., p. 67.

30. Snead and Company, Snead Bookstacks, 1940, p. 24.

31. University of Illinois Library, The Library Building (Urbana, Illinois: The University, 1929), [p. 7].

32. Correspondence between the Library and Snead and Company, August 28, 1929, and May 15, 1930, and invoice of September 10, 1930. (Photocopies in author's files).

33. Snead and Company, ["Catalogue"], Sweet's Catalogue File (Architectural), (1934), p. C391.

34. Snead and Company, Snead Bookstacks and Stack Room Equipment. (New York: Snead and Co., 1931), p. 14a.

35. "Notes on the Construction of the Charles Deering Library," Charles Deering Library, Northwestern University, Bulletin, no. 2 (June, 1932), p. 4.

36. U. S. Patent Office, op. cit., CDXVII (April 12, 1932), p. 572, and CDXLIII (June 5, 1934), p. 85.

37. Ibid., XDIII (August 2, 1938), pp. 49-50.

38. Snead and Company, Snead Bookstacks, (1940), p. 23.

39. Snead and Company, ["Catalogue"], Sweet's Catalogue..., (1934), p. C391.

40. Angus Snead Macdonald, "The Library Bookstack; Capacities and Details" in Joseph L. Wheeler and Alfred Morton Githens, The American Public Library Building... (New York: Charles Scribner's Sons, 1941), p. 426.

41. Letter of Angus Snead Macdonald to Donald B. Gilchrist, May 28, 1926, pp. 1-2.

42. Macdonald to Bond, April 28, 1928, letters to Herbert Putnam, Librarian of Congress; James M. White, Supervising Architect, University of Illinois and others, May 3, 1928. In the letter to White he urged that the American Society of Heating and Ventilating Engineers be represented.

43. W. E. Emley, "Ventilation of Book Stacks and Its Effect on Books," 10p., unpublished report (in Macdonald papers).

44. George K. Burgess, Director, National Bureau of Standards, to Members of the Committee on Library Book Stacks, February 16, 1929, (in Macdonald papers).

45. See U.S. National Bureau of Standards, "Miscellaneous Publications," nos. 128, 140, 142, 144, 154, 1931-1937. The research was also reported in a number of articles in various journals.

46. B. W. Scribner, "The Preservation of Records in Libraries," Library Quarterly, IV (July, 1934), p. 371. Lydenberg was included in the 1928 Committee at Macdonald's request, letter of Macdonald to W. C. Bond, September 19, 1928.

47. U. S. Patent Office, op. cit., CDLXI (December 24, 1935), p. 797.

48. Ibid., CDLXIV (March 17, 1936), pp. 597-8.

49. Robert H. Muller, "College and University Library Buildings, 1929-1949," College and Research Libraries, XII (July, 1951), p. 264.

50. Robert S. Orr, "Financing and Philanthropy in the Building of Academic Libraries Constructed Between 1919-1958," (unpublished Master's thesis in library science, Western Reserve University, 1959), p. 73. (Muller's list arranged by year.)

51. Letter of A. S. Macdonald to Monsignor Eugene Tisserant, Librarian, Vatican Library, January 9, 1934.

52. Macdonald to Tisserant, March 22, 1934, p. 1, (microfilm copy in author's files).

53. Macdonald to Tisserant, July 23, 1936, p. 1. The branch plant was actually established in Orange, Virginia, not Maryland, although a site in Maryland did receive consideration.

54. Macdonald to Tisserant, November 3, 1936.

55. Allowing for some variation in classification, about 160 academic, 90 public and 80 special and school libraries. Snead and Company, Snead Bookstacks, pp. 38-41.

56. American Library Directory, 1942..., comp. by Karl Brown, (New York: R. R. Bowker, 1942), p. 7. 7,800 public, 1,600 academic libraries.

57. Based on a comparison of the Snead list and the list of libraries in Helen Margaret Reynolds "University Library Buildings in the United States, 1890-1939," (unpublished Master's dissertation, Library School, University of Illinois, 1946).

58. Robert H. Muller, op. cit., pp. 262-263.

59. World Almanac and Book of Facts for 1942, ed. by E. Eastman Irvine, (New York: World-Telegram, 1942), p. 596.

60. Interview with Donald L. Bean, July 20, 1967.

61. Snead and Company, Snead Bookstacks..., (1931), p. 25.

62. A fair share might be thought of as one-fourth of the library stack installations or one-fourth of the dollar volume, since there appears to have been at least three active competitors at any one time.

63. William I. Fletcher, "Library Buildings," American Architect and Building News, XXIV (December 1, 1888), p. 198.

64. Bernard R. Green, "The Building of the Library of Congress," op. cit., p. 631.

65. Snead and Company, Library Planning, pp. 153, 161.

66. Bernard R. Green, "Library Buildings and Bookstacks," Library Journal, XXXI (Conference no., 1906), p. 55.

67. Bernard R. Green, "A Library Book Stack in the Dark," Snead and Company, Library Planning..., 1915, pp. 118-9.

68. Snead and Company, Library Planning, p. 216.

69. Joseph L. Wheeler and Alfred M. Githens, op. cit., p. 320.

70. Ibid., p. 144.

71. Angus Snead Macdonald, "Bookstacks," Columbia University Library, South Hall (New York: The Library, 1935), pp. 39-40.

72. U. S. Patent Office, op. cit., DX (January 2, 1940), p. 119.

73. Martin A. Roberts, The Annex of the Library of Congress (n. p., n. d.). Reprinted from the Annual Report of the Librarian of Congress for fiscal year ending June 30, 1937.

74. U. S. Patent Office, op. cit., VIID (August 2, 1938), pp. 49-50.

75. Earle Rugg, "Planning a College Library," American School and University, 21st ed. (New York: American School Publishing Company, 1950), p. 173.

76. Earle Rugg, "A Library Centered Program of Teacher Education," College and Research Libraries, 11 (December, 1940), p. 42.

77. Ibid., p. 43.

78. Letter of Earl Rugg to Angus Snead Macdonald, February 14, 1939, carbon copy in the Colorado State College Library files.

79. Rugg to Macdonald, June 4, 1940, carbon copy in Colorado State College Library files.

Chapter V

Macdonald Develops a Theory of
Library Planning and Construction

In March, 1933, Macdonald received a letter from Helge Kragemo, Förstebibliotekar of the University of Oslo, which announced:

> On October the 20th this year the director of our University Library, Mr. Wilhelm Munthe, completes his 50th year.
>
> On this occasion some of his colleagues here and abroad would like to present him a volume published in his honor. [1]

Kragemo, as editor, went on to invite Macdonald to contribute an article "on any subject and in any language." Macdonald accepted the invitation and elected the topic, "Library Architecture of the Future." Further correspondence settled details of deadlines, page size and illustration.

Before going further, it may be helpful to provide the reader with some background on the broader social events that were, undoubtedly, on Macdonald's mind. When Kragemo's invitation arrived, America was, of course, in the depths of the great depression. The spectacular stock market decline that began in October, 1929, did not reach bottom until July, 1933. One-fourth of the nation's labor force was unemployed, more than 1400 banks had failed in 1932, and more continued to fail in the early months of 1933, before a bank holiday was declared. General business volume was less than half of normal. [2] As Harold Faulkner, an economic historian, has written, "it would be difficult to exaggerate the utter economic collapse and the dark pessimism of the nation when Franklin D. Roosevelt became President on March 4, 1933."[3]

The construction industry and the architect were especially hard hit. Burchard indicates that almost 4,000 architectural firms failed. The 5,000 firms that survived "lived to see the end of an era of plenty. They were forced to reflect upon a wider social basis for architecture."[4] The splendors of Greece and Rome seemed suddenly out of place in American architecture. The depression gave a new opportunity for critical voices to be heard.

The Plight of Libraries

Librarians too suffered from this "pause" in the economy's expansion. As already indicated in the previous chapter, library construction nearly came to a halt in the mid-1930's. Even more serious, "budgets were reduced and services were curtailed. Branches were closed in many cases, and bookmobiles were discontinued, or services to children reduced."[5] Unemployment among librarians in July, 1933, was estimated at 2,000 to 2,500.[6] Some argued that most of these were young, inexperienced persons, and there is some indication that at least 20 per cent of that number would have been unemployed under any circumstances. Nevertheless, the profession was concerned and cries were heard to limit library school enrollment.[7]

Library Journal reported in 1932 that the Fall River, Massachusetts, Public Library budget had been cut 40 per cent,[8] and the Rochester, New York Public Library, 30 per cent, but few seem to have suffered as greatly as the Chicago Public Library. With genuine despair, the librarian, Carl Roden, described his plight in Library Journal. He had, apparently for some time, feared that the library, as an "unessential" service, might be "eliminated entirely" and confessed that:

> I have heard it said, and seen it written, that the present economic situation offers the public libraries of this country a large field of new opportunities for usefulness. I have even heard it said that the public library had, or should have, an important role to play... in the solution of the crisis that envelopes the world. I admit that after some thought, I have been totally unable to discover any clue to the trails leading to either of these fields.[9]

At the same time, public libraries were forced to cope with an unprecedented volume of use. The unemployed flocked to the libraries, seeking either recreational reading or books that would improve their vocational skills.[10] While this brought to the library a somewhat broader cross section of the population, the Syracuse, New York, Public Library reported that the largest occupational group among its registered borrowers were students.[11] Although the enforced leisure of the depression caused concern for many, it was recognized that leisure generally was a product of an industrialized society, and could be a blessing as well. "The most important thing that our industrialism will give us will be Leisure," said the Literary Digest, quoting from a book by C. C. Furnas[12] of Yale's Sheffield Scientific School. What man was to do with this leisure, how he was to keep out of trouble, were questions raised but not answered by Furnas. Instead, he "nominated" the educational system to provide the solution.[13] This same issue of the Literary Digest, incidentally, included an article on the Vatican Library with pictures supplied by Snead and Company, and quoting Angus Macdonald.[14]

The President of the American Library Association, Harry Miller Lydenberg, suggested, in October, 1933, in a speech before the first general session of the association's annual conference, that man's constructive use of this new leisure should be the library's concern.[15] In reporting on this conference, Library Journal stated "Throughout all the sessions this note of leisure and the library was sounded."[16]

There have always been those who decried America's excessively materialistic society, but the depression provided an especially attentive audience. David Lawrence charged in a radio speech that the world had passed through a "decade of debauchery," that "the worship of gold begot a reckless indifference to all codes, corporate or personal, in an orgy of unrestrained sin."[17] Macdonald, in much more restrained tones, observed:

> I ... find our people taking a more serious view of life than has been the case for many years. Many feel that our highly commercialized civilization is distinctly on trial and much will have to be done before it can be fully justified.[18]

A Library of the Future

All of these themes, the depression, leisure time, materialism, the social justification of architecture, the narrowness of the public library's popular appeal, and a new and more vital role for the library, were concerns of the time which found their way into Macdonald's thoughts. These thoughts, expressed in an article entitled "A Library of the Future," were published in a festschrift for Wilhelm Munthe in October, 1933. [19] It was a time that encouraged experimentation with social and public institutions. It is probably not entirely accidental that this article should appear in the same year as the inauguration of Franklin D. Roosevelt as president. Much of the same desire for change that elected Roosevelt can be found in Macdonald's writing.

Precisely why Macdonald should have received the letter from Kragemo, inviting him to contribute to the festschrift, is not clear. Only five of the 41 contributors were Americans. They included Herbert Putnam (Library of Congress), Andrew Keogh (Yale University), J. C. M. Hanson (University of Chicago), William Warner Bishop (University of Michigan), and of course Macdonald. All except Macdonald were distinguished library directors. Hanson, Bishop and Macdonald had in common their participation in the rejuvenation of the Vatican Library.

Macdonald had made a trip to Norway several years before, an indirect result of the Vatican experience, and apparently was befriended by Munthe. Macdonald had also contributed an article to Library Journal in January, 1932, in which he described the University of Oslo Library, and Munthe's plans to expand the building. [20] Munthe was in New York in early October, 1933, apparently unaware of the preparations for the festschrift. Macdonald acted as Munthe's weekend host at his home in Connecticut. [21] It appears, then, that Munthe and Macdonald not only knew each other but were friends. Macdonald also seems to have acquired a certain amount of prestige in Europe as a result of Snead and Company's management of the stack installation at the Vatican Library. [22]

Macdonald's article, as it appeared in October, 1933, took

the reader on an imaginary tour of a public library of the future.
In an earlier, unpublished draft in Macdonald's files, dated August
24, 1933, the future was defined as 25 years hence, or about 1958.
Upon the recommendation of one critic, who reviewed the manuscript,
he dropped the specific time reference. Another critic, Milton J.
Ferguson, of the Brooklyn Public Library, suggested he "end positively." This advice he took in revising the final paragraphs.
There is a certain buoyant quality about this and other writings by
Macdonald--a certain overstatement perhaps, a lack of scholarly
reserve, a "Sunday Supplement" approach that probably was deeply
ingrained from long years of selling Snead products. One critic
of the manuscript actually suggested placing the article in a "Sunday paper."[23]

This article, which has been described "as a turning point
in library architecture,"[24] is one of Macdonald's best known contributions, and may be examined from at least three viewpoints. There
are those features of the article which concern the architecture and
furniture of the future library, the most accurate and important
features; those which broadly concern the library's role and administration; and, finally, those features which, especially when
related to other writings, provide a glimpse of Macdonald's ideas
and values in general.

An Analysis of the Article

Macdonald begins by criticizing the New Deal's attempts to
solve the economic crisis. It is a case "of applying more materialism as a cure for too much materialism."[25] The final outcome of
the depression was difficult to foresee but he was convinced that
the industrial base of our society would remain, bringing with it
much more leisure time for everyone. In order to provide the
average man with an alternative to materialism, to "aimless automobiling," he proposed that libraries "so demonstrate their social
value that they will be given equal consideration with public schools
instead of being looked upon as mere luxuries for the book-loving
few."[26] In order to accomplish this, the library was to be given
far greater financial support, staffed by a team of experts compa-

Macdonald Develops a Theory

rable to university professors, and provided with equipment (e. g., drafting machines and a pantograph) and samples, as well as books. The library he pictured was used far more actively by business and professional men. Books were also to be used in relation to vocational and avocational materials of all kinds. The library might be called a "resource center" for the community. The purpose was to further democracy through a happier, better informed citizenry. This is Macdonald's answer to Roden's despair, and a far more worthy project, in his eyes, for "pump-priming" the economy than endless highway construction programs.

    Macdonald obviously enjoyed speculating about the future. As the reader "tours" this library, he witnesses the establishment of a Nuclear Power Department and observes "calculating machines" in the Mathematics Department that appear to be computers. If some of these things have found their way into the library, they have usually done so in a way different from that envisioned by Macdonald. The 50 subject departments, the staff of experts, the park location, the means of financing have all proved to be little more than speculation. This is an area where Macdonald had least experience and least opportunity to influence the future course of events.

    The elaborate roof garden and restaurant he pictured has not generally found favor either. Use of the roof for gardens and reading terraces is a favorite Macdonald theme. He had suggested a reading terrace for the roof of the Sterling Library's stack tower at Yale,[27] and incorporated the idea in his own home at Orange, Virginia.

    His comments on the architecture and furniture of the building, however, are another matter. They are most perceptive and reveal a man who has given a great deal of thought to the way libraries function. Basically, he believed that the library could not assume a more vital role in society because it was inhibited by an architectural straight jacket:

> We must admit at the outset that the use of traditional library architecture will not solve the problem. It has three fundamental faults: lack of intimate charm,

> inadequate accommodation, and narrow class interest... .
> Our library buildings still follow traditions of regal display at the expense of utility and good reading conditions; of chained books in their arrangements for close supervision; and of student class exclusiveness in their failure to appeal to the man in the street.[28]

Placed near this passage is an illustration of the enormous (and beautiful) reading room of the New York Public Library. This room (even though supported by Snead stacks) was a frequent target of Macdonald, as an example of wasted space and "regal display."

Macdonald sought more intimate surroundings for the reader. He favored much lower ceilings, small tables, lounge chairs, secluded alcoves, and reading areas where the reader could find a measure of privacy approximating a nicely furnished home. For the serious library user, access to the book stack was total. Reading areas and stack spaces were mixed throughout. The economy of such an arrangement in reduced square foot costs seemed obvious. In addition, Macdonald proposed the elimination of most "interior dividing walls and the total absence of any light courts, skylights, and other difficult expedients to obtain natural light."[29] The building was to be illuminated by "softly glowing tubes on the ceiling [which] give out light of such quality that we cannot tell where the natural daylight ends and the made daylight begins."[30] The ventilation system provided totally conditioned air of a quality comparable to "a fine autumn day." Careful attention was also given to sound conditioning to avoid the distractions of the large reading room.

Apparently three-fourths of the building was made up of "interchangeable stack space" supported by "slender stack columns spaced about nine feet apart in both directions." Tier height was increased from seven feet, six inches, deck to deck, to eight feet, "just enough to prevent such spaces ... from seeming oppressively low." This implied a thin stack deck of about four inches. With the exception of the 25 per cent of the space devoted to the lobby, a popular two-tier high reading room, mechanical equipment, etc., all the building was composed of these units of space nine feet by nine feet by eight feet. All of these spaces could be used by readers, staff or for the storage of books. This flexible unit of space, which he later called a "module," was to become a basic principle of library planning.

While it is apparent that some of the basic engineering problems had not yet been thought through in detail by Macdonald, all had known solutions at the time. Perhaps most startling is the confidence he placed in artificial illumination and ventilation, particularly the glowing tubes in the ceiling. Fluorescent lighting was not actively developed in this country until 1935 and not introduced commercially until 1938.[31] However, as Burchard points out regarding the Chicago World's Fair of 1933, "the buildings were ... windowless, they assured the people of the advancements in interior lighting and filtered ventilation; gaily colored, they were ultra-modern and glorified mercury and sodium tube lighting."[32] The July, 1933, issue of Architectural Forum was devoted to this Exposition, including material on the lighting.[33] Also, the July issue of Scientific American in 1932, which carried an article by Macdonald on the Vatican Library,[34] included notice of a sodium vapor lamp.[35] Information about advances in artificial ventilation was also readily available, and in fact, Snead and Company shelving and partitions were being used at this very time for the air conditioned stack in the Butler Library at Columbia University (described in the previous chapter).

Macdonald, of course, had had a great deal of experience in building stacks, and the "convertible" stacks Snead and Company erected later in the decade at Colorado State College, Rockford College and elsewhere, bear a strong resemblance, structurally, to the library of the future. The slender columns shown in the article's illustrations were probably not heavy enough to carry the electrical conduit and ventilating ducts. Just how the air was to be distributed throughout the many floors or tiers of the building was not made clear, nor does it really matter. Macdonald's chief points were that the building, in order to permit the library to assume a more vital role, must be much more comfortable and flexible than in the past, and hopefully, more economical as well. Unlike most previous critics, he offered the beginnings of a plan of how this might be accomplished.

Of Macdonald the man, the article reveals little, although it is probably his longest literary effort. Certain statements are obvious, such as the remarks about "too much materialism," "aimless automobiling," and his opinion of traditional monumental architecture in libraries. Other remarks, especially when related to other facts about the man, reveal a person who is continually excited by new things and ideas (the "glowing tubes," the "capacious wrap checking machine"). There is also a strong streak of Jeffersonianism within him, which is only hinted at in the article. For example, the view from the roof of the library that interests him most is not of an impressive skyline or busy airport, but of "the park, suburb, farmland and forest covered hills... ." While he mentions, elsewhere, "a fine view over the city," it is only the view of the country that is given any detail or depth. Near the close of the article he refers to the importance of reading and education in developing "human individuality ... one of the best balance wheels possible for the successful operation of a democracy."[36]

While plans were being made for the article to be published in Europe, Macdonald also approached Library Journal. Although the editor, Miss Bertine E. Weston, had no suggestions for improving the article, she had, as the correspondence reveals, a great deal of difficulty accommodating the article's length to the periodical's publication schedule.[37] Macdonald cut 67 lines from the article as it appeared in the festschrift version, and it was finally published in the December 1st and 15th issues.[38] All illustrations but one were eliminated from this revision. Macdonald ordered 500 copies of reprints of the article with most of the illustrations restored.[39]

Actually, this was not Macdonald's first effort as a critic of library architecture. In March, 1931, he wrote disapprovingly of library lighting in Library Journal and, in the June, 1932 number of Architectural Forum, he charged that "the chief cause for insufficient lighting was the apparent sacrifice of utility for beauty," and recommended greater reliance on artificial light and an end of light courts.[40] Precisely what effect his writings had at the time is difficult to determine. Library building generally declined sharply during the middle 1930's, and those buildings that were built made only minor innovations. However, the English publication, Year's Work in Librarianship, gave "A Library of the Future" considerable attention in 1935. In its "buildings" section it began by complaining about the lack of a characteristic, functional architecture for libraries, and then continued:

> Nowhere in the literature under review, has this idea been more forcibly expressed than by Mr. Angus Snead Macdonald in a Library Journal article. Mr. Macdonald has for so long been one of the major prophets of good library architecture that there could be no more appropriate opening than to refer to this article.... The "Library of the Future" is an imaginative and yet practical vision of library development.[41]

The author then devoted two pages to a review of Macdonald's ideas.

"Some Engineering Developments..."

Closely related to "A Library of the Future" of 1933, which suffered from a lack of truly adequate illustrations in the festschrift version and practically none in Library Journal, was a well illustrated talk he gave before the American Library Association's Buildings Round Table in June, 1934. This talk, later published in the Association's Bulletin,[42] was illustrated with 23 slides made from the skillful, even dramatic, drawings of Alfred Morton Githens, a well-known library architect. The Githens' drawings appear in Appendix 1. The secretary of the Round Table approved of Macdonald's presentation as "perhaps the most significant talk" of the session.[43]

In this case Macdonald was given what amounted to a program for a teachers college library, and for this he and Githens adapted the type of construction outlined in "A Library of the Future." In some respects this is a more useful article because it limits itself more closely to library architecture, particularly when combined with the unpublished illustrations. The building was composed of "flexible units" (not yet modules) defined by the floor, the ceiling, and the columns on nine feet by nine feet centers. The same eight-foot floor to floor dimension and four-inch deck were envisioned as in "A Library of the Future." These units could be manipulated in all three dimensions. When added interior height was desired for dignity and spaciousness, columns and deck might be omitted. The economy of this type of construction permitted greater investment in better lighting, ventilation, and more comfortable, colorful furniture. All this is familiar from the earlier article. The columns were hollow in order to carry air and electrical services. They also supported book shelves, movable partitions, tables and, as revealed in the drawings, many of the luminaires.

These hollow columns were to become a trademark of Macdonald's most frequently advocated version of the modular plan. At this time, he limited the distance between them to only nine feet in both directions. This dimension, of course, was based on the three-foot shelf and the four-foot, six-inch stack range spacing. It is, essentially, the dimension of the convertible stack which was being developed by Snead and Company at this time. If the economy of this construction was to be realized, the floors must remain thin and the ceiling height low. This, in turn, forced the columns to serve as the ventilating units. There was no room for the space-consuming and expensive overhead ductwork. Without overhead ducts, we can imagine that the need for a close spacing of the hollow columns was virtually a necessity in order to ventilate the large interior area broken by partitions, stacks and furniture.

An examination of Githens' drawings shows how cramped the nine feet by nine feet column spacing actually was for the multiple purposes of the entire library. In the classrooms, on the mezzanine floor, for example, the spacing was increased to 18 feet by omitting a column in the center. In other areas too, such as the conference room, a column was removed from the regular pattern. Presumably, in order to avoid the inconvenience of the columns in some areas, the columns were enveloped by the tables and served as the latter's support.

However, the major break with the stack construction is

Macdonald Develops a Theory

seen in the large area on the main floor set aside for the browsing room, lobby area and reserve book room. This area is two tiers or about 16 feet high. The large reference room on the second floor, with its clerestory, also uses the larger column spacing. From these drawings it is apparent that Macdonald's idea is not nearly so revolutionary. He was not actually advocating a uniform ceiling height of less than eight feet. Approximately one-half of the main and second floors had relatively high ceilings. His use of a mezzanine floor suggests more the public library of the post-World War II period than the modern teachers' college library. The closed stack, reserve book room, and certain other features were undoubtedly specified in the hypothetical problem given to Macdonald.

Many years later, Githens summed up these articles of 1933 and 1934 as follows:

> ... both essays [decried] the complication of library buildings, the rigidity of interior masonry walls that defied re-arrangement, and above all the absurdity of vast and lofty reading rooms, whose readers would much prefer sitting in the bookstack among the books: therefore, it would be logical to build the library as one great bookstack... elastic in its uses, convertible, flexible and... economical. [44]

World War II Intervenes

For the remainder of the decade he wrote no more about the "flexible unit" plan, although there is evidence that he continued to talk about it informally and at least once gave a formal talk on the subject. [45] Since most of the libraries built in the late 1930's and early 1940's continued to follow the traditional architectural patterns requiring separate stack and reading rooms, he began to despair that his ideas would ever be adopted. It was not until after World War II that he wrote again and then there was such a barrage of articles, speeches, informal talks and meetings that one wonders how he found time for anything else.

But before 1945 the war absorbed all his energies. He threw himself into it with a genuine, patriotic sense of duty. The need to defeat Hitler was a responsibility he seems to have taken personally. Fear of another war he recognized and expressed as early as 1936:

> Your foreboding remarks about danger from Germany serve to confirm my own convictions. It seems only a question of time as to how soon a new and colossally disastrous war will start. Personally, I cannot defend this country's attitude and action toward world affairs. Looking back on it now, we should never have gone into the European war unless we were prepared to take a similarly strong stand in securing the peace that followed... .[46]

In March, 1941, after reporting that he was hard at work on a pontoon bridge contract for the Army, he added:

> I think our people realize that essentially human rights are at stake which are worth every sacrifice to preserve and that the forces of moral distintegration must be checked and ultimately destroyed. Hitler is the anti-Christ and cannot be tolerated by a free people.[47]

The war effort at times was an all consuming activity. He wrote to Ellsworth in 1943 that he was working "60 to 70 hours a week on our war jobs."[48] A few months earlier he had described the war activities of Snead and Company for the stockholders as follows:

> The year 1942 has been one of change and readjustment brought about through entire stoppage of the company's peacetime business by Government order and conversion to a 100 percent war basis. This left considerable amounts of working capital tied up in inventories and other unused assets... .
>
> During part of the year the company continued to make with great success aluminum alloy, ten-ton pontoon bridges for the U.S. Army Engineer Corps. This work has fallen off... in order to conserve aluminum for airplanes.
>
> During the year 1942 the company developed at its Orange, Virginia plant, facilities and personnel for making aluminum alloy aeronautical sub-assemblies. The Jersey City plant has been converted to the fabrication of steel sub-assemblies for aircraft carriers, escort ships and other marine work.[49]

Iowa and Further Development of the Modular Library

In the late fall of 1943, Macdonald's interest in libraries was stirred again by a series of letters from Ralph Ellsworth. The latter was about to become Director of Libraries at the State

University of Iowa and was seeking help in planning a new building. In this fascinating exchange of letters between Macdonald and Ellsworth, extending over a period of several years, the form, typical of many modern academic libraries, is gradually revealed.

The mood in experimenting with the college curriculum and methods of teaching, which is described in Chapter VII, was also present on the campus at Iowa. Iowa was hoping to carry out a number of changes, particularly, as Ellsworth described it, in the instructional methods used in the "Lower Division." These changes were to have an important effect on the library, and hence the library building must be considerably different from the libraries of the past. In his letter of November 27, 1943, Ellsworth pictures a library that includes space for advisors of the Lower Division teaching departments and their offices, "for consultation and small group meetings...[and for] group demonstrations." He then adds:

> The central part of the floor would be divided between tables and stacks.... I am assuming, of course, that the nine foot columns would exist everywhere and that the ceiling heights throughout the building would be eight foot six inches except possibly in the all-service area.[50]

Such a library would look very much like the Snead convertible stack in the Colorado State College of Education Library, described in the previous chapter, except for a neater interior finish.

In a letter dated February 18, 1944, it is evident that Macdonald is suggesting a hollow ventilating and supporting column for Iowa with a spacing of 10 feet by 10 feet on center. The extra foot was undoubtedly necessary to allow nine feet or three shelves clear between the relatively large box columns. In this letter, he assures Ellsworth that, based on a report by Charles Leopold, a ventilating and lighting engineer occasionally employed by Snead and Company, the columns would be capable of carrying an adequate supply of air.

Then, on July 19, 1944, Ellsworth reported:

> As you undoubtedly know, we had Mr. Githens and Mr. Leopold out here at the same time for a three day conference... we are keeping the essentials of the unit plan, although we had to do considerable adapting. In the first

place, we realized that to get a ceiling fixture that would
be flush with the ceiling we would have to give up the
idea of a four or six inch floor. We are all inclined to
agree that in a building as big as ours, it would be an
aesthetic tragedy to have the light fixtures protrude... .
In the second place, we found that the ten by ten unit
with hollow columns carrying the air would not work very
well in this big a building, primarily because... it would
be difficult to achieve any economy of arrangement... .

This led us to... the idea of running rows of columns
twenty feet apart in one direction and ten feet apart in
the other.... . These columns would be supporting columns
only.[51]

Ellsworth then went on to describe the proposed location of vertical
ventilation shafts along a center corridor from which horizontal
ducts between the floor and the ceiling would inject fresh air and
exhaust the vitiated air.

This change in the column spacing and the ceiling to floor
measurement was a major concession to the reality of designing a
building for multiple use. The economical stack structure was
simply too limited to accommodate all of the activities of a modern
library within the generally accepted limits of comfort and convenience. The record is not precise as to which man, Ellsworth,
Leopold or Githens, was responsible for this major change. It
is, however, part of the long term trend toward an ever larger
column spacing. Although the finished building did not incorporate
Macdonald's version of the hollow column, its small, separate
ventilating ducts were fitted against the columns achieving, thereby,
a "vertical" method of air distribution and many of the space economies advocated by Macdonald. Except for a somewhat lower ceiling, the building frame took on, at this point, a greater resemblance
to the modern warehouse or office building than to its stack progenitor.

"New Possibilities in Library Planning"

Macdonald was not content with the 10 feet by 20 feet column
spacing and separate duct work. In August, 1944 he wrote to Ellsworth reporting that new drawings had been made which were "a
considerable departure from the construction which he discussed

last January in Iowa City."[52] At a meeting in New York in the autumn of 1944 with Ellsworth and the Iowa architects, Keffer and Jones, Macdonald recommended a system of hollow, box columns of welded steel plate, box beams and hollow steel floor pans. The column spacing he proposed was 19 feet by 13 feet six inches on center. Shortly after this meeting Ellsworth, realizing that the basic plan was becoming fixed, stated, "before too much time has elapsed, the whole idea should receive publicity."[53] Ellsworth's literary contributions at this time will be discussed in another chapter; Macdonald's, based on this and other experiences produced another major article, "New Possibilities in Library Planning," which was not published until December, 1945.[54]

Nineteen forty-five, of course, saw an end of World War II. It also witnessed considerable dislocation as American industry shifted from the production of war material to products for the peaceful consumer. The effect of the War's sudden end on Snead and Company and Macdonald was unexpected:

> On VJ-Day we were on a 100% war basis with $5,000,000 worth of contracts and nearly 600 employees. Three days afterwards all the war work was cancelled and we had to let out about 500 people. It hurt like hell to have to do it but orders were to stop work absolutely, we couldn't drive another rivet or even put a final coat of paint on pontoons that were otherwise ready for shipment.[55]

However, this letter concluded with an optimistic view of the peacetime business just ahead for Snead and Company

Unlike "A Library of the Future" which incorporated comments on many of the social and economic problems of the day, "New Possibilities in Library Planning" made reference only to the fact that "librarians of this country are now undertaking the most important library building program ever financed..."[56] The victory, the problems of reconstruction, the formation of a world government, all of these and many other problems were ignored as Macdonald wrote a shorter and a more tightly reasoned article.

If "A Library of the Future" seemed to have little effect at the time it was published, "New Possibilities in Library Planning" received immediate attention. The Library of Congress Information Bulletin noted that the writers in The Year's Work in Librarianship seemed most interested "in Fremont Rider's microcards and Angus Snead Macdonald's modular construction,"[57] and Year's Work itself observed:

> Although mention has already been made... of Angus Snead Macdonald's article, "New Possibilities in Library Planning," it is necessary to quote at some length from this important contribution because practically all the papers on library planning and most of the more important projects for new buildings are influenced by its proposals.[58]

The article contained many of Macdonald's familiar criticisms of the traditional library buildings, their frozen, monumental rooms, their separate, inaccessible bookstacks, their expense and lack of comfort for the reader and staff, and finally, of course, their lack of flexibility. But the article also contained a number of new ideas concerning his recently developed loft or warehouse frame, with hollow columns, girders and floors. It was well illustrated and it introduced the reader to the term "modular." It also contained a very clear, simple statement which defined the "modular system" as:

> ... [a] system of construction wherein the cubage between the exterior walls, foundations and roof is divided in equal, rectangular prisms of space, bordered on top and bottom by floors and ceilings and on the edges by structural columns. Aside from the columns, there would be nothing to interfere with the free use of space except for such things as main stairways, elevators and lavatories.[59]

Macdonald believed that the module or bay could be square or rectangular, and that column spacing should be based on "whatever best suits the site," although this dimension should be kept between 18 and 24 feet for reasons of economy and adaptability.[60]

He also believed that ceilings should be flat and that great precision should be employed in construction to permit partitions and shelving to be moved from one location to another with minimum difficulty. The article went on to propose a building that would be well lighted (35 foot candles), and fully air-conditioned, freeing the design of libraries from their dependence on unreliable natural light and ventilation.[61] These regular prisms of space, when combined with "dry" or movable walls, low ceilings, adequate artificial light, ventilation and other services, formed the basis of the modular plan. He believed such a system would permit greater use of "very accurate mass production methods" and would free the architect and librarian from compromise plans that forced them "to guess the future" instead of concentrating on the present. On a somewhat personal note, he added:

> And finally, with apologies to the shades of my ancestors for the admission, there will be no multi-tier book stacks! Instead, the books... will be shelved in single-tier movable stacks close to the points of greatest use... .[62]

In this article Macdonald did not fail to point out that this type of construction had been used in other building types for some time. However, its application to libraries offered "new possibilities" and those aspects of the system that combined the ventilating and structural elements in the same building members were, in part, an original idea.

Other Writings

In retrospect, Library Journal apparently considered this article of prime importance in shaping libraries built after World War II, for on December 1, 1955, ten years later, it published an "interview" with Macdonald. In the interview, he was asked to "re-evaluate 'modular construction'."[63] He pointed out that:

> Modular construction... involves more than rows of regularly spaced columns, and some confusion that developed... The term is not purely physical; it should be directed by a philosophy which aims toward the removal of constrictions on library functions and provides for future expansion.[64]

On the basis of experience he questioned the use of columns spaced as closely as 18 feet because "this results in an excessive number of columns" and this space, he found, did not subdivide well. Instead he now advocated modules as large as 27 feet square, exactly three times as large as his original proposals in the 1930's. This interview concluded Macdonald's pronouncements on library architecture, and was actually based on an article he had written in March, 1955, for the American Library Association's Library Building Plans Institute.[65] He wrote to Joseph Wheeler, in the summer of 1956,

after founding Everdure, Inc.:
> I felt that I had shot my bolt in the library field and wanted to take up something new and challenging.... On that account I do not intend to write anything more about libraries, at least not in the immediate future. [66]

At this time Angus Macdonald was almost 73 years old.

Apparently he kept his word, for he wrote no more, at least for publication, about libraries. In the ten-year period 1945 to 1955 he had contributed at least eight articles plus one privately published pamphlet. All of these articles dealt with some aspect of library architecture and most made mention, at least, of the modular plan. One of these articles, "Building Design for Library Management," is one of his better efforts. It originated with an invitation from Ralph Shaw, the issue editor of Library Trends. He then used the material he had prepared for this article in a speech before the Canadian Library Association in the summer of 1953, and in slightly revised form it was published in Library Trends a few months later. [67] It is much more general in scope than his other writings, dealing with virtually all aspects of the library building. It contains the familiar criticism of traditional library architecture, and makes a number of practical suggestions ranging from the advantages of a written building program to the disadvantages of wall shelving. It represents a life-time of thought and experience concerning libraries. It is also important because it reveals a further development in his thinking about the modular plan. In this paragraph he describes three types of construction: (1) the conventional plan with reading rooms with high ceilings and a separate stack room, which results in wasted space in small rooms and corridors; (2) modular construction in which "book storage is somewhat more costly than with multi-tier stacks"; and (3) a combination of the two in which part of the building floors would be 16 feet high and the remaining "50-60 percent" composed of multi-tier, convertible stacks. The stack area would accommodate the book storage functions as well as small reading areas, and study and work rooms. "The contrast between the high- and the low-ceiling sections is attractive, and the over-all

Macdonald Develops a Theory 137

square foot cost of the building is moderate."[68]

In part, he probably considered the compromise desirable because the economy of the bookstack type of construction had been lost in many of the new modular buildings, but also because he had always been concerned about the poor aesthetic effect of large interior spaces with uniformly low ceilings. It will be recalled that the Library of the Future, described in 1933, contained provision for higher ceilings in a limited number of public areas. Regarding one of his last associations with library buildings he wrote: "They [the architects of the Louisiana State University Library] did not accept my suggestions and are building a library with enormous floor areas that will inevitably be monotonous and uninteresting."[69]

With this in mind, it might be fair to conclude that the St. Louis University Library, or many of the newer public library buildings such as the one at Vancouver, B. C., come closer to the Macdonald ideal than do the libraries at Washington State University, Pullman, or Louisiana State University or even North Dakota Agricultural College, Fargo, which are often thought to be the epitome of the modular plan.

This review of Macdonald's writings reveals his dissatisfaction with library architecture up to, and even after, 1940. It was, in his view, too inflexible and too limited in its appeal. As an alternative, he developed the modular plan in a series of published articles, beginning with "A Library of the Future" in 1933. Actually, he had hinted that libraries should rely less on natural ventilation and illumination as early as 1931 and 1932 in two articles on library lighting.

It is evidence that, as the modular idea achieved greater clarity, a well-controlled artificial environment was an essential component of the plan. Macdonald also advocated, as part of the typical modular library, free-standing stacks and radically lower ceilings. This latter feature, however, he always tempered with higher ceilings in a small portion of the building.

Notes

1. Letter of Helge Bergh Kragemo to Angus Snead Macdonald, March 13, 1933, in Macdonald Papers.

2. Harold Underwood Faulkner, American Economic History, (7th ed.; New York: Harper & Brothers, 1954), p. 646.

3. Ibid., p. 654.

4. John Burchard, op. cit., p. 385.

5. Elmer D. Johnson, A History of Libraries in the Western World (New York: Scarecrow Press, 1965), p. 329.

6. Rebecca B. Rankin, "Unemployment Among Librarians," American Library Association Bulletin, XXIX (March, 1935), p. 148.

7. "Unemployment in the Profession," American Library Association Bulletin, XXVI (February, 1932), p. 88.

8. "Budget Cuts," Library Journal, LVII (January 1, 1932), p. 25.

9. Carl B. Roden, "The Library in Hard Times," Library Journal, LVI (December 1, 1931), p. 984.

10. Elmer D. Johnson, loc. cit.

11. Paul M. Paine, "Survey of Borrowers by Occupation," Library Journal, LVI (September 15, 1931), p. 755.

12. C. C. Furnas, America's Tomorrow; An Informal Excursion Into the Era of the Two-Hour Working Day, (New York: Funk & Wagnalls, 1931).

13. "Coming: The Age of Leisure," Literary Digest, CXII (January 18, 1932), p. 26.

14. "Worms Imperil Vatican Treasures," Literary Digest, CXII (January 16, 1932), pp. 17-18).

15. Harry Miller Lydenberg, "Unanswered Questions," American Library Association Bulletin, XXVII (December 15, 1933), pp. 557-568.

16. "Editorial," Library Journal, LVIII (November 1, 1933), p. 878.

17. "The Way Out of the Debauch," Literary Digest, CXIII (January 23, 1932), p. 17.

18. Letter of Angus Snead Macdonald to Monsignor Eugene Tisserant, October 12, 1931, microfilm copy of an initialled carbon copy in author's files.

19. Angus Snead Macdonald, "A Library of the Future," Overbibliotekar Wilhelm Munthe på Femtiarsdågen, 20 Oktober 1933... (Oslo: Grøndahl & Søns, 1933), pp. 168-184.

20. Angus Snead Macdonald, "The University Library at Oslo," Library Journal, LVII (January 15, 1932), pp. 69-72.

21. Letter of Angus Snead Macdonald to Helge Kragemo, October 6, 1933.

22. Paul Remond, "Les Magasins de Livres et les Rayonnages Métalliques dans les Bibliothèques," World Congress of Universal Documentation, 1937, Communications (Paris: the Congress, 1937), p. 286. Remond lists the Vatican along with other important European library book stacks and "depots."

23. Letter of "G. T." addressed "Dear Angus", undated, but attached to manuscript dated August 24, 1933, in Macdonald papers.

24. Ralph E. Ellsworth, "Library Architecture and Buildings," Library Quarterly, XXV (January, 1955), pp. 66-75.

25. Angus Snead Macdonald, "A Library of the Future," p. 168.

26. Ibid.

27. "Notes of Plans for Sterling Library," April 7, 1927, p. 1 (typed copy in Macdonald papers).

28. Angus Snead Macdonald, "A Library of the Future," p. 169.

29. Ibid., p. 173.

30. Ibid., p. 177.

31. "Electric illumination," Collier's Encyclopedia... ed. by Louis Shores. (New York: Crowell-Collier Publishing Co., 1962), p. 724.

32. John Burchard, op. cit., p. 384.

33. "Century of Progress Issue," Architectural Forum, LIX (July, 1933), p. 54.

34. Angus S. Macdonald, "The Disaster in the Vatican Library," Scientific American, CXLVI (April, 1932), pp. 226-227.

35. New Sodium Lamp is 70 Percent Efficient," Scientific American, CXLVI (April, 1932), p. 233.

36. Ibid., p. 184.

37. Correspondence between Angus Snead Macdonald and Miss Bertine E. Weston, various dates between September 6, 1933 and March 1, 1934.

38. Angus Snead Macdonald, "A Library of the Future," Library Journal, LVIII (December 1 & 15, 1933), pp. 971-5, 1023-5.

39. Letter of Angus Snead Macdonald to Miss Bertine E. Weston, March 1, 1934.

40. Angus S. Macdonald, "Effective Library Lighting," Architectural Forum, LVI (June, 1932), p. 631, and "Library Lighting," Library Journal, LVI (March 1, 1931), pp. 203-10.

41. E. J. Carter, "Library Building, 1933-34" Year's Work in Librarianship, VII, 1934 (London: The Library Association, 1935), p. 95.

42. Angus Snead Macdonald, "Some Engineering Developments Affecting Large Libraries" American Library Association Bulletin, XXVIII (September, 1934), pp. 628-32. Githens' drawings were not published with the article.

43. Ibid., p. 628.

44. Alfred Morton Githens, "The Evolution of a Library," Library Journal, LXXVIII (December 15, 1953), p. 2132.

45. Letter of Angus Snead Macdonald to Cardinal Tisserant, June 26, 1940, film copy of carbon copy in author's files, tells of speaking in Colorado on "A Library of the Future" before a "library group" in June, 1940.

46. Macdonald to Tisserant, May 1, 1936. Author's microfilm copy.

47. Macdonald to Tisserant, March 27, 1941, pp. 1-2. Author's microfilm copy.

48. Letter of Angus Snead Macdonald to Ralph Ellsworth, December 27, 1943. Photocopy in author's files. Original in University of Iowa Library files.

49. Angus S. Macdonald "To the Stock Holders of Snead and Company, April 5, 1943" in Report for the Heirs of the

Estate of Udolpho Snead, (Snead and Company, 1943) duplicate copy. p. 1.

50. Letter of Ralph E. Ellsworth to Angus Snead Macdonald, November 27, 1943, p. 1-2. Carbon of original in files of the State University of Iowa, photocopy in author's files.

51. Ellsworth to Macdonald, July 19, 1944, p. 1. (Photocopy in author's files. Original in the University of Iowa Library).

52. Macdonald to Ellsworth, August 7, 1944. (Photocopy in author's files.)

53. Ellsworth to Macdonald, October 21, 1944.

54. Angus Snead Macdonald, "New Possibilities in Library Planning," Library Journal, LXX (December 15, 1945), pp. 1169-74.

55. Macdonald to Ellsworth, August 21, 1945.

56. Angus Snead Macdonald, "New Possibilities...," p. 1169.

57. "[Review of] the Year's Work in Librarianship, 1939-1945, 1946," Library of Congress Information Bulletin, IX (March 20, 1950), p. 18.

58. Edwin F. Patterson, "Library Buildings," Year's Work in Librarianship, XII, 1946 (London: The Library Association, 1946), p. 122.

59. Angus Snead Macdonald, "New Possibilities..." p. 1171. This definition is also quoted by Georg Leyh in Handbuch der Bibliothekswissenschaft, 2 aufl. (Wiesbaden: Otto Harrassowitz, 1961), II, p. 997.

60. Ibid.

61. Ibid., p. 1174.

62. Ibid.

63. Angus Snead Macdonald, "Modular Construction," Library Journal, LXXX (December 1, 1955), pp. 2718-30.

64. Ibid., pp. 2728-29.

65. Angus Snead Macdonald "Some Comments on Modular Libraries," American Library Association, Association of College and Reference Libraries, Building Committee, Fifth and Sixth Library Buildings Plans Institutes Proceedings, A. C. R. L.

Monograph 15 (Chicago: Association of College and Reference Libraries, 1956), pp. 155-7.

66. Macdonald to Joseph L. Wheeler, August 3, 1956. Microfilm copy of carbon copy in author's files.

67. Angus Snead Macdonald, "Building Design for Library Management," Library Trends, II (January, 1954), pp. 463-9.

68. Ibid., p. 467. Actually he had proposed a similar compromise at least as early as February, 1949, in a letter to Bail, Horton & Associates, architects for Florida State University, and also in the Canisius College Sketches of 1950 which are reproduced in Appendix 1.

69. Macdonald to Wheeler, op. cit.

Chapter VI

The Module is the Message:
Macdonald as Consultant and Publicist

The theoretical libraries that Macdonald built in the minds of his readers and listeners between 1933 and 1955 were not entirely spun from his imagination. As has been demonstrated, his earlier ideas, those concerning the public and teachers college libraries of 1933 and 1934, were rooted in his experience in bookstack construction, and, in a very limited way, soon became a reality in the Snead Convertible Stack. There were either readily available, or in the developmental stage, various improvements in building materials and methods, of which Macdonald was aware and about which more will be said in Chapter VII.

Developing the Hollow-Column System

Tied to his idea of modular construction, especially as it developed in the 1940's, was the hollow-column feature.[1] This method of construction, he was convinced, would prove more economical and more flexible. He also argued that it would result in less stair-climbing because, by eliminating duct-work, ceiling to floor dimensions were shortened. For a time, in the late 1940's and early 1950's, there seemed to be a strong possibility that the hollow column would vie in popularity with traditional steel and reinforced concrete as the framing system of the new modular libraries. Because it is so closely allied with his promotional activities, it may prove useful to discuss Macdonald's association with the hollow-column idea.

There was, to be sure, much more behind Macdonald's theories, particularly the hollow-column system, than "mere thought," Githens, perhaps a little overgenerous in his praise, noted that "most types of plans gradually evolve, but the principles underlying this [hollow-column modular plan] were thought out by one person."[2] Macdonald had indeed given a great deal of thought to a new structural frame for libraries, as his correspondence and sketches demonstrate, but he had no genuine prototype to follow. After the general concepts concerning the framework of the University of Iowa library were settled, Macdonald felt some tests were needed to determine the ability of the columns to withstand heavy library loads. Following basic ideas supplied by Macdonald, Gilbert D. Fish, a consulting engineer, designed light steel columns based on theories drawn from aeronautical practice.[3] The sample columns were manufactured in Snead's Orange, Virginia, plant and tested in the spring of 1945 at Columbia University.[4]

The system, as it emerged shortly after the tests, is shown by the two isometric drawings, Figures 24-25. It is presumed that the indentations on each face of the column in Figure 24 were made to eliminate the need for spot welding internal stiffeners in place and, at the same time, to provide support for movable partitions. Later versions of the columns employed two heavy "U"-shaped steel channels welded together. Through a system of dampers, the amount of air distributed to and exhausted from each bay or module was controlled. In most versions of the scheme, alternate columns served as plenum and exhaust ducts. For a more detailed description, see the Gilbert Fish letter of January 30, 1947, in Appendix I. With some variations, the steel hollow-column system was used at the Hardin-Simmons Library (1947), North Dakota Agricultural College Library (1950), and the University of Georgia Library (1953). Other libraries, such as those at the State University of Iowa, Princeton University, and more recently the Queens Borough Public Library, have employed what appears to be the hollow-column principle, but these actually make use of separate duct-work within or adjacent to the column. The three buildings that employed the Macdonald-Fish scheme were not fireproofed, although provision for a vermiculite covering had been made by Macdonald.

The Module is the Message

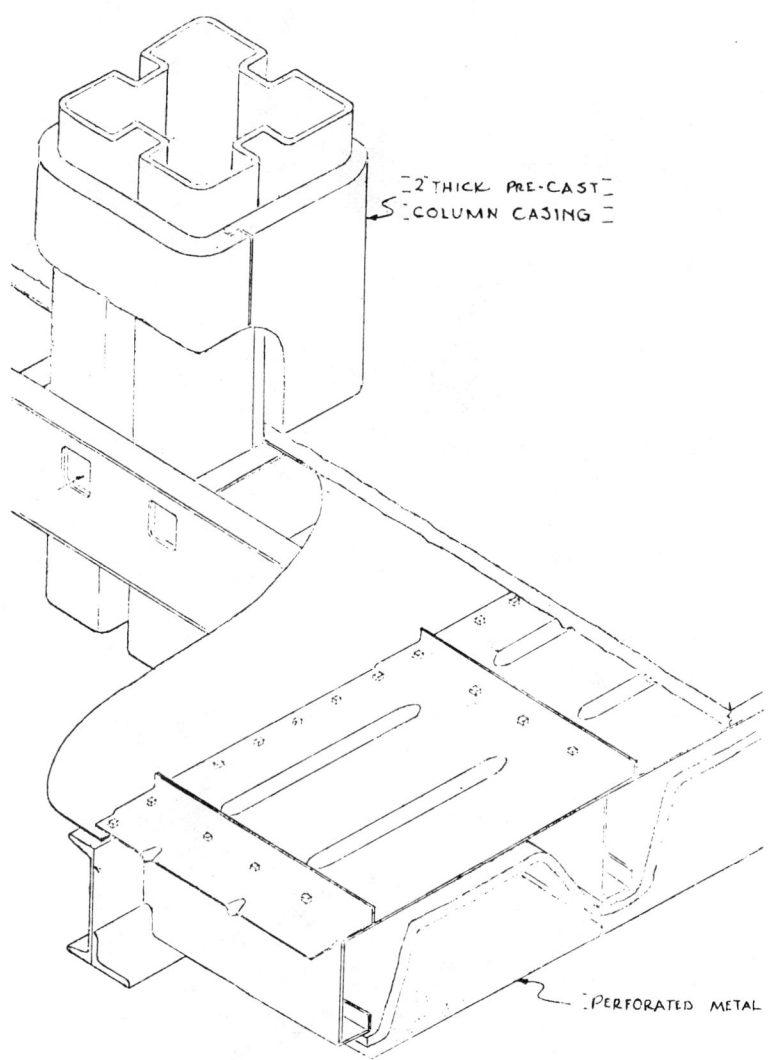

Figure 24. Modular construction, detail.

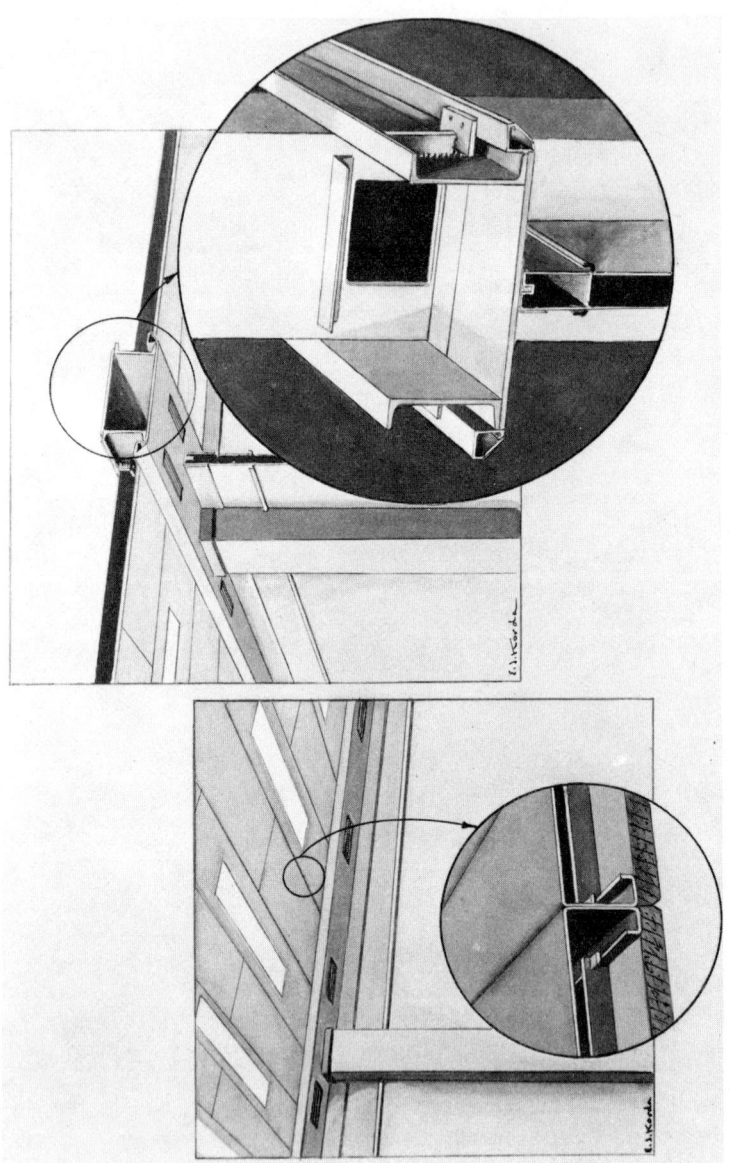

Figure 25. Modular construction, later version.

The Module is the Message   147

It is quite probable that Macdonald had placed much of his hopes for the future of Snead and Company on this construction method. The hollow-column, perhaps, was to become as synonymous with the Snead name in the future as the open-bar shelf and cast-iron shelf support had been in the past. However, from the number of libraries listed above, it is obvious that the idea was far less successful. The reasons for its lack of success are numerous, but the following paragraphs describe briefly some of the problems.

Objections to the System

The chief objection to the hollow-column system seems to have come from those who were concerned about its safety in the event of fire. Apparently insurance companies, and especially architects who were sensitive to fire codes and insurance restrictions, felt the columns should be fireproofed internally as well as externally. External fireproofing Macdonald recognized as a necessity, but internal fireproofing would have made the columns excessively bulky and costly. Those who opposed the system argued that, should a fire start in the ventilating system, it would spread through the columns, which would act as flues, thereby weakening them to the point of collapse. Macdonald, and others, argued that such a fire was highly improbable and devices could be installed to eliminate the danger.

Some architects argued that condensation would form inside the columns and girders and would cause rust which would eventually weaken them. They felt this would be particularly true in an air-conditioned building.[5] William Kurke, the architect who eventually employed Macdonald's ideas in the North Dakota Agricultural College Library, was concerned about static pressure building within the columns, thereby increasing the load on the fans. To guard against this possibility, he insisted that the inside of the columns be as smooth as possible.[6]

During the 1940's and early 1950's, except for a brief period in the late 1940's, America experienced a more or less chronic steel shortage due to the involvement in World War II and the Korean War.[7] Gilbert Fish observed in 1947:

> This form of construction [i.e., the steel hollow-column] was considered for the Princeton Library a year ago with fireproofing included. The general contractors reported that it was the most inexpensive construction of the four types considered, but certain delays to be expected in obtaining steel would prevent immediate construction. To avoid this delay, reinforced concrete was adopted...[8]

In the summer of 1947 Macdonald noted that West Coast architects preferred concrete "both because steel is scarce and expensive and because they are used to that construction and like it,"[9] and in 1950 Fish reported a return of the "gray market" in steel.[10] These steel shortages reduced the chances for buildings being framed in steel, and thereby reduced the opportunities for architects to experiment with Macdonald's idea.

Having encountered difficulties with steel, Macdonald, as early as 1946, indicated an interest in developing the hollow-column idea in reinforced, pre-cast concrete for "such jobs as the new Harvard undergraduate library... ."[11] However, after considerable effort, Gilbert Fish concluded that the scheme was impractical, or at least of limited value, chiefly because of the excessive weight of concrete.[12]

Undoubtedly one of the greatest factors in checking the development of the idea was the loss of the manufacturing facilities of Snead and Company in August, 1946. This loss was the greatest tragedy in Macdonald's career. Although the sales and engineering units of the Company survived for six more years, the loss of the Company's manufacturing plants and equipment was a serious blow. None of the stack or structural parts of any of the buildings in which Macdonald was involved, after World War II, were manufactured by Snead and Company. Assuming an architect had managed to overcome all of the preceding difficulties, where would he turn for the manufacture of the hollow columns? They could not be bought "off the shelf" from any of the major steel companies, and although they could be easily fabricated, it nevertheless would have required special effort on the part of the architect and the contractor, and clearance on Macdonald's patent rights.

In a recent letter to the author, Robert O'Connor, architect for the Princeton Library, listed most of the reasons above, plus one more: fear of union jurisdictional disputes.[13] Was Macdonald's column a structural support or a ventilating duct? If the former, one union would have jurisdiction; if the latter, another would claim the right of installation.

Applications of the System

For all his efforts, and those of his associates, the Snead hollow-column system was generally forgotten after the first flurry of interest following World War II. Only three library buildings[14] had employed the system and on all of these Macdonald waived his patent rights.[15] On only one, North Dakota Agricultural College, was he likely to have realized any personal gain, since Snead and Company had the contract for supplying and erecting its framework. Alfred Morton Githens, in writing about his experiences as architect of the Ilah Dunlap Little Library, University of Georgia (1953, the largest and last of the hollow-column libraries to be built), observed:

> All went wrong. I had to overcome one unexpected trouble after another. These had nothing to do with the type of design...but it has made the Georgia Library undesirable to boast about as the first great example of the type.[16]

Precisely what Githens means by "All went wrong" is difficult to understand; however, Georgia did present problems. On the basis of test borings he had assumed the building was being built on bedrock, and designed the foundations accordingly. Githens wrote, "Actual excavation showed no bedrock at all; each of the borings had struck a large boulder."[17] His first ventilation and air conditioning engineer became "visionary" and had to be replaced.[18] Even after the building was opened the air conditioning was not entirely satisfactory,[19] and some complained of excessive vibration from fans in the penthouse.[20] Finally, Macdonald himself conceded that the column spacing, 18 feet on center in both directions, was too close for an ideal arrangement.[21]

With architects generally reluctant, often for good reason,

to combine the structural and ventilation systems, and without a really outstanding example of the system in operation, the hollow-column version of the modular plan was doomed to oblivion. The important issue, however, for the library world, was not the method of air distribution but the modular plan itself.

Probable Sources of Macdonald's Ideas

As has already been established, Macdonald's theory of a modular library grew out of his tinkering with bookstack design in the 1930's. Clearly, this is the primary source of his ideas; however, as the modular library took on more of the characteristics of the loft building and less of the bookstack, it is probable that there were other building types that provided inspiration. While it is unlikely that Macdonald could have graduated from the School of Architecture at Columbia University without learning about modern warehouse or loft construction, there was, for him, a more practical demonstration of the advantages of this type of building. In 1910 Udolpho Snead, Macdonald's uncle, organized the Snead Manufacturing Building Company whose sole function seems to have been to build and rent a large building (total area 130,911 square feet) on the site of the old Snead and Company Iron Works in Louisville. In time Angus S. Macdonald became president of the Snead Manufacturing Building Company, and in 1943, pending sale of the property, he described the building in these words:

> The Snead Manufacturing Building was made of reinforced concrete, without permanent interior walls except around elevators and toilets so as to permit the various floors being divided to suit the tenants. This was the first building of the kind ever constructed in Louisville... [22]

Although Macdonald had advocated flexibility in library design long before, Snead and Company was involved in supplying movable partitions for the landmark research building on the Bell Telephone Laboratories at Murray Hill, New Jersey (1942). This building placed special stress on ease of rearrangement to meet changing research needs. To carry several services (various gases, air, water, steam and electricity) to the laboratory benches, hollow floor panels housed a variety of pipes and conduits, and Snead metal partitions were used to permit quick and inexpensive alterations for room sizes. The architects, Voorhees, Walker, Foley, and Smith, had erected a full-scale model before the laboratory was actually built.[23] From reports and correspondence in his papers it is obvious that Macdonald was well aware of the features of this building, and, perhaps, became more firmly convinced that similar flexibility in library design was equally desirable.

Macdonald's Techniques as Publicist and Consultant

Often, it is difficult to determine when Macdonald was acting as a publicist and when he adopted the role of a consultant. Obviously, in his published writings he is a publicist, with the one consistent theme being a plea for more flexible and economical library buildings. In his correspondence, he also seems to have taken an opportunity, when called upon to give advice, to spread the modular "gospel." Because he frequently adopted both roles simultaneously, little attempt will be made to separate the two.

It is apparent from the correspondence that remains that Macdonald was well known among the leaders of the library profession. The good will and respect that accrued to him after successfully building one large bookstack after another gave him a prestige that remains unique among manufacturers of library equipment.[24] He had the energy to attend many, probably most, of the American Library Association meetings and to participate occasionally in the programs. Snead and Company usually held a cocktail party that annually brought together Macdonald and many librarians, particularly those who had an interest in library buildings. Evelyn Steele Little wrote, in 1967:

> We met at A. L. A. conferences [in the 1930's and 1940's] and as I was dreaming of a new building he readily converted me to the modular idea, and we drew endless plans on the backs of envelopes.... He was a dynamic man and when he talked about modules you saw them and knew it was the only way to build.[25]

By virtue of his training as an architect, his interest in buildings, the prestige of Snead and Company, and his popularity among librarians and some architects, Macdonald was in a strong position to influence library design.

The techniques Macdonald employed to bring his ideas to the attention of librarians and architects were varied.

Public Speaking

He addressed a number of professional groups, beginning with a lecture before the Library Buildings Round Table of the American Library Association on June 26, 1934.[26] On June 28, 1940 he addressed a group of Colorado librarians on "The Library of the Future,"[27] and used the same title for a speech before the Canadian Library Association in June, 1948. The talk was published in the Association's Bulletin.[28] He also spoke before the Cooperative Committee on Library Building Plans on several occasions, the American Theological Library Association on June 21, 1949,[29] and to at least one library school class.[30]

A speaking engagement that seemed to cause Macdonald much concern was his luncheon talk to the New York Chapter of the American Institute of Architects on January 4, 1949. Some of the more influential architects of the time were likely to be in attendance. The title, "The So-Called Modular Library," was chosen by Alfred Morton Githens, but Githens requested that his friend, Macdonald, give the talk. Fearing some heckling from Ralph Walker and others, Macdonald requested that William Randall be present to lend support.[31] In his talk he stressed the beauty but impracticality of the monumental building, and the advantages in flexibility, operation, and economy of the modular building.[32] (While records are not clear, it appears that the speech was received reasonably well.)

Coining the Term

The recognition of any new idea is aided by a term that is easy to remember. In the 1930's Macdonald referred to this new type of library design as the "flexible unit plan,"[33] and in his letter of December 12, 1946, to Macdonald, Alfred Morton Githens proposed "interchangeable, convertible, adaptable, adjustable, and mutable, as well as flexible." But Macdonald, drawing upon his architectural training, decided to call the blocks of space "modules," meaning units of measure, which according to Githens, he drew from Vignola.[34] The word appears to have been first used in print by Macdonald in his "New Possibilities in Library Planning" in 1945.[35]

Githens objected to the term since, at this time, "module" was also being applied to the building industry by the American Standards Association as meaning something different. In September, 1947, Macdonald received an unexpected, but quasi-official, "blessing" in the use of the term from Modular Grid Lines, a periodical devoted to "the advancement of ASA Project A62." After referring to Macdonald's usage, Modular Grid Lines stated:

> We do not take exception to Mr. Macdonald's use of the term 'modular,' realizing that it conforms to the correct and generally understood usage; we do suspect that some confusion may arise from the inexactness of our terminology. Probably the A62 method [reference to American Standards Association Project A62] is better described as 'Dimensional Coordination.'
>
> ...The large planning module is applied to the overall design of buildings, whereas the four inch module [basic dimension of the A62 project] is used primarily for the design and coordination of building parts.[36]

On September 24, 1947, Macdonald acknowledged the article in Modular Grid Lines as "quite generous," and indicated that he too was "not at all satisfied with the term 'module.'" He stated that he was hoping to establish "Adaptive Modular Plan" in its place,[37] but after using this awkward phrase for a year or two in correspondence, he apparently realized that "module" and "modular" were too firmly entrenched, and abandoned the effort. The library world too had some disagreement over what the word meant, as the early discussions of the Library Buildings Plans Institute bear out,[38] but even Githens, in his article on the University of Georgia Library, published in 1953, accepted Macdonald's term.[39] Eventually Macdonald came to be known as "Mr. Module."[40]

The Canisius Sketches

Snead and Company, like other major equipment suppliers, were frequently called upon to render advice on library planning problems. Macdonald's writings and reputation probably made the

Company's advice especially popular. Many librarians, and occasionally an architect, wrote for assistance; in his replies Macdonald would rarely miss an opportunity to suggest the modular plan. One of the librarians seeking this free service was Father Andrew L. Bouwhuis, of Canisius College in Buffalo, New York. Out of a series of letters and meetings that began in May, 1948, and continued into the early 1950's, Macdonald made a number of suggestions. These suggestions were incorporated in a group of sketches, drawn by Snead and Company, in May, 1950, and revised several times, (Appendix I).

The sketches, although not accepted by Canisius College, were sent to a number of other librarians in the early 1950's. [41]

Travel

In addition to writing, speaking and corresponding, Macdonald traveled a great deal, speaking informally to individuals and small groups of librarians in the United States and Canada. Virtually all of this traveling was done as part of the efforts to obtain new business for Snead and Company, or, as Snead's business expanded after World War II, to supervise work in progress. As noted in Chapter V, he had traveled to Iowa City and to New York to confer about the library building at the State University of Iowa. His appointment calendar shows that he traveled, in 1946, to Chicago (A. L. A. Midwinter Meeting) in January, to New York in March, and to Iowa City again in December. In 1947 he made two extended trips, going as far north as Edmonton and as far south and west as San Diego. [42] While in Canada in October, he stopped at Winnipeg, and wrote to Gilbert D. Fish, his consulting engineer, that "The architects, the leaders in this section, and engineers in the C. E. Department of the University here are keen about our adaptive modular system.... They see applications far beyond libraries... ."[43]

After attending the American Library Association's Midwinter Meeting in late January, 1948, it appears that he made another trip to the West Coast with appointments in Los Angeles on February fifth through ninth, then flew north to San Francisco, Seattle, and Vancouver, and returned to Orange after making several stops in the Midwest. His appointment calendar for March first bears the note, "in Peoria with Robert H. Muller, President Owen, architect Briggs." The meeting probably concerned the new library being planned for Bradley University. In late April Macdonald was traveling in the South and in May he was on the West Coast and in Canada again. He spoke before the Canadian Library Association in Ottawa in early June and made a number of calls along the way. Later that month he attended the American Library Association Annual Meeting in Atlantic City. During the summer he made a number of trips to the Midwest, including Fargo, North Dakota (North Dakota Agricultural College), and in the fall he visited New York on at least two occasions, once concerning the 43-station conveyor in the United Nations building. In December he took a "vacation" to Miami but called at the public and university libraries there, making a note to forward information on the modular plan. The record for 1949 is much the same. The entry for August 14th notes that he conferred with Father J. P. Donnelly at St. Louis University, and includes a sketch that suggests the mezzanine library that was built a decade later. On October 27th he met with N. Orwin Rush and the Library Planning Committee at the University of Wyoming.

To save time traveling and to avoid the inconvenience of conforming to the schedules of public transportation, he decided to take instruction as a private airplane pilot. There is evidence that he had had an interest in flying for several years, and his son Avery was already a licensed pilot. He began his study of this new mode of travel in the summer of 1949, squeezing an hour or two out of his busy schedule to practice every Saturday morning. After his solo flight in September he quickly gained confidence and used the plane for the vacation-business trip to Miami in December. He continued to fly in 1950 and in February, 1951, he wrote to Baron Moens de Fernig of Belgium about the joys of flying and the new friends he had made: "With every trip that Mrs. Macdonald and I take together, we find ourselves enriched with the experience and youth [of other flyers]."[44] He had just returned from an "island-hopping" trip to the West Indies and was planning another to South America. He was 67 at the time.

If the airplane provided speed and convenience, it also presented some serious problems. On May 15, 1952, while he was attempting to land at his farm near Orange, Virginia, a gust of wind carried his plane into a wooded area. The resulting crash and fire caused serious injury to his passenger, Walter Downs, a business acquaintance. Macdonald managed to pull him out of the plane, but Downs was confined to a hospital for several months; he later brought suit, unsuccessfully, against Macdonald.[45] A second crash, at Oaxaca, Mexico, on March 24, 1953,[46] resulted in serious injury to Mrs. Macdonald and brought an end to his exploits as a pilot. By this time he had sold the remaining assets of Snead and Company and was active only as a library consultant. The ability to travel extensively and quickly was less important. The airplane, however, had added a colorful chapter to his life.

Snead and Company Staff

In the years immediately following World War II, Macdonald was not the only Snead and Company employee to carry the modular message. It is apparent that, late in World War II, Macdonald had plans for an enlarged Snead and Company, one which would provide a wider type of service to libraries. Perhaps his old yearning to be an architect, perhaps his desire to make libraries better places than they were, and, undoubtedly, the hope for greater profits, spurred him to expand the officers of the company. Apparently, with the hollow-column modular plan he hoped that Snead would build the entire structure of the library, not just the bookstack, since this type of building no longer required a bookstack, in the old sense of the term.

J. Russell Bailey

In October, 1945, he added J. Russell Bailey, an architect, who assumed certain responsibilities that Macdonald had borne; this also permitted the company to offer a far broader planning service than had been possible in the past. Bailey was a graduate of the University of Michigan School of Architecture and had

The Module is the Message   157

studied under Eliel Saarinin at Michigan's Cranbrook Academy. He
later designed a number of modular library buildings, including Converse College (1950) and DePauw University (1956). Since his Snead
experience, he has been associated with the planning of well over
100 library buildings.[47] He is also the architectural advisor of
the American Library Association.

William Randall

In addition to an architect, Macdonald felt the need for a
closer relationship with the library world. He needed someone
with genuine stature in the profession as well as an interest in
buildings. In the latter part of 1945 he approached William M.
Randall. Randall had been one of the "bright lights" of the library
profession before World War II. A scholar (Ph.D. from Hartford
Theological Seminary in Arabic, 1929), he had been one of the four
American librarians sent by the Carnegie Endowment for International Peace to assist in recataloging and classifying the Vatican Library in 1929. Before entering the Army Air Corps in World War
II, he had held the rank of full professor in the Graduate Library
School of the University of Chicago, had been a consultant for the
Carnegie Corporation, the General Education Board, and the North
Central Association in the area of academic libraries.[48] He also
had an extensive record of published writings. In addition to writing books and articles, he had been the first editor of <u>Library
Quarterly</u> and the author (with F. L. D. Goodrich) of <u>Principles
of College Library Administration</u>.[49] In this work he warned the
reader to beware of the architect and called for a functional building with a plan "rather different from the old idea of reading room,
periodical room, delivery desk, and stack."[50] The selected references at the end of the chapter on buildings included reference to
Macdonald's "A Library of the Future." Just before entering the
service, Randall had completed most of the research for a "definitive volume" on academic library buildings.[51]

Although the professorship at Chicago was waiting for him,
he accepted Macdonald's offer, joining Snead and Company in November, 1945. Randall remained with Snead until June, 1947, when

he accepted the position of Director of Libraries at the University of Georgia. During that time he served the Company as Vice President in charge of the Library Division, and remained active in library affairs. At the annual meeting of the Association of College and Reference Libraries in Buffalo, New York, in June, 1946, Randall delivered a paper on library planning which was published in College and Research Libraries a short time later.[52] Although he refused to use the term "modular" and substituted his own "adaptive," it employed, nevertheless, many of the same arguments found in Macdonald's writings on the subject. Two months later he delivered a similar paper at the Library Institute of the University of Chicago.[53]

Precisely what effect Randall had on persuading the library and architectural professions to abandon their old ways is impossible to assess, but it is probable that his endorsement of the scheme had some influence with his former pupils of the Graduate Library School.

The Model

One of the most effective devices employed by Macdonald to publicize the idea of modular planning for libraries was the full-scale, two-story model he built at Orange, Virginia. The basic structural design of this model was described earlier in this chapter. The model had been discussed as early as the fall of 1944,[54] but due to steel shortages (even the shelves that went into the model were borrowed from a nearby library) and other problems, the project was not completed until late in the following spring. As Figure 26 illustrates, the interior was furnished in the informal manner Macdonald had advocated in 1933. Julian Boyd, Librarian at Princeton University, who was one of the early visitors, wrote, "Your model is an exciting landmark in library architecture. I hope that you will be able to eliminate the overhead noises, for I think that is about the only criticism I have to offer."[55] In the late summer the noisy steel floor of the second story was replaced by sections of pre-cast vermiculite-asbestos which did much to correct Boyd's complaint. The model as it stood at this time had a main floor of 12-gauge steel (with asbestos tile covering), relatively

The Module is the Message

Figure 26. Interior of Snead model, first floor.

low eight-foot ceilings, and movable partitions.[56] The column spacing, 13 1/2 feet by 19 1/2 feet, was chosen to duplicate that being planned for the State University of Iowa,[57] but, as Macdonald was quick to point out, these dimensions could be easily increased to 20 feet by 25 feet.[58]

After attending several meetings of librarians and architects at which he had apparently been describing the virtues of the modular plan, Ellsworth stressed the importance of the model. He wrote to Macdonald:

> The sooner the "mock up" is finished the better off we will be...
>
> It becomes increasingly clear to me that from now on, you are going to be swamped with all kinds of people interested in the type of construction you are planning. As near as I have been able to find out, everyone puts the burden of proof on you and us... . We have got to be able to show them that lighting, air conditioning, sound deadening, and structural aspects of this plan are sound and economical.[59]

The model's purpose, of course, was to demonstrate the advantages and economies of this type of library construction, and to facilitate study of related engineering, architectural and planning problems.

In October, 1945, the model was the scene of the Orange Conference of the Cooperative Committee on Library Building Plans.[60] All eleven institutional members of this influential committee were represented. Membership in the committee was deliberately kept small: it consisted of those academic institutions planning to build new libraries as soon as funds and materials were available. Among the librarians present were Julian Boyd of Princeton, John Burchard of the Massachusetts Institute of Technology, and, accompanied by President Virgil Hancher, Ralph Ellsworth of Iowa. Also present were a number of influential architects, most in the employ of the members, including Robert B. O'Connor, Edgar Albright, Alfred M. Githens, and Ralph Walker. Walker was not especially fond of the modular idea and criticized the model for its low ceilings. He argued that the skimpy vertical dimension might have an undesirable effect on the young individual's sense of freedom. He compared the model to solitary confinement.

"Solitary," he said, "is a six-foot cube in which a single light is burning."[61] Others defended the model as "a rather pleasant solution," but Walker's concern about the radically lower ceilings was to be voiced many times in the early post-war period. Both Iowa and Princeton soon built less elaborate models of their own.

Snead and Company had invited a number of engineers to the Conference, including G. D. Fish, Charles Leopold, and the Deputy Commissioner of the U. S. Public Buildings Administration, George Howe. Howe's unit was interested in the model for government office buildings. Perhaps with an eye for greater Snead business, Macdonald stressed, in his opening remarks to the Conference, the advantages of prefabricating as much of the building as possible. This would, he argued, produce "shop accuracy" and reduce overall costs.[62]

The model itself, of course, was an expense to Snead. The original estimates of the cost were set in May at $10,000, including $750 for furnishings,[63] but Macdonald soon requested a trimmer budget of $7,500. Engineering costs, the new flooring for the second story and other expenses revised the budget upward to $25,000,[64] and a December report set the final cost at $47,000.[65] It is virtually certain that Macdonald never recovered the cost of the "bread he cast upon the water" in 1945, but according to Ellsworth, this model "was responsible for convincing librarians and architects that the idea had possibilities."[66]

Morrow's Library and the Beaux-Arts Design

Ironically, in spite of Snead and Company's heavy commitment to the academic field, Macdonald expressed genuine interest in and concern for America's public libraries. Morrow's Library,[67] a pamphlet he published privately in March, 1948, treated the modular plan, as did "A Library of the Future," as a subordinate theme. The chief emphasis, in the former treatise, was placed on the financial plight of many public libraries (and municipal governments generally) after the war, and offered, as a solution, a library with added revenue from rented space. The pamphlet, in style similar to that of the 1933 article, pictured an office building of 26 floors and 643,000 usable square feet of which the library occupied four floors and 128,000 square feet of space. The rented floors provided a handsome income for the library. The building was of modular construction, and the floors devoted to offices were to provide ample expansion space for the library. Macdonald "pushed" the idea in correspondence, distributing the pamphlet to leaders of the library profession, both at home and abroad. The pamphlet also formed the basis for an enthusiastically received talk before the Canadian Library Association, [68] and somewhat later, an article in Library Journal. [69]

To publicize further the idea of a library in an office building, he sponsored an architectural competition through the Beaux-Arts Institute of Design. A total of 161 student architects from eight institutions participated, with the University of Illinois and Oklahoma Agricultural and Mechanical College providing the six winners. [70] The judging was done in May, 1950, as part of the Beaux-Arts Institute's annual meeting. Robert O'Connor and O'Neil Ford, both architects who were involved in modular library buildings, and Malcom Wyer, of the Denver Public Library, were among the judges. [71]

Librarians found other answers to their financial problems, (larger units of service, state and federal aid) and, after a flurry of interest in Macdonald's proposals in the late 1940's and early 1950's, dismissed them. Generally they found legal hurdles, opposition from real estate groups, and the fear of being abandoned altogether by the taxpayer, too great to overcome. From his correspondence, it is obvious that Macdonald was sincere in his efforts to make public libraries of greater service to their communities. For several years the Morrow idea served to keep him in the "limelight." Joseph Wheeler thought the idea "sensible," if difficult to achieve because of opposition;[72] Milton Ferguson thought the scheme would become popular if only one large library would accept it;[73] and librarians from Vancouver and Sudbury in Canada to Kalamazoo and Washington, D.C. in the United States seriously considered it. And always included in his writings and talks on the subject was

The Module is the Message 163

the modular plan. Indeed, the office building skyscraper and the
modular library were merged (in theory, at least.)

Compact Storage

Macdonald's endeavors to develop special compact shelving
for the Midwest Inter-Library Center, [74] for a time at least, served
to bring him still further attention within the library world. For
the March 6, 1950, meeting of the Center's Board of Directors,
Snead and Company erected, on the campus of the Illinois Institute
of Technology, a model of a new type of shelving. Unlike the compact storage developed by Snead for the Toronto Reference Library,
which employed rolling compartments, this new model featured
swinging cases. These cases were eventually installed in a large
portion of the Center's 2,000,000 volume bookstack (Figure 27).
For a time, studies made by the Center and others indicated that,
for this type of facility, the Snead design achieved a real economy
in book storage costs. [75]

Macdonald's development of compact storage, according to
Ellsworth, spurred other American manufacturers to develop their
own versions. [76] It also came at a time when the Swiss-German
Compactusingold motorized compact stack was developed, and when
Fremont Rider was arguing that, granted an edition of 25, microcards were cheaper than the most economical storage methods. [77]
The interest in these new approaches to an age-old library problem
appears to have been keen, and Macdonald again found himself involved in one of the vital library issues of the time.

As work progressed in the late summer of 1950, relations
between the Center and Snead and Company were very cordial. In
September Ralph Esterquest, the Director, congratulated Macdonald
on the handsome brochure describing the compact shelving, and
declared "it makes me feel proud to be associated with the whole
enterprise."[78] But America's problems in supplying both guns and
butter during the Korean War began to place a strain on the project.
Because of the steel shortage Macdonald turned to Snead's French
franchise, Forges de Strasbourg, for shelves. When the shelves
arrived, they were rusty. Troubles began to mount, compounded,

Figure 27. Compact storage.

The Module is the Message 165

no doubt, by Macdonald's own slender financial resources. Tempers grew short on both sides: there were charges and counter-charges. The arbitration clause of the contract was finally invoked by Snead and Company, and the basic issue, one involving $26,048.36, was decided in favor of Snead.[79] Nevertheless, Macdonald claimed to have lost over $39,000 on the job,[80] and maintained that these losses were largely responsible for forcing Snead and Company out of business in the summer of 1952.[81]

Macdonald early modified his view of the modular library to provide for compact storage, and his article "Building Design for Library Management," advocated the use of three types of shelving--conventional, readily accessible shelving with "wide aisles...and superb lighting," a closed area with shelving for rare items, and, for the "very inactive stock...compact storage, where economy dominates rather than visibility."[82] Compact shelving, however, has had only limited applications. In spite of its potential economy, the heavy floor loads and the need for special bracing contradicted the trend toward flexibility that many librarians were building into their modular libraries.

Macdonald's Influence Abroad

Since the involvement of Snead and Company in the Vatican Library in the late 1920's, Macdonald was known in Europe. As was established earlier, his "Library of the Future" was written for a European festschrift, and it is Macdonald's definition of modular planning that is cited in such standard European works as Milkau[83] and Thompson.[84]

J. P. Lamb, the librarian of the Sheffield (England) Public Library, delivered a paper before the Library Association's Brighton Conference in June, 1947, in which he drew heavily on Macdonald's ideas. Lamb, after reading "New Possibilities...," wrote to him requesting further details. Macdonald obliged, and had Githens send sketches of the University of Georgia Library, then in the planning stage.[85] Lamb gave Macdonald full credit for the substance of his paper and referred to the 1933 article, "A Library of the Future," as one of "extraordinary inventiveness."[86] From the discussion that followed Mr. Lamb's presentation, it is obvious that his ideas stimulated considerable interest among the audience, particularly the matter of low ceilings (10 feet) in the reading areas. [87]

Another example of Macdonald's influence abroad is found in a long article by G. Liebers-Kassel. Struck by the emphasis on flexibility in post-war American libraries, he described, in 1952, Macdonald's theories and gave him credit for advocating the application of new (modular) building techniques to libraries as early as 1933. Liebers-Kassel, after a general description of the modular plan, discussed in some detail the four libraries at the State University of Iowa, Princeton University, the Massachusetts Institute of Technology and Harvard's Lamont Library. [88]

Consulting: Two Hollow-Column Buildings

During the years that Macdonald was associated with Snead and Company he naturally adopted the role of a consultant, a service provided without cost, but usually with the hope that Snead would obtain the stack contract. Later, after selling the remaining assets and good will of the company to Globe-Wernicke, in August, 1952, he adopted the role of consultant on a professional basis. However, in the period just after World War II, Macdonald exerted considerable influence on the design of two buildings in the role of unpaid consultant and, later, contractor.

In the summer of 1945 Miss Thelma Andrews completed work on her Master of Arts thesis at the University of Chicago. Miss Andrews was librarian at Hardin-Simmons University; and her thesis was a study of 30 small academic library buildings built in the past 20 years. [89] This work demonstrates that she was aware of a number of the transitional buildings of the pre-war period, such as the Babson Institute (1939), and the convertible stacks at Colorado College of Education (1939) and Rockford College (1940). She also stressed the need for flexibility in a time of changing curriculum and methods of instruction, and wrote of the plans for the State University of Iowa library to provide this flexibility. Among the articles cited by Miss Andrews were four by

The Module is the Message

Ralph Ellsworth, including his "Buildings and Architecture,"[90] in which he described the Iowa plan. She wrote of the advantages of the "unit" construction proposed for Iowa, and it is not surprising that the Hardin-Simmons University Library was built in this manner.

Macdonald and Snead and Company were deeply involved in the building. The hollow structural framework, shelving, and lighting were contracted to Snead. Unfortunately, while this building was under construction, Snead and Company's plant was acquired by Virginia Metal Products Corporation, and some inevitable delays and confusion resulted. From a telephone conversation with Miss Andrews[91] and correspondence with Miss Mabel E. Willoughby,[92] the present librarian, it is clear that the hollow-column structure was suggested by Macdonald. As important, perhaps, as the structure, was the lighting. Miss Willoughby still regards it as "very good indeed." Alfred Morton Githens, after visiting the library in 1950, wrote to Macdonald:

> In fact the lighting was so good that, studying the architect's plans with Miss Andrews in the library, I was not aware that it was growing dark outside. Congratulations... Miss Andrews... is very pleased with the building.... As you suggested, Georgia [Githens was designing the University of Georgia Library at this time] might try some revisions along these lines.[93]

Based on recommendations Macdonald was making for North Dakota in the late 1940's, it is probable that a lighting intensity of 35 foot candles was provided by a luminous ceiling using a louverall grid. Hardin-Simmons may have been the first library to use a louverall ceiling on such an extensive scale. In a response to Githens' letter, Macdonald indicated he was not entirely satisfied with the lighting there and hoped to design an improved louver that would eliminate all glare.[94]

While the Hardin-Simmons University Library was under construction, in December, 1946, Macdonald's office received a letter from William F. Kurke and Associates, architects, in Fargo, North Dakota.[95] In his letter, Kurke recalled that he had had a "satisfactory" experience working with Snead and Company on the North Dakota Historical Building. His December letter concerned plans for a library at North Dakota Agricultural College in Fargo. The letter was accompanied by a one-sixteenth inch scale architectural drawing, and requested suggestions for equipment. The drawing was of a typical "T"-plan college library, with a conventional stack at the rear, reserve and periodical reading rooms on the main floor, a double staircase up to a delivery hall, and a great reading room (70 feet by 145 feet) on the second floor, extending across the front of the building. Thus began a close association between Macdonald and this North Dakota building. Macdonald, the architect, and H. Dean Stallings, the librarian, met at the American Library Association meeting in Atlantic City, New Jersey, in June, 1948. After the meeting Stallings wrote, "Our architects are redrawing the plan in line with many of the suggestions we received," and requested that Macdonald visit Fargo during the summer. [96]

By November, 1948, Macdonald had arranged for Gilbert D. Fish to cooperate with Kurke on the engineering and specifications. It is clear from the letter that a second hollow-column, modular library was being planned. [97] Somewhat on a note of triumph, Macdonald stated, in another letter:

> They are using the ideas we recommended pretty much all the way through, including the modular plan, the hollow structure... louverall ceiling lighting, and sound-absorption pads serving as concrete forms. They also accepted my suggestions about eliminating main windows except those necessary for psychological purposes. [98]

The building, when completed in 1950, employed the hollow columns spaced on 22 1/2-foot centers in both directions. Since it enclosed only 44,000 square feet, it was still a relatively small building. Like Hardin-Simmons which was also small, it could not be the great example of its type that would set the architectural world astir. However, the librarian was pleased with the building and boasted of its extremely low cost. Even in its time it was something of a wonder, providing 555,000 cubic feet of furnished space on a budget of $500,000. [99]

Macdonald's reformed Snead and Company won the bid for the structural framework, the lighting and some of the furniture. None of this material was actually manufactured by Snead, but was awarded to sub-contractors. Ironically the book shelving was awarded to Remington Rand's Library Bureau. If there had been delays at Hardin-Simmons, the North Dakota library seems to have been completed with relative ease. The librarian observed that only 10 working days were required to erect the framework. [100]

Other Buildings Influenced by Macdonald

Probably no other structures, with the exception of numerous stack rooms and the stack portion of the Midwest Interlibrary Center (now Center for Research Libraries), bore more completely the Macdonald stamp than the two just described. However, the librarians or architects of a number of other modular buildings readily acknowledged their debt to Macdonald.

The librarian at the State University of Iowa (now University of Iowa), Ralph Ellsworth, repeatedly and generously acknowledged Macdonald's assistance. In the previous chapter Macdonald's involvement in the planning of the Iowa building was described as part of the evolution of the modular idea. While the Iowa library rejected the hollow-column principle, it did incorporate all other precepts of the modular plan. The column spacing was a uniform 19 1/2 feet by 27 feet, ceilings were low (8 feet 2 inches), partitions could be easily moved, and lighting, ventilation, and floor loads were such that any part of the building could be used for reader spaces, offices or book storage. [101] The columns, although of the standard "I" beam type, had ventilating ducts and electrical raceways fitted into them (Figure 28). If the columns themselves were not hollow, they achieved virtually the same objective: vertical distribution of air. This method of construction occupied approximately the same space as the column itself, permitted smaller horizontal ducts in the ceiling (hence, smaller ceiling to floor dimensions and less stair-climbing) and avoided the large air shafts, found in many later buildings, which consume almost as much space and interfere with library operations almost as much as the old light courts.

While this building was being planned, Macdonald traveled to Iowa City or Des Moines, where the architects' offices were located, and met with the architects and Ellsworth on a number of occasions.

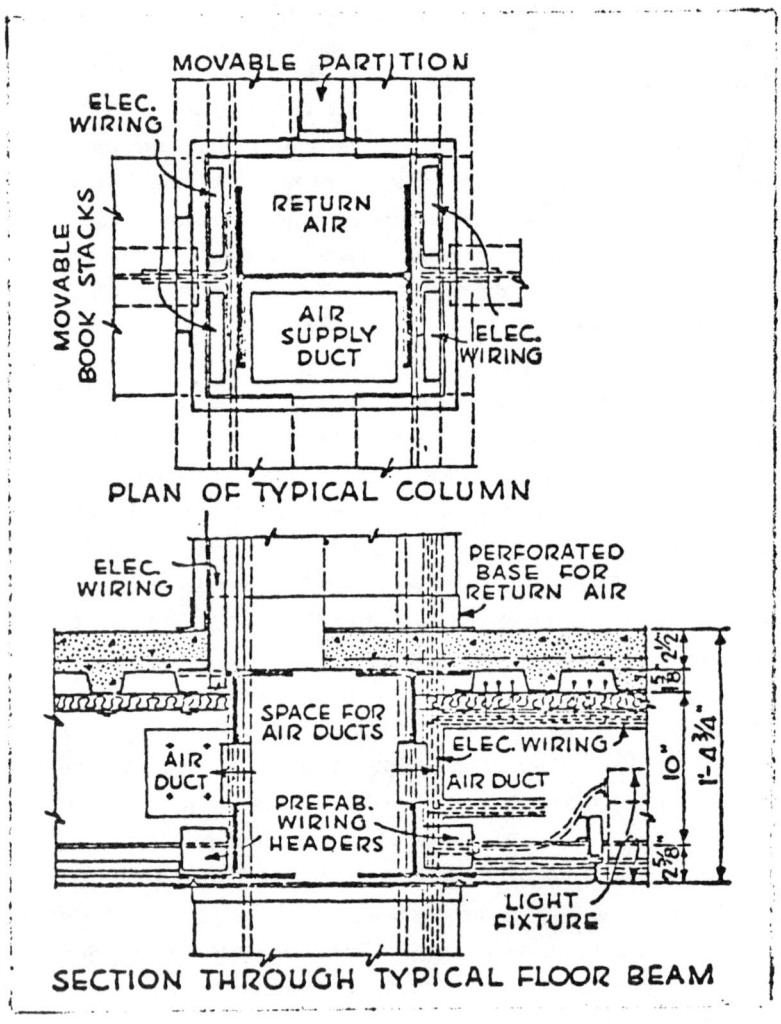

Figure 28. Column and beam design, University of Iowa as designed in 1946.

The Module is the Message

It is fair to conclude that Macdonald's influence on the Iowa library extended to the modular plan plus the other aspects listed in the previous paragraph, and even to some of the furniture. He also probably had some influence on the system of ventilation adopted. However, as documented in the previous chapter, the column spacing, fortunately, did not conform to his earlier ideas of 10 feet.

The University of Georgia Library is another that bears Macdonald's mark. There was a close association, both personal and professional, between Alfred Morton Githens, the architect for Georgia, and Macdonald. As already noted, Githens visited the Hardin-Simmons Library while Georgia was being planned; he examined the Snead and Company model in Orange on at least one occasion, [102] and, in his article in Library Journal, graciously acknowledged Macdonald's assistance. [103] While Georgia was the last of the three hollow-column libraries to be completed (November, 1953), it was actually designed before the one at the North Dakota Agricultural College was completed in 1950. Column spacing for the Georgia library was fixed at 18 feet in both directions. [104] Again, neither Iowa nor Georgia purchased their bookstacks from Snead and Company.

Beyond these buildings, the influence of Macdonald as a consultant becomes less clear. However, it is safe to say that other buildings were affected by him. For example, the Library at New Mexico Agricultural and Mechanical College, completed in 1953, was a modular building. Its regular column spacing, 22 1/2 feet by 18 feet, and its relatively low ceiling and flexible interior were becoming familiar features. In an article describing the building, the librarian, Chester H. Linscheid, acknowledged Macdonald's help in arriving at a "basic design of the building and for certain [other] ideas incorporated in it."[105] Macdonald had begun consulting with Linscheid before the plans were drawn. [106]

A little less clear is Macdonald's involvement in the library at Washington State College (now University). It was one of the first large buildings of the modular type to be completed after World War II. Constructed between 1948 and 1949, it was designed by John W. Maloney, architect, and the librarian, G. Donald Smith. It too bore the usual features of the modular plan, but relied upon the horizontal distribution of air (a few large vertical air shafts distributing air to relatively large ducts between the floor and ceiling.) Like North Dakota State, its columns were regularly spaced on 22 1/2 foot centers, but were of reinforced concrete. It was a large building with over 200,000 square feet and a budget of $2,500,000.[107] Smith stated that Macdonald had "very little" to do with the final planning of the building, but he did add, in a letter to the author:

> [Macdonald] and a few other individuals, did see and comment on our plans once or twice during their development, and he visited the campus once. He also spent part of a day with our architects in Seattle. On the other hand, this building does reflect many of his ideas and concepts for college library architecture... I was familiar with his writings on the subject, and had talked with him frequently in previous years before I came to Washington State. There is no doubt, therefore, that he did have a great influence on the design of this building...[108]

The West Virginia State College at Fairmont, West Virginia, appears to have been affected by Macdonald's writings rather than his work as an unpaid consultant. In 1948 the librarian, Harold D. Jones, requested 10 copies of the reprint of Macdonald's "New Possibilities in Library Planning" which were given to the Faculty Library Planning Committee and the architect. Four years later Jones reported that the "final plans are vastly different from the original ones proposed by the architects... I believe your article did much to clarify our thinking."[109] At the time Jones complimented Macdonald he requested 20 more copies for the planners of the Brooklyn College Library addition. Jones, at this time, was Chief Circulation Librarian at the New York college, and in 1953 he presented the plans for the addition to the Library Buildings Institute.[110] In 1961, it was reported that, in contrast to the original monumental, Georgian-style building, the new addition achieved "flexibility through modular design..."[111]

Macdonald's success as paid consultant is not dramatic. Although he received a number of commissions, few of them were big enough to keep him occupied for more than a few days. After Macdonald sold what remained of Snead and Company to Globe-Wernicke in August, 1952, Library Journal announced that he was "now free to pursue a long-standing ambition of serving professionally in the library field as a consultant and advisor to architects, librarians and trustees."[112] He was approaching his seventieth birthday as he embarked on this new, but short-lived, career.

The Library at Louisiana State University, in Baton Rouge, was probably his largest commission as a consultant. Both intellectually and emotionally he became very involved in the building. Macdonald arrived on the scene before the architect was selected, and the situation seemed to present an ideal opportunity: Louisiana was ready for a large, modern library, and an old friend, Guy Lyle, was librarian. Another friend, Mrs. Calvin K. Schwing, had recently been appointed to the University's Board of Supervisors and was a member of the Library Operating Committee. Before the building was completed, Lyle had moved to Emory University and Macdonald had resigned as consultant. While these two events were not related, they undoubtedly complicated the planning of the library.

Although a reasonably complete correspondence file remains, it is difficult to establish Macdonald's influence. It is probable that he was responsible for the selection of the site and for the general, modular plan. His attempts to convince the architects of the advantages of the hollow-column design were not successful, and his original cost estimates were somewhat optimistic. He had originally proposed a four-story building,[113] but the $3,500,000 budget bought only three stories five years later.[114] Nevertheless, the site, the general plan and the column spacing of 24 feet by 27 feet were adopted as Macdonald had suggested in his program.

Macdonald's resignation in 1955 was occasioned by his disagreement with the architect, Ralph Dodman, over certain structural and aesthetic aspects of the building. Almost from the beginning, there seems to have been some difference in opinion between Macdonald and Lyle over the use of a bookstack-supported mezzanine.

Lyle was opposed to the idea on the grounds that it limited flexibility. He preferred unbroken floors with 8 to 10 feet ceiling heights, "if the effect is not too utilitarian looking." In December, 1953, Macdonald agreed that the "saving in costs of a typical mezzanine floor construction as contrasted with a main floor construction is hardly enough to warrant the loss of complete flexibility of space use."[115] However, in the intervening period between this statement and his resignation he must have had second thoughts, for the first reason given in his letter of resignation concerns the architect's failure to incorporate the mezzanine idea. He feared that a modular building as large as the one planned for Louisiana State University (almost 190,000 square feet), while functionally successful, would have the "effect... of a glorified warehouse."[116] Macdonald also objected to the use of horizontal instead of vertical air distribution as unnecessarily expensive, but Lyle had been to the University of Georgia and had not approved of the air-conditioning there.[117] The matter of settling the final plans of the building was left to the architects, to Sidney Smith, Lyle's replacement, and to Keyes Metcalf, whom Macdonald had recommended as a consultant. The building was large, and to some, apparently, the epitome of modular planning.[118]

Of special interest to Macdonald was the project he hoped to develop with Edgar Robinson, the Librarian at Vancouver, British Columbia. The public library needed a new library building, but found it difficult to obtain sufficient support from the city government. Edgar Robinson was favorably impressed with Macdonald's plan for a library-office building. In 1948 Robinson requested 50 copies of "Morrow's Library,"[119] and for several years the two revised plans at conferences and through correspondence. In October, 1953, Robinson thanked Macdonald for what he "had done to date. It has been costly for you," he wrote, "and I only hope we can repay you by consultation work...."[120] On December 11, 1953, Robinson cabled that a $2,000,000 bond issue had been approved. By this time, the dreams of a generous income from wealthy office tenants had vanished. The city fathers preferred the tried and true method of the bond issue and continued public support, but Macdonald still served as consultant. In November, 1954, Robinson and Macdonald met in Los Angeles and San Diego concerning the new building, and they consulted with lighting, structural and ventilation engineers in the area.[121] The building, when completed in November, 1957, was of modified modular design with a mezzanine over a large part of the main floor. The second and third floors had relatively low ceilings. Two levels of bookstacks, with a capacity of 700,000 volumes, occupied the basement. Some of its features, such as the two-level stack beneath the main floor, the location of the administrative offices on the third, and even the electrically driven sun shields or louvers, suggested the Cincinnati Public Library, completed three years before. However, with a book capacity of 850,000 volumes, approximately one-half of Cincinnati's, it avoided the "layer cake" design of placing stack levels between service floors.[122] Robinson, who had devoted so much energy to convincing Vancouver of its need for a new building, died of a heart attack one week before the building was formally opened to the public.

Many other buildings, particularly in the college and university field, benefited from Macdonald's ideas or were influenced by the early post-war modular buildings. Macdonald brought G. Donald Smith and T. N. MacMullan together in his home in Orange, which undoubtedly resulted in some of the Washington State College experience being passed on to Louisiana State University.[123] The University of Wyoming Library Planning Committee visited the Colorado State College of Education, early in its planning, and later the buildings at Washington State College, State University of Iowa and North Dakota Agricultural College. N. Orwin Rush, the Librarian at Wyoming, expressed his gratitude to Macdonald and his admiration of the Washington State College Library in a letter of November 17, 1950. How many other librarians and architects were influenced by these buildings is impossible to determine. As the rings of Macdonald's influence spread from the early modular buildings his personal role became less distinct. Other forces, operating more or less parallel to Macdonald, became more important.

Macdonald's activities as a publicist or consultant are not always easy to separate and sometimes not easy to document. His influence on such library buildings as those at Hardin-Simmons University, North Dakota Agricultural College and the University of Georgia is clear. His role at Iowa, New Mexico State, West Virginia State College and other libraries can be readily established, although in some cases his involvement was impersonal, through his published writings. It seems fair to conclude that many buildings, not simply those cited in this chapter, were influenced by his writings, travels, talks, the model, the Beaux-Arts competition, and other devices he employed to publicize his modular "gospel."

Notes

1. "Hollow-column" is used in this discussion as a means of referring to that system of construction described in his "New Possibilities in Library Planning," and which involved not only hollow columns, but hollow beams, girders and floor panels as well. These hollow members took the place of the conventional, separate ventilating duct-work.

2. Alfred Morton Githens, op. cit., p. 2131.

3. Most likely this inspiration came from Macdonald who had been involved in the production of aircraft sub-assemblies and gliders during World War II.

4. Gilbert D. Fish, "Report to Snead and Company on Tests of Bookstack Columns," unpublished report, May 28, 1945. 4p.

5. Apparently Keffer and Jones, architects for the University of Iowa Library, had such fears, as borne out by an exchange of letters between Ralph Ellsworth and Macdonald, August 17 and 21, 1945, in the University of Iowa Library files.

6. William F. Kurke to Meinecke-Johnson Co., May 19, 1949, p. 2, carbon copy in Macdonald papers.

7. See Eliot Janeway, "Balancing America's Metal Requirements," Harvard Business Review, XXIX (November, 1951), pp. 92-102, in which the "inventory recession" of 1949 and early 1950 is described as the only period between 1942 and 1951 in which "customer demand on rolling schedules eased." With the Korean War (June, 1950) steel was

again in short supply, and by 1951, Janeway depicts the economy as "bottlenecked for lack of structural steel," p. 95.

8. Gilbert Fish to Kaufmann, Lippincott and Eggers, January 30, 1947, p. 2, see Appendix L

9. Macdonald to Fish, July 25, 1947, p. 1.

10. Fish to Macdonald, February 15, 1951.

11. Macdonald to Fish, September 26, 1946.

12. Fish to Macdonald, August 14, 1947 and March 12, 1948. The two men had considered a joint patent on the concrete version of the system.

13. O'Connor to the author, April 16, 1968, attached memorandum for Walter H. Kilham, Jr.

14. Hardin-Simmons University (1949), North Dakota Agricultural College (1950), and University of Georgia (1953).

15. U. S. Patent Office, Official Gazette, DCLXIV (November 4, 1952), pp. 191-192. Macdonald applied for patent protection on October 5, 1945, but only after considerable delay was Patent Number 2,616,529 finally granted on certain aspects of the system. The correspondence with J. Preston Swecker, a Washington patent attorney, gives details, and reveals that other inventors, as early as 1887, had begun patenting various aspects of the system (damper controls and hollow columns). It is also obvious from the correspondence that Macdonald was unaware of most of these earlier attempts.

16. Letter from Alfred Morton Githens to the author, December (i.e., January) 18, 1967, p. 2.

17. Alfred Morton Githens, "The Evolution of a Library," op. cit., p. 2137.

18. Ibid., p. 2134.

19. Guy R. Lyle to Angus S. Macdonald, December 11, 1953 (Louisiana State University Library file in Macdonald papers.)

20. Concern over excessive vibration in the penthouse and the top floor or floors is born out by correspondence between Macdonald and Githens on September 25th and 30th, between Githens and C. Barton Albright, architectural engineer, on September 16th and 21st, and Githens' letter

to John E. Sims, of Georgia's University System Building Authority, of September 25th, 1953. Microfilm copies in author's files.

21. Macdonald to Alfred Morton Githens, October 1, 1953 (Louisiana State University Library file in Macdonald papers.)

22. Angus S. Macdonald, "To the Stockholders of Snead and Company," op. cit., p. 1.

23. "A Research Laboratories Building," Engineering News Record, February 26, 1942, p. 344, and Don Graf, Convenience for Research (New York: Voorhees, Foley and Smith, 1944), 56p.

24. William Warner Bishop paid tribute to the Vatican Library installation, in 1946, calling it "the most successful installation of modern library shelving and furniture... into an old palace of which I have knowledge. Great credit is due... the Snead Company [which] furnished the engineering skill which overcame all obstacles." See Bishop's "The Historic Development of Library Buildings," Herman H. Fussler, ed., Library Buildings for Library Service (Chicago: American Library Association, 1947), pp. 2, 3.

25. Letter from Mrs. Evelyn Steele Little to the author, January 15, 1967, p. 1.

26. Angus Snead Macdonald, "Some Engineering Developments Affecting Large Libraries," p. 628.

27. Letter of Earl V. Rugg to Macdonald, June 4, 1940, p. 3. (Colorado State Library files).

28. Angus Snead Macdonald, "A Library of the Future," Canadian Library Association Bulletin, V (July, 1948), pp. 11-13, 29.

29. "Planning, Adapting and Equipping the Library Building," American Theological Library Association [Conference Proceedings, 1949.] (Evanston, Ill.: Garrett Biblical Institute, 1949), pp. 40-4 (mimeographed).

30. Addressed Physical Problems Class and Colloquium, University of Illinois, Graduate School of Library Science, May 5, 1949. Correspondence between Macdonald and Herbert Goldhor.

31. Letter of Macdonald to William M. Randall, a former librarian, but at the time Dean of the U.S. Merchant Marine Academy, Dec. 21. 1948.

32. Angus Snead Macdonald, "The So-Called Modular Library," unpublished notes, January 4, 1949.

33. "Some Engineering Developments Affecting Large Libraries," op. cit., p. 269.

34. Alfred Morton Githens, "The Evolution of a Library," op. cit., p. 2132.

35. Angus Snead Macdonald, "New Possibilities in Library Planning," op. cit., p. 1171. Edward L. Tilton had recommended the use of "a module [of] approximately 12 feet" for planning purposes in his "Scientific Library Planning," Library Journal, XXXVII (September, 1912), p. 501. This article was reprinted in Snead and Company's Library Planning... in 1915.

36. "What is a Module?" Modular Grid Lines, 1 (September, 1947), p. 7.

37. Letter of Macdonald to Frank C. Burke, Editor of Modular Grid Lines, September 24, 1947.

38. "A New Fangled Word for an Old Fashioned Principle: Modular," Library Buildings Plans Institute, 2nd, Chicago, 1953, Proceedings, ed. Donald C. Davidson (Chicago: Association of College and Reference Libraries, 1953), pp. 6-7.

39. Alfred Morton Githens, "The Evolution of a Library," op. cit., p. 2131.

40. Alvin Toffler, "Libraries," Educational Facilities Laboratories, Bricks and Mortar Boards... (New York: The Laboratories, 1964), p. 76.

41. Among the libraries receiving the sketches were those at Colgate University, the Universities of Maryland and Manitoba, New Mexico College of Agriculture and Mechanic Arts, state teachers' colleges at St. Cloud, Minnesota and Towson, Maryland, and Virginia Polytechnic Institute. (Based on notes in Snead and Company's prospect file).

42. Macdonald to Cardinal Tisserant, November 19, 1947.

43. Macdonald to Gilbert D. Fish, October 19, 1947, pp. 1-2.

44. Macdonald to Baron Moens de Fernig, February 8, 1951 (carbon copy in Macdonald papers.)

45. "Jury Returns Verdict in $100,000 Damage Suit in Favor of Defendent Angus S. Macdonald...," Orange Review,

April 8, 1954, p. 1.

46. Macdonald to Mrs. Calvin Schwing, April 23, 1953, p. 1 (Macdonald papers, Louisiana State University file).

47. In a letter to the author, May 6, 1968, Bailey listed 140 libraries for which he had served as architect or consultant.

48. University of Georgia, News Bureau, ["William Randall"] News Release, May 20, 1947, p. 1-2 (copy in Macdonald papers).

49. William M. Randall and F. L. D. Goodrich, Principles of College Library Administration, (2d ed., Chicago: American Library Association, 1941).

50. Ibid., p. 170.

51. Letter of William M. Randall to Macdonald, October 29, 1945, p. 3.

52. William M. Randall, "Some Principles for Library Planning," College and Research Libraries, VII (October, 1946), pp. 319-325.

53. "The Constitution of the Modern Library Building," Library Buildings for Library Service, ed. Herman H. Fussler (Chicago: American Library Association, 1947), pp. 182-205. Randall is identified as Director of Libraries, University of Georgia, p. xii, but at the time he delivered the paper, he was employed by Snead and Company.

54. Exchange of letters between Alfred Morton Githens and Macdonald, October 9 and 11, 1944, and letter to Ralph E. Ellsworth, October 14, 1944.

55. Boyd to Macdonald, July 6, 1945.

56. Cooperative Committee on Library Plans, The Orange Conference, (Philadelphia: Printed by Stephenson Brothers, 1946), p. 2.

57. Ralph E. Ellsworth, "A Modular Library for the State University of Iowa," American School and University, 18th ed. (1946), p. 98. A larger column spacing was later adopted by Iowa.

58. Cooperative Committee on Library Plans, op. cit.; p. 3.

59. Ralph E. Ellsworth to Macdonald, May 4, 1945, (carbon copy in University of Iowa Library files).

60. For a colorful description of the Conference, see John Ely Burchard, "A Signpost in Virginia," American Institute of Architects Journal, V (January, 1946), pp. 23-7.

61. Cooperative Committee on Library Plans, op. cit., p. 32.

62. Ibid., p. 2.

63. Snead and Company, Shop Order XO-401, May 16, 1945, May 24, 1945; and September 20, 1945, respectively.

64. Snead and Company, Shop Order XO-401, May 24, 1945 and September 20, 1945.

65. Snead and Company, "Estimate of Quick Assets Available, December 31, 1945," unpublished, processed report, p. 3.

66. Ralph E. Ellsworth, "Library Architecture and Buildings," Library Quarterly, XXV (January, 1955), p. 70.

67. Angus Snead Macdonald, Morrow's Library, (Orange, Virginia: privately printed, 1948), 16p.

68. Angus Snead Macdonald, "A Library of the Future," Canadian Library Association Bulletin, V (July, 1948), pp. 11-13, 29.

69. _____, "Libraries Unchained," Library Journal, LXXVIII (January 15, 1953), pp. 77-84.

70. "A Library and Office Building - Angus Snead Macdonald Prize," Beaux-Arts Institute of Design Bulletin, XXVI (May, 1950), [p. 1-3].

71. "Texas Architects Will Judge Design Institute Competition," Dallas Daily Times Herald, May 19, 1950, Sec. 4, p. 5, col. 1-3.

72. Letter of Joseph L. Wheeler to Macdonald, May 24, 1953.

73. Macdonald to Helen Wessels, ed. of Library Journal, January 23, 1953.

74. Now the Center for Research Libraries.

75. "Midwest Inter-Library Center Considers its Shelving Program" Library Journal, LXXV (April 15, 1950), pp. 726-7. Robert H. Muller later demonstrated that such shelving was not economical except where land or building costs were excessively high. See his "Compact Storage Equipment: Where to Use it and Where Not," College and Research Libraries, XV (July, 1954), pp. 300-307.

76. Ralph E. Ellsworth "Library Architecture and Buildings,"

op. cit., p. 74.

77. Fremont Rider, "Warehouse or Microcard?" Library Journal, LXXV (April 15, 1950), pp. 927-31.

78. Letter from Ralph T. Esterquest to Macdonald, September 5, 1950, (copy in files of Dixon, Todhunter, Knouff and Holmes, Lawyers, Chicago.)

79. American Arbitration Association, Administrator, "Commercial Arbitration Tribunal in the Matter of the Arbitration between Angus Snead Macdonald Corporation d/b/a Snead and Company and the Midwest Interlibrary Corporation; Award of Arbitrators" Case C-10812 CH1-C-4-53, February 9, 1954.

80. Macdonald to the Board of Directors of the Midwest Inter-Library Center, June 27, 1952.

81. Macdonald to Ralph E. Ellsworth, September 21, 1954.

82. Angus Snead Macdonald, "Building Design for Library Management," op. cit., p. 468.

83. Fritz Milkau, ed., op cit., II, 997.

84. Anthony Thompson, Library Buildings of Britain and Europe (London: Butterworths, 1963), pp. 22-24.

85. Macdonald to Githens, March 19, 1947 and Githens to Lamb, March 24, 1947. Microfilm copy in author's files.

86. J. P. Lamb and C. G. Stillman, "Public Library Buildings of the Future," Library Association Conference, Brighton, 1947, Papers (London: The Association, 1947), p. 97.

87. Ibid., pp. 103-4.

88. G. Liebers-Kassel, "Der Gedanke Der 'Flexibility' in Neueren Amerikanischen Bibliotheksbau," Nachrichten für Wissenschaftliche Bibliotheken V (Dezember, 1952), pp. 225-242.

89. Thelma Andrews, "Trends in College Library Buildings," (unpublished Master's thesis, Graduate Library School, University of Chicago, 1945), 91 p.

90. Ralph E. Ellsworth, "Buildings and Architecture," College and Research Libraries, VI, no. 3 (June, 1945), pp. 279-81.

91. Telephone interview with Miss Thelma Andrews, January 15, 1967.

92. Letter of Mabel E. Willoughby to the author, January 18, 1967.

93. Githens to Macdonald, February 22, 1950 (microfilm copy in author's files.)

94. Macdonald to Githens, May 11, 1950 (microfilm copy in author's files).

95. Kurke to Macdonald, December 9, 1946, 2 pp. and drawing.

96. Stallings to Macdonald, June 22, 1948.

97. Macdonald to Kurke, November 26, 1948.

98. Macdonald to E. W. Bartley, Snead and Company's agent in Minneapolis, November 15, 1948.

99. H. Dean Stallings, "A New Pattern for Economy, Utility and Beauty...," College and Research Libraries, XI (April, 1950), p. 135. (In an unpublished analysis for Louisiana State University, Macdonald reported the cost as $525,000, but still under $1.00 per cubic foot. Macdonald included $25,000 for additional furnishings.)

100. Ibid., p. 135.

101. Ralph E. Ellsworth, "A Modular Library for the State University of Iowa," op. cit., pp. 98-105.

102. Cooperative Committee on Library Building Plans, The Orange Conference, op. cit., p. 1.

103. Alfred Morton Githens, "Evolution of a Library," op. cit., p. 2132.

104. Ibid., p. 2133.

105. Chester H. Linscheid, "New Mexico A & M to Move into New Library Building Next Fall," New Mexico Library Bulletin, XXI (January, 1952), p. 12.

106. Ibid.

107. John W. Maloney, "Modular Library Under Construction...", Architectural Record, CIV (July, 1948), p. 102.

108. Letter of G. Donald Smith to the author, January 27, 1967.

109. Letter of Harold D. Jones to Macdonald, October 10, 1952.

110. "Brooklyn College Library," Library Building Plans Institute, 2nd, Chicago, 1953 Proceedings, (A. C. R. L. Monograph

no. 10, Chicago: Association of College and Reference Libraries, 1953), pp. 64-9. Architect-critic of the presentation was J. Russell Bailey, formerly of Snead and Company.

111. H. G. Bousfield, "Brooklyn College Triples Size," Library Journal, LXXXVI (January 1, 1961), p. 78.

112. "Angus Snead Macdonald to be Consultant," Library Journal, LXXVII (October 15, 1952), p. 1790.

113. Angus Snead Macdonald, "A Suggested Program for the Louisiana State University Library Building," unpublished, typewritten report August ?, 1954, p. 5.

114. Sidney B. Smith, "New L. S. U. Library in Action," College and Research Libraries, XX (May, 1959), p. 194.

115. Exchange of letters between Lyle and Macdonald, November 30, 1953 and December 4, 1953, respectively.

116. Macdonald to Charles E. Smith, Dean of the University, June 3, 1955.

117. Lyle to Macdonald, November 30, 1953.

118. Fritz, Milkau, ed., op. cit., p. 998-1001.

119. Macdonald to Forrest D. Spaulding, Librarian, Des Moines, Iowa, Public Library, April 6, 1948.

120. Robinson to Macdonald, October 22, 1953.

121. Notes in Macdonald's "Memindex" appointment calendar, November 14-20, 1954.

122. Edgar S. Robinson, "Canadian Landmark," Library Journal, LXXXII (December 1, 1957), pp. 3021-24 and Carl Vitz, "Pleasantly Functional," Library Journal, LXXIX (December 15, 1954), pp. 2360-64.

123. Notes in Macdonald's "Memindex" appointment calendar, September 22, 1954.

Chapter VII

Other Forces Responsible for Change

Although this study has focused on the contributions made by Macdonald and his company, there were many other forces and individuals responsible for making the new library architecture possible. Changes in building technology and taste, in educational methods, in the role of the library in the community or campus, and the impress of individuals all played an important part. Some of these forces were in motion before Macdonald was born, and others were more important than the work of any individual.

It should be obvious that certain improvements in building technique and material were necessary before modular libraries could be built. Clearly, a library such as the one built at Princeton University in the mid-twentieth century was not possible for Oxford University in the seventeenth century. Nevertheless, a few of the more important technological improvements will be discussed.

The Building Frame

The most apparent feature of a modular library is, generally, its regular column spacing. The use of cast iron in English textile mills toward the end of the eighteenth century initiated this important feature. The further development of rolling mills in the 1840's and the development of steel processes made first iron and then steel available in ever increasing dimensions suitable for structural use.[1] Henri Labrouste's use of iron in the Bibliothèque Ste-Geneviève (1843) is a well-known early example, although the building can hardly be classified as "modular."

The warehouse is a building type that made early use of regularly-spaced, iron columns. The multi-storied warehouses designed by William Fairburn (English) and James Bogardus (American) in the mid-nineteenth century were forerunners of the American department store.[2] The flexibility of a large unbroken space, that could be subdivided to suit varying demands of the tenants, was well known to a few librarians, such as John Cotton Dana,[3] to architects, and, as has already been established, to Angus Macdonald.

As early as 1863 department stores were making use of regularly-spaced iron columns. The A. T. Stewart (later Wanamaker's) store, built in New York in that year, employed a regular column grid and attempted to bring light to the interior by a large, central, skylighted court (Figure 29). The Magasin au Bon Marche (Paris, 1876) is another well-known example of an early department store using structural iron. Welch has pointed out that these "large, specially built structures with open plans were discovered more efficient in handling crowds and... for display of merchandise."[4] The success of the department store, not only because of its structure, but for its many other popular features, has had an important and well-known influence on American libraries.[5]

Developing a little later than the structural use of iron and steel, but offering similar advantages in avoiding load-bearing walls and partitions, was the reinforced concrete frame. Although the American Portland cement industry did not begin until 1875,[6] Ernest Ransome and others quickly improved upon the techniques developed in Europe during the third quarter of the nineteenth century. Ransome's machine shop for Kelly and Jones, Greenburg, Pennsylvania (1903-4), was four stories high and employed reinforced concrete columns placed on approximately 20-foot centers in both directions.[7]

A building employing regularly-spaced columns, either of steel or reinforced concrete, does not make a modular library, even if it shuns the monumentality that irritated Dana. A warehouse, although solidly built and capable of accommodating heavy floor loads, could not serve as a modular library until highly sophisticated systems of illumination and ventilation had been developed. It is these two improvements that provided the final and crucial impetus toward change. To be truly effective as a substitute for the traditional library, which after all was, and in many cases still is, reasonably efficient, the modular library demanded truly effective substitutes

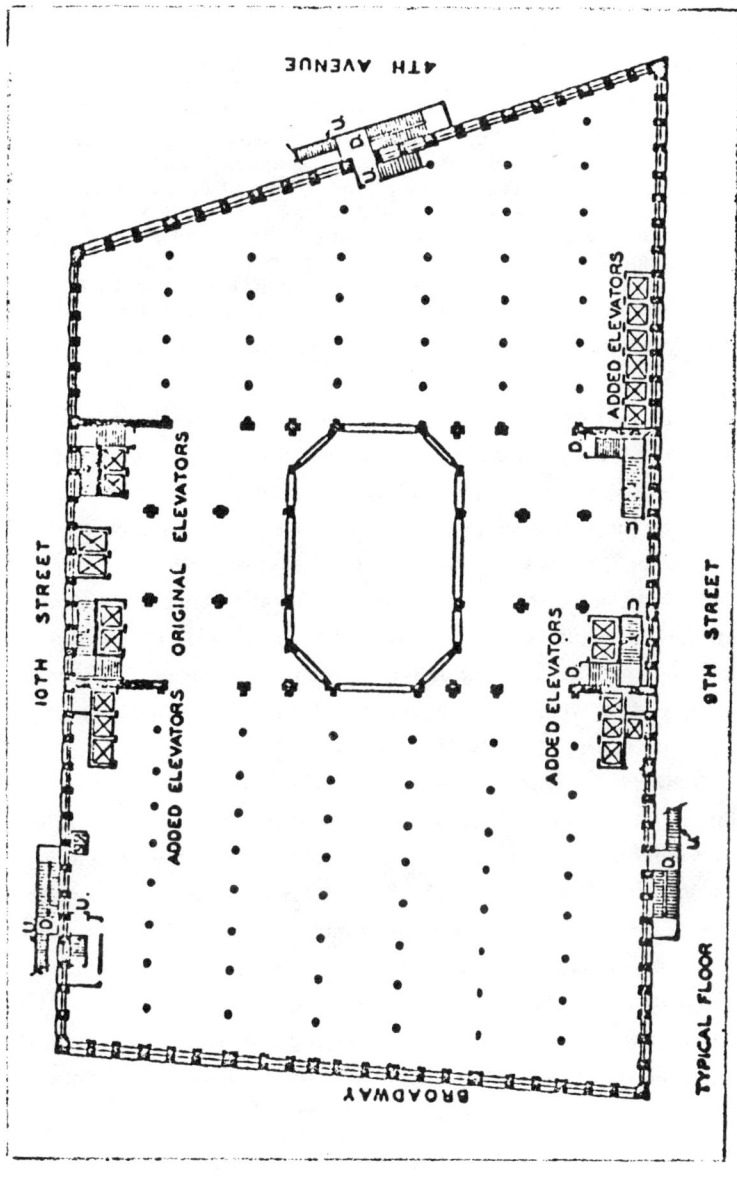

Figure 29. A. T. Stewart store, 1863.

for natural light and ventilation.

Natural and Incandescent Light

In 1927 the chairman of the American Library Association's Committee on Ventilation and Lighting, Samuel H. Ranck, wrote:

> ... we have trained our eyes to require a great deal more light than was satisfactory to the average user 25 or 30 years ago. There was a time when 4- or 5-foot candles on the reading plane (that is to say, an ordinary library table) were considered adequate lighting. Today 10-foot [candles are] very generally required and some of the newer library buildings have as high as 14- or 15-foot candles, although they seem to me to be overlighted. [8]

Apparently without knowing why, Ranck went on to state that "natural light is, of course, to be preferred."

It is well known that, down to the present, illumination experts have not been content to accept the "overlighted" effect of 14- or 15-foot candles, but have continually called for higher ratings. [9] Even though the output of incandescent lamps gradually increased throughout the 1920's and 1930's, and their initial cost and operating cost gradually declined, [10] authorities on library planning continued to call for an abundance of natural light. In addition to Ranck's remark, quoted above, many other authorities throughout the period up to the end of World War II (and after) continued to place heavy emphasis on natural light for the reader.

Edward L. Tilton, an architect to whom reference was made earlier in this paper, advised library planners "to follow the school house requirement and make the total glass area of the reading rooms equal to 20 percent of their floor areas." He also suggested the use of another popular rule-of-thumb; that "light from the windows will be effective in the room for a distance equal to about one and one-half times the height of the top window from the floor."[11]

Gerould in 1932, presented essentially the same recommendations,[12] and three years later McComb observed that "it is indeed difficult to provide too great an area of window openings."[13] Evenden[14] in 1938, and Hanley[15] and Lowe[16] both writing in 1939, stressed the importance of natural light and most referred to the "school house" standards. In 1941 Wheeler and Githens increased

Other Forces for Change

the recommended intensity of artificial light to 20-foot candles (Evenden had recommended this figure for college libraries) and presented to the reader a clear explanation of the problems of artificial illumination. However, they observed that "no library has been bold enough to do away with natural light" and conceded that "daylight is preferred."[17] As late as 1945 A. Gordon Lorimer declared, "It is obvious that the reading rooms should have an abundance of natural light... ."[18] However, Kraehenbuehl, in 1941, minimized the value of natural light because of its unreliability. He also abhorred the library table lamp, and recommended general illumination of 30-foot candles.[19]

Lyle, publishing three years later, generally followed Kraehenbuehl's recommendations and devoted very little space to the problems of natural light, simply referring the reader to earlier authorities. Regarding the choice between filament and cathode artificial lighting, he expressed a preference for the "more adequate" fluorescent.[20]

Up to this time, with a few exceptions such as the carrels in Columbia's Butler Library, the Treasure Room at the Virginia State Library, and the children's room at the London, Ontario, Public Library, virtually no reader spaces in libraries required artificial illumination, except after daylight hours. A survey of the literature on library buildings of this period (see Appendix II) tends to confirm this observation. Although the cost of lamps and electricity was declining, librarians still remembered the time when a 100-watt lamp cost between $1.00 and $2.00, and, with the depression, were reluctant to become entirely dependent upon "the electrical age."

Fluorescent Light

Complicating the problem for the library planner just before and after World War II was the introduction of fluorescent lighting. Spurred by the two World's Fairs of 1938-1939, and then temporarily retarded by pressure from utility companies (presumably because of its more efficient use of electricity), fluorescent lighting had a faltering introduction.[21] Before the war interrupted civilian production, a few libraries, recognizing its superior qualities, installed the new light source. Harvard's Houghton Library, Tulane's Howard-Tilton Library, and the Toledo Public Library, all completed in late 1940 and 1941, installed some fluorescent equipment. However, all three, fearing to trust the new source completely, included a large number of incandescent fixtures also. The Skidmore College Library (1940) happily discarded the conventional lighting for the "much superior" fluorescent. [22] Although Skidmore's crude troffers poured 35-foot candles on the table below, the reading areas were adjacent to the tall, 15-foot windows.

But the trial for fluorescent light in libraries was not yet over. Out of the experience of numerous fluorescent installations in war plants came reports of eye fatigue and irritation, and some authorities were concerned about excessive ultra-violet light reaching the workers' (or readers') eyes. [23] The work of Le Grand Hardy and Barbara Rand, both at the Columbia University Medical Center, caught the attention of librarians and architects. These researchers implied that there was a clear danger of irritation to the cornea and conjuntiva from prolonged exposure to ultra-violet light. They also listed flicker, high intrinsic brightness, lag of emission in the blue-green-yellow portion of the spectrum and the stroboscopic effect as disadvantages. [24] One of the frequently cited sources on library planning, the November, 1946, issue of the Architectural Record, which was devoted to libraries, began its article on lighting as follows:

> Opinions and recommendations on the subject vary widely, with recent assertions by ophthalmologists as to the possible harmful effects of flicker and ultra-violet radiation adding fuel to the controversy of filament vs. fluorescent systems. [25]

The article, although limiting itself to general lighting principles, could hardly be called an endorsement for fluorescent lighting and made no further reference to it.

At this time the Firestone Library for Princeton University, which incorporated a large modular "stack" section under the more conventional reading rooms, was already under construction. Julian Boyd reported the reasons for rejecting fluorescent lighting for the Firestone Library:

Other Forces for Change

> We objected to the stroboscopic effect, the humming noise, the delayed [start]... the color and the fact that, in a large number of fixtures, one or several are irregularly incandescent. Also there is some evidence that direct exposure to a fluorescent fixture is harmful to the human eye... .[26]

As a result, the Firestone Library is handsomely (if expensively) lighted by semi-direct and other incandescent fixtures.

The issue seemed to resolve itself quickly, however, when Rand withdrew her objections at the Second Princeton Conference, June 12-14, 1946, provided that the fixtures were properly shielded.[27] Fluorescent lighting rapidly became the standard light source in many libraries that were built in the post-war building boom (see Appendix II). The efficiency and generally superior quality of fluorescent lighting made possible the illumination of large interior areas at a considerable economy, even though the initial cost was greater. A power consumption ratio of from 2:1 to 4:1 in favor of the fluorescent source was generally reported.[28] The conferees at the second Princeton meeting of the Cooperative Committee seemed to agree that windows were necessary for psychological purposes only.[29]

Ventilation

Although its benefits as a light source were readily recognized, the fluorescent tube had another important advantage for the modular library--its low heat output. Radiated heat, especially important in relation to human comfort, has been shown to be considerably less under the fluorescent source. Claims varied but Kraehenbuehl, in 1951, reported 47 percent radiant energy from the cathode lamp as compared to 81 percent from the filament.[30]

The installation and operation of mechanical ventilation machinery as standard equipment in libraries is a relatively new concept. The early use of ventilation equipment was generally concerned with the bookstack and preventing damage to the books by mold and heat. In the late 1920's and early 1930's, the work of the Committee on Library Ventilation and the National Bureau of Standards (discussed in Chapter IV) attacked the problem of paper deterioration and the harmful effects of soot and chemicals in libraries in urban areas. The thought of ventilation for people was, until the 1920's, concerned with meeting any legal requirements regarding possible suffocation.[31] Virtually all public and staff rooms were provided with large windows that could provide the necessary ventilation as well as natural light. Even in the below-grade stacks of the "open plan" libraries, Githens questioned the need for mechanical ventilating equipment and reported that those libraries that had installed it, rarely used it.[32]

For the low-ceilinged modular library, at least in many parts of the United States, mere ventilation during the hot summer months would not be adequate. The work of Willis Haviland Carrier for the Sackett-Wilhelms Publishing Company in 1902 is credited as the first attempt to control mechanically both humidity and temperature.[33] Air conditioning, which includes the control of temperature, humidity, motion and quality of the air, was an important ingredient in making the modular library usable. Prior to 1911, the installation of air conditioning equipment was generally limited to special industrial uses in printing and textile plants, and tobacco curing warehouses. After 1920 large installations for public comfort began to make an appearance,[34] and by 1935 most large theaters and better restaurants were air-conditioned.[35] Throughout the 1930's and early 1940's the application of air conditioning (at times improperly used to mean simply mechanically cooled air) spread to many types of commercial and industrial buildings.

The April, 1935, issue of Library Journal carried four articles on the application of air conditioning equipment to libraries. Of the three large libraries discussed, only the Library of Congress Annex, not to be completed for three more years, was to be fully air conditioned. The other articles concerned a small, partial system for the Ponca City, Oklahoma, Public Library, the air conditioning equipment for the stacks of Columbia University's Butler Library (described in Chapter IV) and the Silica-Gel system at the Enoch Pratt Library. Enoch Pratt's system extended to the stacks and public reading rooms only (about 3/4 of the building's

Other Forces for Change

total cubage). It employed Silica-Gel to dry the air, and, operating in the days before Freon, a compressed carbon dioxide system to cool it. Whether due to poor design, maintenance, or inexperienced operators, Enoch Pratt's system proved ineffective and by 1946 was beyond repair. [36] During the depression years it was too expensive to operate, except on the warmest days, and after that period it was largely inoperative.

Gerould, in 1932, advocated air conditioning equipment for the stack room, particularly for humidity and dust control, but left the reader with the impression that full air conditioning for the entire building was impractical because of cost and "those who... demand open windows."[37] Dana McComb, writing three years later, questioned the high initial cost and observed that "day-by-day operation is also unduly expensive."[38] Hanley in 1939, and Wheeler and Githens, in 1941, both recommended full air conditioning for libraries operating in warm climates, or if it was beyond the library's budget, that the necessary duct work be provided to permit easy installation at a later date.[39] Clearly, by the beginning of the 1940's, air conditioning had been accepted by the leading authorities on library planning.

Rather than advocating a new idea for libraries, these authorities seemed to be simply following a trend that was beginning to develop. In addition to Enoch Pratt (1933) and the Library of Congress Annex (1937) at least two academic libraries, Columbia University (1934) and Brooklyn College (1937), had fully air-conditioned stacks before the end of the decade. Although Tulane claimed to be "the first completely air-conditioned university library" in 1941,[40] Eastern Washington College of Education and the Toledo Public Library, both 1940, were also "fully" air-conditioned. Harvard's Houghton Library (1942) was equipped to maintain, throughout the year, a constant 70 degrees F. temperature and 50 percent relative humidity.[41] Metcalf points out that it was not until after World War II that certain governmental agencies, such as the City of New York and the State of North Carolina, removed the prohibition (because of the expense) on air conditioning in publically financed buildings.[42] Nevertheless, in spite of the expense and official bans, air conditioning, like fluorescent lighting, was finding its way into libraries in the years just prior to World War II, and after the War gained rapidly in popularity. However, its acceptance was neither as rapid nor as complete as the new lighting device.

Up to this point, the discussion has focused on "complete" or "total" air conditioning. In spite of the observation by Githens, referred to above, and by Macdonald in an earlier chapter, that in the 1920's and early 1930's most libraries did not make use of the ventilating equipment which had been installed, the literature of the 1930's and early 1940's indicates that many new libraries continued to be equipped with some type of ventilating machinery which did not involve artificial cooling. A few libraries, such as the Fort Worth Public Library and the University of Wichita Library, both 1939, planned their ventilating systems in such a manner that cooling equipment could be added later.

The development of reasonably efficient ventilating systems, without cooling apparatus, but with controls to maintain at least a constant minimum temperature, is important. Without it a modular library of any size is unthinkable and in some areas would be illegal. It should be remembered too that most of the library buildings erected just after World War II, including those on the modular plan, were not fully air-conditioned. Neither Hardin-Simmons, Georgia, North Dakota, Princeton, nor Iowa, all referred to in earlier chapters, were equipped with cooling equipment on opening day, although most had plans for adding it to the ventilating system later. While complete air conditioning obviously made modular libraries more comfortable, and it might be possible to establish a vague correlation between the growing popularity of both after World War II, it is obvious that artificial cooling, like fluorescent lighting, is not an absolute necessity. Better artificial lighting and air conditioning systems did, however, virtually eliminate the dependence on natural light and ventilation, thus making the large interior spaces of modular libraries more comfortable.[43]

Other Forces for Change   195

Administrative Influences

No less important than technological advances in bringing about a change, were changes in the philosophy of library service. If one believed that books and readers were to be kept separate, then obviously, libraries would look a great deal different than if he believed readers should browse freely among the libraries' collections.

Public Libraries

In Chapter II the development of the open plan, open access, and the divisional arrangement of public libraries prior to World War II was mentioned. Lowell Martin, in 1955, pointed out that after the central buildings, at Los Angeles (1926) and Baltimore (1933) "every large central building constructed thereafter had this concept [divisional plan] prominent... ."[44] All of these trends continued after World War II, but unlike colleges and universities, few municipalities or counties built large library buildings immediately after the War. Obviously the number of cases available for study is limited. One might expect these three influences to support the adoption of the modular plan for public libraries. However, certain other factors counteract these forces. Common to all open-plan libraries, and most other large public libraries, is a separate stack area for the less frequently used materials. The five early open-plan libraries described in Chapter II all placed fixed, multi-tier stacks beneath the main floor. This plan was also adopted by the public libraries at Rochester, New York (1936) and Toledo, Ohio (1940). After the war it can be seen with only slight modification in the Dallas (1955), San Diego (1955), Denver (1956), Vancouver (1957) and Seattle (1960) public libraries. Cincinnati (1954) adopted the unique "layer cake" design, interspersing stack levels and public service floors. The public libraries, then, rarely embraced wholeheartedly the modular philosophy of complete interchangeability of space. Almost always there was a stack space somewhere that would forever remain a stack space, or be exceedingly expensive to modify for reader use.

The reason for this arrangement can be stated simply, and

is basic to the philosophy of large public library management: merchandise the books that are in demand and remove from the general public view those which are useful for research purposes only. There is pressure to place on the main floor as much of the new materials as possible, and to make the main floor as attractive and accessible as possible. By removing to closed or restricted stack areas the less frequently used materials, the "resultant reader frustrations" in the public areas are reduced, since only the new or more popular materials remain. [45]

Academic Libraries: A New Curriculum

Changes in educational philosophy and curriculum that occurred in the late 1920's and the 1930's are of vital concern to theories of library administration, which in turn affected library building design. Unlike the public libraries which retained a large portion of their collections in closed stack areas, the academic libraries, after World War II, placed virtually all materials on open shelves.

The rapid growth of graduate enrollment and library collections was noted in Chapter II. The graduate student, generally granted stack privileges, cozy in his carrel and surrounded by his books, was not likely to cause any concern on the part of the library administrator. It was, primarily, changes in undergraduate teaching methods and curriculum that forced certain changes in the library. The rise of the elective system, the "compartmentalization of knowledge" and the reliance on the lecture-textbook method of instruction in American colleges in the period prior to World War I are well known. [46] Beginning with the general education movement and the introduction of the survey course, Social and Economic Institutions, at Amherst, in 1914/15, a gradual trend was established that attempted, for the undergraduate, to return a measure of unity to the college curriculum. Fortunately for the library, both the Progressive educators, who earlier had supported the elective system, and those favoring a return to the discipline of the humanist or classic tradition agreed on the abuses of the elective system. The complex battle that raged among John Dewey, Mortimer Adler, Robert Hutchins and others now seems almost beside the point. [47]

Other Forces for Change

The experiments with the curriculum at Minnesota, Princeton, Colgate, Chicago and elsewhere had, according to writers at the time, a profound effect on library use. Gerould, in 1932, observed:

> Except as it provides a skeleton which the new student may clothe with living flesh of his own creation..., in the more progressive institutions, the textbook has largely passed out of use. Even in his Freshman year, the student is expected to gain some conception of the relativity of truth, to compare views of one authority with those of another.... . The library is a necessary part of the process... . On its richness and variety, on the convenience, attractiveness and accessibility of its housing, depends, in no considerable degree, the success of the student in securing an education. [48]

By 1932 the University of Chicago's New Plan, which appears to have attracted a great deal of attention, had been in operation for one year. This curriculum stressed broad survey courses (those that involve two or more departments) instead of the former departmentalized arrangements in the freshman and sophomore years. [49] It drew on the experience of Columbia University with a broad course in Contemporary Civilization, on Harvard's experience with comprehensive examinations, and hoped to provide "the freedom and intellectual responsibility which [had] been given to the student of the continental European university."[50] The New Plan stressed reading, and a carefully planned relationship between the curriculum and the library. A new book collection and expert advisors were added to the library. [51]

Randall, after completing a two-year study of college libraries for the Carnegie Foundation, noted that "the disappearance of the 'textbook method' is forcing the college library to the forefront." Astutely he added, "Most college libraries have been designed in terms of functions quite different from the services now expected of them."[52] Danton, in 1937, claimed an "almost complete displacement of the textbook method of teaching" and suggested that the new philosophy had its roots in the graduate seminar introduced before the turn of the century. [53] However, Ruth Walling observed, five years later, that "a surprisingly large number of courses rely entirely upon a textbook." Walling's study, which examined the curricula of the nation's 653 liberal arts colleges, revealed that about two-thirds of them offered no survey courses, and she estimated that 32 percent of all courses in the sciences, 27 percent in the social sciences and 9 percent in the humanities employed the textbook exclusively.[54] While there is no necessary association between departmentalized courses and use of the textbook, the survey course, apparently, tended to break down dependence on both. In spite of Walling's qualification, there was a clear trend away from reliance on the textbook. Survey courses of the time, such as those at the University of Chicago, required far more books (50-200 titles) than the typical "textbook" course, but still no great depth in book collections was necessary.

Frequently associated with these curriculum innovations were undergraduate seminars and honors courses which required "the development of library resources along intensive as well as extensive lines."[55] In support of this view, one survey found that the honors programs for undergraduates involved students in a wide range of materials and obligated them to become familiar with the library's bibliographic resources. It also forced the library to adopt new loan procedures, special stack privileges and reading facilities.[56]

Reeves and Russell cited a number of changes in the pattern of higher education which were contributing to dissatisfaction with the older form of library service. In addition to the movements discussed above, they added increased enrollment in the social studies. They pointed out that in the period between 1915 to 1930 total college enrollment doubled; and while enrollment in mathematics and foreign languages remained constant, that of social studies quadrupled. They observed that book production and library use for the social studies were heavy while both of these factors were relatively light for mathematics and foreign languages.[57]

Most of the writers cited above declared that these curriculum changes were forcing upon the library increases in influence, size and, most important, use. Branscomb's influential <u>Teaching With Books</u> stressed the dilemma that the closed stack library posed for the college student in this new curriculum. "What the closed shelf does is thus to interpose between the student and his reading the necessity of a definite and exact knowledge of the book which is wanted,"[58] Branscomb declared. He called for an open stack arrangement for the undergraduate student, and noted that such a movement was already under way.[59] Evenden, in 1938, cautiously advocated a building that could be adapted to an open stack policy "which is becoming increasingly popular,"[60] but both Evenden and Carter Alexander presume a separate stack structure in their guides for library planners.[61]

Effect of Curriculum Changes on Library Design

Even before World War II some colleges recognized the need for a different type of library to suit the changing curriculum. The case of the Colorado College of Education (1940) was discussed in Chapter IV. In an attempt to meet the educational needs of the University of Colorado, Ellsworth, drawing upon Enoch Pratt, adopted a divisional plan. This plan not only included the three familiar divisional reading rooms for science, humanities and social sciences, but also a lower division reading room designed to coordinate the program of the first two years.[62] Rockford College, in Illinois, adopted a similar divisional plan in order to accommodate "the character of the teaching done" and to preserve the informality of the smaller, older quarters.[63] While all of these libraries retained separate stack structures, the Colorado College of Education and Rockford combined the open stack policy with Snead convertible stacks, and the University of Colorado placed most of the heavily used volumes on open shelves in the divisional reading rooms.

In spite of the fact that Princeton had, from 1920-1938, a distinguished librarian in James Thayer Gerould, a librarian who had written a book on library planning referred to earlier in this chapter, the basic philosophy of Princeton's Firestone Library is generally ascribed to C. Rufus Morey, the equally distinguished chairman of the Department of Art and Archaeology.

Gerould had called attention to the inadequacy of Princeton's library buildings in 1920, and studies were made in the 1920's by Charles Z. Klauder which concluded that expansion of the existing facilities was not practical.[64]

Princeton had long prided itself on its emphasis on individual study and in 1923 implemented a new program for upperclassmen which required concentrated study in a major area and a thesis. Use of the library increased dramatically.[65] In 1932 Morey issued a document which called for a library that would give to the departments concerned with the humanities and social sciences the same facilities that the sciences enjoyed in their laboratories. Appropriately, he called this statement "A Laboratory Library," and envisioned a close association of the staff of the teaching departments, their students and books in the library.[66]

By 1940 Princeton was planning, for this unconventional program, a more or less conventional stack-at-the-rear building but with three stack levels extending under the reading rooms.[67]

In 1944, however, a brochure was issued which described the laboratory library as a major step in the development of Princeton's curriculum and predicted a further shift in the responsibility for the student's intellectual development away from the faculty member to the student himself.[68] This brochure is especially important because it envisioned an interchangeability of stack and reader or "educational" space, drawing upon the "device of interior flexibility already successfully tested in commercial office buildings and industrial laboratories."[69] Basic also to the philosophy of the new building was the open stack policy which had been introduced during Gerould's administration and which was considered important for the Princeton method of education. Princeton claimed to be the first large university library to abandon the closed stack[70] and, in its new building, looked forward to a "stack" that was roomier, more inviting and more flexible, where "space for human occupancy and space for book storage are, in other words, interchangeable in the modular plan..."[71] The huge modular stack structure was placed below grade with reading rooms, departmental offices and certain areas requiring "monumental" treatment superimposed.

Relating to the general education movement, and following closely Princeton's report of 1944, came Iowa's <u>The Library as a Teaching Instrument</u> in 1945. In the introduction, President Hancher

Other Forces for Change

viewed the future library at Iowa as a laboratory, providing the same facilities for the humanities and social sciences that the sciences already enjoyed.[72] The program envisioned a library in which, particularly for the lower classmen in the Arts College, all types of media would be made available and much of the instruction, especially that involving small groups or individuals, would take place.

In attempting to unite the compartments of knowledge for these students, Iowa placed on the first floor the Heritage Library which arranged materials chronologically. This area also provided seminar and visual aid rooms and offices for instructors and counselors.[73]

To permit this new type of library to function, to permit books and readers to mingle freely, Iowa adopted the modular plan in its entirety. Some of the details of the building's planning have already been presented. Iowa became closely identified with the modular plan and is frequently cited as an early example of the type. With the exception of variations in column spacing, structural details and lighting, Iowa is a replica of Princeton's stack, without any of the high-ceilinged reading areas placed on top. The objectives of both library programs were very similar and the solutions were remarkably alike.

The program for the new library at M. I. T. expressed some ideas similar to those of Iowa and Princeton. The building was to be the humanities center for the campus, and was to include offices for the teaching staff in the humanities "not so much for the purpose of luring students to the library as for the reason that a substantial portion of the instruction in these courses [best] takes place in office or other conference... near to the books."[74] But, although M. I. T. was attempting to relate its library more closely to the educational program, particularly in the humanities and social sciences, its solution was considerably different from that worked out at Princeton or Iowa. The program repeatedly called for flexibility, but neither the librarian nor the architect considered the "total" flexibility of the modular plan worth the price. While conceding that the University of Iowa's planned library offered greater flexibility, John Burchard, Director of Libraries and later Dean of Humanities, questioned, to some extent, the need for it. He wrote, "only the most amorphous activities can proceed with equal efficiency in universal space. In seeking universal flexibility we run the risk of creating universal mediocrity."[75] Burchard favored a compromise between the old "foundation-to-roof stacks" and the completely modular building. The final plan at M. I. T. interrupted the five-level bookstack at every other level with a structural floor, but assumed the bookstack would "remain more or less permanent."[76]

Any discussion of the early post-war buildings would not be complete without including the Lamont Library at Harvard University. Opened in January, 1949, this library was smaller than those discussed above, and was designed especially for the undergraduate men of Harvard College. It was planned for reading, not research, and its well-known book collection was chosen with undergraduate reading needs in mind. The building, a modified modular design, provided conference rooms for the general education program, and placed a "bookstack" in the center which featured reading alcoves. Grouped around the center stack were reading rooms generally two stack levels high.[77] Because of the unusual column spacing and use of mezzanines, the stack space tends to be fixed.

Not all of the colleges and universities that built new library buildings after World War II were sufficiently concerned about the new trends in undergraduate education to permit them to affect the library structure. The University of Wisconsin, for example, was much more concerned about the cost of modular construction, and the heavy emphasis on the relation of the library to graduate education. Affecting the cost, in view of the planners, was the site. Louis Kaplan wrote recently:

> We decided against a modular building for a number of reasons. Most important among these was the site, which did not offer sufficient expansion horizontally. It is my belief that modular construction, from the viewpoint of book capacity, is unfavorable unless horizontal space is available to make up for the loss vertically.[78]

Other Forces for Change

Nevertheless, Wisconsin was also concerned about bringing books and readers together and opened its ten-tier, conventional stack to lower classmen for limited periods, and to all upperclassmen and graduate students. [79]

On the other hand, North Dakota Agricultural College did adopt the modular plan without undergoing any drastic change in its educational philosophy. Stallings makes no mention of the library's involvement in new educational programs (though it certainly was in the traditional sense) in his writings, [80] nor did the building provide offices for faculty or counselors as did Princeton, Iowa and M. I. T. North Dakota, apparently, adopted the modular plan for other reasons, as the titles of Stallings' writings imply, for economy, for flexibility in future arrangement and for aesthetic reasons.

Flexibility

If there is a single, consistent motif in the voices of library planners over the years, it is the call for greater flexibility in library buildings. [81] A number of the early writers, such as Dana and Bertram, have already been mentioned in preceding chapters. Others, such as Charles C. Soule in 1912[82] and Chalmers Hadley in 1924, [83] made pleas for flexible interiors free of structural partitions. Virtually all writers on library planning made some protest against the inflexible designs of the past. This inflexibility was due in part to the construction methods employed at the time, but in large measure it was also a result of the popularity of the floor-to-ceiling bookstack. So long as the library building incorporated a separate stack structure, its flexibility was limited. Even where bookcases were a single tier in height and were used as partitions the problem was not always solved. Librarians at Enoch Pratt, for example, were frustrated by the major repairs that were required on the floor when the "free standing" cases were moved. [84]

In addition to the experiences of the past, which demonstrated the desirability of keeping the library's interior as free of permanent obstructions as possible, there was another compelling reason for demanding flexibility: the uncertainty about the future. In addition to the changing functions of libraries caused by the new curriculum, in the case of academic libraries, and the departmentalization of public libraries, the entire picture of the library and and its relation to the book was undergoing scrutiny. Microfilm had begun to find its way into libraries before World War II and Fremont Rider pictured micro-text as the research library's salvation.[85] Vannevar Bush's article in 1945 caused considerable concern about even more drastic changes. Bush revealed the new wonders of facsimile transmission and micro-micro-photography coupled with new indexing techniques which would place a sizeable library at any researcher's fingertips.[86] Burchard was one of many who were obviously influenced by Bush's ideas. After acknowledging his debt to Bush, he wrote, "Accordingly, no [library] building can be profitably contrived which will freeze any one of these activities either in form or scale."[87]

Viewing American libraries from abroad in 1952, a German writer, Liebers-Kassel, wrote:

> One main concept becomes more and more evident; this concept influences present-day American library construction a great extent and is automatically included in almost every design. This is the concept of "flexibility," that is to say the idea of mobility or interchangeability of all rooms and furnishings within the library.[88]

The persistence of the demands for greater flexibility, and the conviction on the part of many that the library would change, leads one to believe that it was simply a matter of time before technology, particularly lighting and ventilation engineering, and changing concepts of library administration were to make it possible.

Changing Taste and Economy

Another common and consistent call in the literature of library planning is for an end to the wastefulness of "class conscious" monumental design. In one manner or another, the writers objected to unnecessarily broad staircases, overly ornate decoration, useless but imposing columns, and the wasted space of unnecessarily high ceilings, broad corridors and grand entry halls. Arthur Bostwick, writing in 1927, was one of many who objected, and claimed that as much as 50 percent of the floor space of some libraries was expended on these features.[89] Certainly none delighted more in pointing out these foibles than Angus Macdonald.

But libraries were simply one type among many public buildings imprisoned by the taste of the times. Until the grip of the eclectic style was broken by the need for economy in the 1930's and 1940's, until the international school of architecture brought new forms, until advertising design and display could effectively relate an urban, industrial society to artistic expression, banks, post offices, railroad stations, court houses, museums and libraries were all expected to have the forms and imposing grandeur of Greece and Rome. Librarians might have been willing to settle for something less in the name of economy, informality and efficiency, but the older generation, the wealthy donor, the city fathers, the established architects had money, influence and tradition on their side.[90]

The earliest examples of libraries embodying the new ideas in architecture appear to be in Europe. Alvar Aalto's famous library and lecture hall at Viipuri, Finland (now in the U.S.S.R.) (1927-34) was a daring departure architecturally, but not a very practical library.[91] The Swiss National Library (1930-31), while more conservative than Aalto's design, is another landmark. It incorporated an early suggestion of the modular plan and, in renouncing all decoration, acknowledged its debt to Le Corbusier.[92] Not so well known perhaps are such examples in the United States as Louis Allen Abramson's design for the 136th Street Branch of the New York Public Library (1939) and the astonishingly modern library at Redwood City, California, by James H. Mitchell (1939). While it is relatively easy to identify early examples of modern design applied to European and other libraries, it is not so easy to trace the influence of these buildings on any of the post-war modular libraries. It is simply an indication of changing artistic taste and evidence that this change was affecting both the exterior and interior appearance. It would seem logical to conclude that in such an atmosphere alteration of the basic structure was also easier.

The Cooperative Committee and Its Members

The Cooperative Committee on Library Building Plans was convened at Princeton on December 15-16, 1944 at the suggestion of Princeton's President, Harold W. Dodds.[93] Its purpose was to bring together librarians, architects and others concerned with the libraries for a number of colleges and universities which were planning to build as soon as World War II ended. Institutions represented at the first meeting were the State University of Iowa, the University of Maine, the Massachusetts Institute of Technology, the University of Missouri, the University of North Carolina, the University of Pennsylvania, Rutgers--the State University of New Jersey, the State College of Washington and, of course, Princeton. Julian Boyd of Princeton was elected chairman.[94] The composition of the group varied during its brief existence but its membership always remained small in order to foster frank and open discussion of the members' building plans as they were presented. The Committee met in various cities, usually the home of one of the members, between 1944 and 1952. A notable exception was the meeting in Orange, Virginia, to examine the model of Snead and Company, discussed in Chapter VI.

Realizing the value of these discussions, the Committee, through John Burchard, applied to the Rockefeller Foundation in February, 1946, for a grant to publish the group's findings. The resulting compilation, Planning the University Library Building, carried the message of flexibility "in which the building is the stack and the stack is the building."[95] Leroy C. Merritt, then librarian at the State Teachers College, Farmville, Virginia, was hired to write the first draft. This draft was reviewed by the Committee and rewritten by Burchard, Boyd, and Charles W. David of the University of Pennsylvania. Ellsworth, Metcalf and Robert O'Connor, Princeton's architect, made a further review before the text was published in 1949.[96] The book was indeed a cooperative effort, but was hardly the success that the committee's work itself had been. American reviewers bestowed no accolades, finding it "disappointingly brief."[97]

Other Forces for Change 207

It is, of course, impossible to separate the actions of the committee from those of its members. Its members were surprisingly active in numerous related affairs. The extensive publications of Ralph Ellsworth have been mentioned previously. Some of John Burchard's publications have also been cited, and the involvement in library planning of Keyes Metcalf, who represented Harvard University on the Committee, is well known. Sixteen years after the Committee's major publication effort had been received coolly, Metcalf produced the guide for planning university libraries that all had sought in 1949.[98] Merritt and Ellsworth had participated in the Library Institute of the University of Chicago in 1946,[99] and Burchard had arranged the third session of the American Library Association's Library Building Institute in San Francisco in 1947.[100]

More important than the committee's publications and the activities of the members were the buildings that they built.[101] Reference has already been made to the library structures at M. I. T., the University of Wisconsin, the State College of Washington and the importance of the one at the State University of Iowa. Although the Firestone Library of Princeton University has already been mentioned, its importance should not be underestimated. The model or mock-up with its variable ceiling height, that O'Connor and Kilham erected in Princeton's Riding Hall, established the minimum desirable ceiling height for the modular stack at eight feet, four inches,[102] which, incidentally, was only a few inches higher than the Snead Model. The Princeton architects went on to design other library buildings, and strongly influenced the plans of the University of Idaho Library.[103]

Finally, the Cooperative Committee inspired the Association of College and Reference Libraries to continue the method of general discussion and criticism of specific plans after the committee disbanded in February, 1952.[104] Unfortunately, as the registration at these conferences grew, the informality of the older body was quickly lost.

The Influence of Wheeler and Githens

No summary of the forces and individuals at work in library

planning after World War II would be complete without at least mention of Joseph Wheeler and Alfred Morton Githens. Their book, The American Public Library Building, originally published in 1941 by Charles Scribner's Sons, was reissued in 1947 by the American Library Association, and remains useful even today. Their building for the Enoch Pratt Free Library has been examined by "unnumbered visitors" and has had an important effect on both public and academic libraries.[105] Wheeler was a popular library surveyor and favored a flexible, if not necessarily a fully modular approach to library design. Githens, after the war, in addition to his regular practice, occasionally served as a consulting architect, as at the Cincinnati Public Library and the early stages of the State University of Iowa Library. Githens, as has already been established, was deeply committed to the modular idea.

To ascribe to Macdonald the full responsibility for bringing about the important change in library architecture which occurred after World War II would be incorrect and would ignore the many other individuals and forces that were also working toward a new library building form. Changing tastes, curricula, and principles of library administration all contributed to the desire for change. The work of certain groups and individuals, such as the Cooperative Committee on Library Building Plans, Ralph Ellsworth and Joseph Wheeler and Alfred Githens, must also be recognized. However, most important were the technological advances which made possible the creation of a reasonably comfortable artificial environment for the reader. It is difficult to identify, much less delineate, all of the forces operating in society in general, and the library world in particular, that were impelling library design in new directions at the end of World War II. The common thread in all of those treated here is the desire for greater flexibility.

Notes

1. The story of the development of the steel or "skyscraper" frame is readily available in many sources. See, for example, Sigfried Giedion, Space, Time and Architecture; the Growth of a New Tradition (Cambridge, Mass.:

Harvard University Press, 1967), 5th ed., pp. 167-290; or Talbot Hamlin, ed. Forms and Functions of Twentieth-Century Architecture (New York: Columbia University Press, 1952), 11, pp. 425-58.

2. Sigfried Giedion, op. cit., pp. 195-196, 236.

3. Dana called for the adoption of "The workshop, the factory, the office building, the modern business structure of almost any kind" in preference to the typical monumental library building. See "The Public and Its Public Library" in his Libraries: Addresses and Essays (New York: H. W. Wilson Co., 1916), p. 22.

4. Kenneth C. Welch, "Department Stores," Forms and Functions of Twentieth-Century Architecture, ed. Talbot Hamlin (New York: Columbia University Press, 1952), IV, p. 37.

5. As early as 1915 Chalmers Hadley objected to attempts to give public libraries "the appearance of a store." See his "Some Recent Features in Library Architecture," A. L. A. Bulletin, IX (July, 1915), p. 126.

6. Richard Shelton Kirby and Others, Engineering in History (New York: McGraw-Hill, 1956), p. 197.

7. Ernest Leslie Ransome and Alexis Saurbrey, Reinforced Concrete Buildings (New York: McGraw-Hill, 1912).

8. Samuel H. Ranck, "Ventilating and Lighting Library Buildings" Architectural Forum, XLVII (December, 1927), p. 532.

9. In 1964, H. Richard Blackwell endorsed the illuminating Engineering Society's recommendation of 70 foot candles with certain qualifications. See his "Lighting the Library--Standards for Illumination," Library Equipment Institute, 1964, The Library Environment (Chicago: American Library Association, 1964), pp. 23-31.

10. Tables on pp. 269, 331 and 361 in Arthur Aaron Bright, The Electric-Lamp Industry ... (New York: Macmillan, 1949) demonstrate that lumens/watt of the 100 watt lamp doubled while lamp and energy prices declined sharply from 1907 to 1946.

11. Edward L. Tilton, "Library Planning," Architectural Forum, XLVII (December, 1927), p. 504. Some later authorities extended the effective distance to double the window height.

12. James Thayer Gerould, op. cit., pp. 92-93.

13. Dana Quick McComb, Public Library Buildings... (Los Angeles: The Author, 1935), p. 43.

14. E. S. Evenden, G. D. Strayer and N. L. Engelhardt, Standards for College Buildings (New York: Columbia University Teachers College, 1938), pp. 131-3.

15. Edna R. Hanley, College and University Library Buildings (Chicago: American Library Association, 1939), pp. 18-19.

16. John Adam Lowe, Small Public Library Buildings (Chicago: American Library Association, 1939), p. 16.

17. Joseph L. Wheeler and Alfred M. Githens, op. cit., pp. 393, 398.

18. A. Gordon Lorimer, "Modern Design in Library Building," Iowa Library Quarterly, XV (July, 1945), p. 26.

19. John O. Kraehenbuehl, "Lighting the Library," College and Research Libraries, 11 (June, 1941), p. 232.

20. Guy Redvers Lyle, The Administration of the College Library (New York: H. W. Wilson Co., 1944), pp. 558-9.

21. Arthur Aaron Bright, op. cit., pp. 399-403.

22. Eulin Klyver Hobbie, "The Skidmore College Library," Library Journal, LXV (December 15, 1940), p. 1059.

23. A well-reported case is by E. B. Ley, "Study of Illumination," Illuminating Engineering, XXXIX (September, 1944), pp. 501-5.

24. Le Grand H. Hardy and Gertrude Rand, "Elementary Illumination for the Ophthalmologist," Archives of Ophthalmology, XXXIII (January, 1945), p. 8. A short time later Russell J. Schunk in his Pointers for Public Library Planners (Chicago: American Library Association, 1945), p. 38, reported a "clean bill of health" from the American Medical Association.

25. "Lighting in Libraries," Architectural Record, C (November, 1946), p. 120.

26. Quoted in Frederick S. Osborne, "New Library 'Humanistic Laboratory'," Library Journal, LXXIII (December 15, 1948).

27. Cooperative Committee on Library Building Plans, The Second Princeton Conference [Proceedings] ... June 12-

14, 1946 (Philadelphia: Printed by Stephenson-Brothers, 1947), pp. 46-59.

28. John O. Kraehenbuehl, "Modern Library Illumination," Library Buildings for Library Service, ed. Herman H. Fussler (Chicago: American Library Association, 1947), p. 155.

29. Cooperative Committee on Library Building Plans, op. cit., p. 61.

30. John O. Kraehenbuehl, Electric Illumination (2d ed.; New York: John Wiley and Sons, 1951), p. 172.

31. Samuel H. Ranck, op. cit., pp. 530-531.

32. Alfred Morton Githens, "The Complete Development of the Open Plan...," op. cit., p. 384.

33. Margaret Ingels, Willis Haviland Carrier; Father of Modern Air Conditioning (Garden City, N.Y.: Country Life Press, 1952), p. 15.

34. "Contributions of Science and Technology to Building Design: 1891-1941," Architectural Record, XIC (January, 1941), p. 51.

35. Minneapolis-Honeywell Regulator Company, This Thing Called Air Conditioning (Minneapolis: The author, 1935), p. 26.

36. Richard Hart, "Enoch Pratt Building Twenty Years After...," Library Journal, LXXVIII (May 15, 1953), p. 867.

37. James Thayer Gerould, op. cit., p. 105.

38. Dana Quick McComb, op. cit., p. 65.

39. Edna R. Hanley, op. cit., p. 18 and Joseph L. Wheeler and Alfred M. Githens, op. cit., p. 410.

40. Robert J. Usher "The Howard-Tilton Memorial Library," Library Journal, LXVI (June 15, 1941), p. 538.

41. William A. Jackson, "Rare Books at Harvard," College and Research Libraries, XII (December, 1943), pp. 31-35.

42. Keyes D. Metcalf, Planning Academic and Research Library Buildings, (New York: McGraw-Hill, 1965), p. 197.

43. Francis Keally, a noted library architect, expressed a similar view, but with less qualification, in his "An Architect's View of Library Planning," Library Journal, LXXXVIII (December 1, 1963), p. 4524.

44. Lowell A. Martin, "Library Service to Adults," Library Quarterly, XXV (January, 1955), pp. 7-8.

45. Joseph L. Wheeler and Herbert Goldhor, Practical Administration of Public Libraries (New York: Harper and Row, 1962), pp. 474-5.

46. See R. Freeman Butts, The College Charts Its Course (New York: McGraw-Hill, 1939), pp. 203-317, and John S. Brubacher, op. cit., pp. 440-452.

47. See Social Frontier, III (December, 1936), January, February and March, 1937) and V (February, 1939), and Fred B. Millet, The Rebirth of Liberal Education (New York: Harcourt, Brace, 1945), pp. 4-77.

48. James Thayer Gerould, op. cit., pp. 5-7.

49. Robert Maynard Hutchins, "The Chicago Plan," Educational Record, XII (January, 1931), pp. 24-5.

50. Beardsley Ruml, "The Chicago Plan," Educational Record, XII (July, 1931), p. 360.

51. Augustus Frederick Kuhlman, "Some Implications in the New Plan... for College Libraries," Library Quarterly, III (January, 1933), pp. 22-31.

52. William M. Randall, The College Library (Chicago: American Library Association, 1932), p. 3.

53. J. Periam Danton, "The College Library: A New Factor in Education," Journal of Higher Education, VIII (October, 1937), p. 379.

54. Ruth Walling, "Book Requirements of Survey Courses," Library Quarterly, XII (January, 1942), pp. 89-91.

55. Robert B. Downs, "College Curriculum Changes and the College Library," Library Journal, LIX (December, 1934), p. 962.

56. Stanford, Edward B., "Honors Work and the College Library...," Library Quarterly, XII (April, 1942), pp. 236-45.

57. Floyd W. Reeves and John D. Russell, "The Relation of the College Library to Recent Movements in Higher Education," Library Quarterly, I (January, 1931), p. 60.

58. Bennett Harvie Branscomb, Teaching With Books (Chicago: Association of American Colleges, American Library Association, 1940), p. 107.

59. Ibid., pp. 108-117.

60. E. S. Evenden, G. D. Strayer and N. L. Engelhardt, op. cit., p. 131.

61. Carter Alexander, Tomorrow's Libraries for Teachers Colleges, Prepared for the Committee on Standards and Survey of the American Association of Teachers Colleges (n. p., 1944?) pp. 52-3.

62. Ralph E. Ellsworth, "Colorado University's Divisional Reading Room Plan: Description and Evaluation," College and Research Libraries, II (March, 1941), pp. 103-106.

63. Jean MacNeill Sharpe, "Rockford College Library," Library Journal, LXV (December 15, 1940), pp. 1064-1065.

64. "Planning the New Library," The Harvey S. Firestone Memorial Library, (reprinted from Princeton Alumni Weekly; Princeton, N. J.: 1948?), pp. 18-19.

65. Ibid.

66. C. Rufus Morey, A Laboratory Library (Princeton, N. J.: Distributed by the Princeton University Store, 1932?), 15p.

67. R. B. O'Connor and W. H. Kilham, Jr., Architects, "A Survey of Requirements for the Princeton University Library," 1945. Unpublished, typewritten copy in Princeton University Library files. Compares libraries at Harvard, Yale and Virginia.

68. Princeton University, Committee on New Library, Laboratory-Workshop: Library for Princeton, 1746-1946), (Princeton, N. J.: 1944), p. 6-7.

69. Ibid., p. 10. Julian Boyd revealed, in an interview with the author on June 21, 1967, that the Bell Telephone Laboratories at nearby Murray Hill had a strong influence on Princeton.

70. "Harvey S. Firestone Library," Princeton Alumni Weekly, p. 1.

71. Julian P. Boyd, "The Harvey S. Firestone Memorial Library," Princeton Alumni Weekly, XLVII (January 24, 1947), p. 6.

72. State University of Iowa, University Library Planning Committee, The Library as a Teaching Instrument (Iowa City, Ia., 1945), p. 1.

73. Ralph E. Ellsworth, "A Modular Library for the State University of Iowa," op. cit., p. 100.

74. John Ely Burchard, A Program for a New Library Building at the Massachusetts Institute of Technology (Miscellaneous Publications on Microfilm No. 1; Cambridge, Mass.: The Technology Press, 1945), p. 25.

75. John Ely Burchard, "Postwar Library Buildings," College and Research Libraries, VII (April, 1946), p. 124.

76. "Library Construction for Interchangeable Use," Architectural Record, C (November, 1946), p. 115. A large basement stack extending under the courtyard is only one level deep.

77. "New Library Opened," Library Journal, LXXIV (February 1, 1949), pp. 166-8 and Keyes D. Metcalf, Planning Academic and Research Library Buildings, various pages, but in particular pp. 50, 69 and 272-3.

78. Letter of Louis Kaplan to the author, May 20, 1968.

79. Lloyd W. Griffin and Louis Kaplan, "Wisconsin's New University Library After Two Years," College and Research Libraries, XVII (September, 1956), p. 391.

80. H. Dean Stallings, "A New Pattern for Economy, Utility and Beauty...," op. cit., pp. 135-136; "Beauty-Efficiency-Economy," Library Journal, LXXV (December 15, 1950), pp. 2109-2112.

81. This is true at least until the introduction of the modular plan. Shortly after that there were those such as Burchard, quoted above, and Metcalf [see his "Spatial Problems in University Libraries," Library Trends, II (April, 1954)], who questioned the desirability for this apparent ultimate in flexibility.

82. Charles C. Soule, How to Plan a Library Building for Library Work (Boston: Boston Book Company, 1912), pp. 169-170, 183-184.

83. Chalmers Hadley, Library Buildings; Notes and Plans (Chicago: American Library Association, 1924), p. 13.

84. Richard Hart, op. cit., p. 865.

85. Fremont Rider, The Scholar and the Future of the Research Library... (New York: Hadham Press, 1944), p. 162.

86. Vannevar Bush, "As We May Think," Atlantic Monthly, CLXXVI (July, 1945), pp. 101-108.

87. John Ely Burchard, "The Library of Tomorrow," American Institute of Architects Journal, (January-February, 1947), pp. 91-92.

88. G. Liebers-Kassel, op. cit., pp. 225-226. (Author's translation.)

89. Arthur E. Bostwick, "The Librarian's Ideas of Library Design," Architectural Forum, XLVII (December, 1927), p. 512.

90. The change in public taste is in itself a fascinating story and one that has been recorded by a number of authorities. See the works by Burchard and Giedion, already cited, for stimulating narratives.

91. Alfred Roth, La Nouvelle Architecture (Zurich: H. Girsberger, 1940), pp. 181-8.

92. Henri Le Maitre, "Swiss National Library at Berne," Library Association Record Ser. 3; III (March, 1933), pp. 76-77.

93. Cooperative Committee on Library Building Plans, The Orange Conference, p. 1.

94. Cooperative Committee on Library Buildings, "[Minutes of the] Meeting Held at Princeton University, December 15-16, 1944," p. 1. Dittoed copy in Princeton University Library files.

95. Cooperative Committee on Library Building Plans, Planning the University Library Building (Princeton, N.J.: Princeton University Press, 1949), p. 60.

96. Based largely on the Committee's "Final Report on Grant Number 46037 Made March 15, 1946 by the Rockefeller Foundation...," April, 1948, carbon copy in Princeton University Library.

97. Herman Fussler, Review of Planning the University Library Building, Library Quarterly, XX (July, 1950), p. 211. See also reviews by Ernest J. Reece, College and Research Libraries, X (Oct., 1949) pp. 483-5, and Victor Bondos, The American Archivist, XII (October, 1949), pp. 422-25.

98. Keyes D. Metcalf, Planning Academic and Research Library Buildings. (New York: McGraw-Hill, 1965).

99. Herman H. Fussler, ed., Library Buildings for Library Service.

100. Ernest I. Miller, "The Library Building Institute," A.L.A. Bulletin, XLI (August, 1947), p. 252.

101. It is interesting to observe that not all committee members erected buildings as soon as materials became available.

Some were painfully slow in breaking ground.

102. R. B. O'Connor and W. H. Kilham, "Full Size Mock-up for Library Planning," Architectural Record, CI (January, 1947), p. 99.

103. Lee Zimmerman, "An invitation and an Opportunity" (Moscow, Idaho: University of Idaho Library, 1956) reprinted from the University of Idaho Bookmark, p. 35, and "Idaho's Ideal," Library Journal, LXXI (December 15, 1956), p. 2757.

104. Library Building Plans Institute, 1st, Columbus, O., 1952, Proceedings (Chicago: Association of College and Reference Libraries, 1952), p. 1.

105. Richard Hart, op. cit., p. 864.

Chapter VIII

Summary and Conclusions

Since medieval times, libraries have witnessed many changes in the policy of restricted versus open access. From the locked cupboards of early monastic and church libraries, the policy changed to open access. This new policy, introduced around the thirteenth century, was made possible by a technological improvement, the chain, and by the alcove arrangement. As both the number of books housed in libraries and the public using them grew in size a more restrictive policy was adopted. It was impractical to chain thousands of volumes, particularly when it became necessary to add a gallery above the first level of shelving. Access to the galleries and, later, the alcoves, was often restricted by railings, but the books were still visible. The introduction of another technological improvement, the bookstack, completed the cycle again to restricted access. Later, assisted by the modular plan, the bookstack, at least in numerous American academic institutions, became the library, and the reader again had free and easy access to the materials. Perhaps in the near future, through the application of computers or such devices as the Rand-Triever, the pendulum may swing to a more restrictive policy.

Snead and Company and B. R. Green

The irony, of course, in the shift from the policies of limited access of the bookstack era to the present one of mixing books and readers, is that Snead and Company, the leader in the large bookstack field, should be one of the leaders in advocating a change in library architecture that destroyed its own specialty. The Snead company had a long history extending back to 1849 when its founder, Charles Scott Snead, organized an iron foundry in Louisville, Kentucky. Snead was an inventive man, and his sons and grandsons, including Angus and Harry Macdonald, continued the family tradition. In the early period, before entering the bookstack field, Snead and Company offered to contract for the entire iron work of buildings in any part of the country. Unknowingly, perhaps, Angus Snead Macdonald hoped for the return of this tradition through his hollow-column design.

With the rapid growth of libraries in the United States in the latter part of the nineteenth century, the bookstack quickly displaced the towering galleries of the alcove library as the preferred means of storing books. Drawing upon European inspiration, the Ware-Winsor design for Harvard's Gore Hall established the basic plan in 1876.

As early as 1885, with the Washington Monument, Snead and Company and Bernard Richardson Green found themselves working on the same project in Washington. Green was a trained engineer with the Army's Corps of Engineers, which was assigned responsibility for erecting many of the government buildings at this time. With the awarding of the contract in August of 1885 for the bookstack in the State, War and Navy Departments building, [1] Snead, executing a design from the Corps of Engineers, began its association with the library world. Most likely this heavy, ornate design originated with Green. Upon the completion of this building in 1888, Green became Superintendent of Construction for the Library of Congress, and two years later developed a much improved stack design for the new library. Snead and Company, after winning the contract, made a permanent association with Green's bookstack by acquiring his patents. Careful workmanship, which had been lacking in earlier stacks, and good design were combined for the first time. The basic supporting columns, in stacks over seven tiers, were of steel, and the shelf supports were cast-iron. The open-bar shelves were of light-weight steel, and were easy to adjust. No rough edges were exposed anywhere to damage the books, and care was taken to leave ample open areas in the shelves and shelf supports to permit air circulation around the books.

Green combined a good basic stack structure with provisions

Summary and Conclusions 219

for ventilation, lighting, communications and book distribution. After the two-tier model was displayed at the World's Columbian Exposition in Chicago in 1893, the Snead-Green association proved a financial success. In Boston another great library was under construction at this time, but its stack design was quickly forgotten.[2] Other manufacturers offered metal stacks, but the elegance of the Snead stack, with its neatly finished metal, embossed decoration, sturdy structure, and white marble floors, can hardly be compared with its competitors of the time.

Although the company was gradually forced to shift its emphasis from cast-iron standard stacks to the cheaper, more versatile, all-steel bracket stacks, it never lost the leadership in the large bookstack field that it had gained from its experience at the Library of Congress. It managed to make the shift from the cast-iron stack at Yale's Sterling book tower in 1930 to Columbia's interior bracket stack in 1934 without apparent difficulty.[3] The important element was not the material but the company's expertise. However, it was ensnared in its own pattern of excellence which, for a number of factors, excluded it from the small library market. This specialty made Snead somewhat vulnerable to a feast or famine type of existence, while its competitors enjoyed a less exciting, but steady, diet of the small to medium-sized library jobs. Its attempts to develop other products, as the various cast-iron specialities lost favor, met with varying success. Most important was its position as a manufacturer of metal movable partitions. Although the "Mobilwall" was a major item[4] it too tended to be vulnerable to the cycles of the building industry. In Donald Bean's view, Macdonald's chief failing was in his inability or unwillingness to adapt Snead's products and sales force to the small library market.[5]

Angus Macdonald

From the beginning there was about the Snead stack, a tradition of excellence that was often the envy of its competitors. This tradition was a part of Macdonald's youthful years in the business and under him this image was perpetuated as long as the company manufactured bookstacks. Macdonald's first association with large research libraries began in his boyhood with a tour of the Boston Public Library in 1894. A proud uncle showed him Snead's decorative iron work as it was being installed in this famous building designed by McKim, Mead and White. Years later Macdonald wrote to a friend, "McKim was aghast at the idea of having such works of art executed in the wilds of the west [Louisville, Kentucky] but he was eminently satisfied with the finished results and was good enough to say so."[6] This sense of excellence, of being a leader, remained with Macdonald throughout his career.

Macdonald was, after all, in spite of his name, a Snead. His association with his father was brief. He grew up under the guidance of his mother, his uncles, particularly Udolpho, and his grandfather, Charles Scott Snead, the founder of Snead and Company. Nowhere in the evidence that remains do we find any strong influence from the Macdonald side of the family.

Macdonald's long involvement in the affairs of Snead and Company gave him some opportunity to exercise his creative abilities. From his first improvements on the Green patents, to the concrete deck, zig-zag ventilation, stack lighting, the convertible stack, and compact storage, he maintained the Snead name as a leader and innovator. It should be remembered however, that he was, deep down, a frustrated architect. It was as an architect that he preferred to be remembered, and for his role in persuading librarians and architects to build a different kind of library, this preference may be justified. There was, in Macdonald, a well developed aesthetic sense, a sense of beauty that often transcended the practical. Thus he could not bring himself to abandon entirely the spaciousness of the high-ceilinged reading room and, therefore, championed the mezzanine as an economical alternative to low ceilings in larger modular libraries. It explains his objection to the Louisiana State University Library as a "glorified warehouse." In a letter to Frank Lloyd Wright, Macdonald expressed his approval of Wright's work and condemned his own training at Columbia which left him uninspired. His switch to business, he told Wright, "became a matter of regret when I finally felt your influence."[7] He was, after all, an architect.

Summary and Conclusions

Macdonald's Personality

In looking at Macdonald's life, there is ample evidence of his continual fascination with new ideas and causes. He appears never to have been afraid of a change that he considered to be an improvement. Whether it was glowing tubes on the ceiling of the Library of the Future, the hollow column of the model, or a fish pond and shrubbery on the roof of his home, he was always stimulated by the unusual. Nor does he seem to have lost this quality in his later years. Even the process employed in his last and surviving business venture involves an unusual copper sulphate pressure bath as a wood preservative. He named the company, which specializes in fences and similar products, Everdure.

In judging the man, this pioneering spirit should always be added in the balance. To a degree this spirit is counter to the qualities necessary for a successful business man. Could plywood gliders win the war? Macdonald's prototypes of 1942 were rejected, but such gliders did play an important part in the Allied invasions of Europe. Could libraries be built differently, based on regularly-spaced, hollow columns? The hollow column, at least Macdonald's particular version of it, was generally rejected, but libraries certainly have adopted a plan based on regularly spaced columns.

In that his outlook was generally sanguine, that he believed things and conditions would steadily improve, that change was to be welcomed, he was typically American. He had, too, a firm belief in himself, in his judgment and his political and social philosophies. On issues that he considered important he was not reluctant to write to his favorite senator, or to use his influence at the Vatican to arrange a private audience with the Pope for his good friend, Margaret Sanger. In domestic politics he was generally conservative, but not easy to stereotype. In matters of foreign policy, he would fall with the more liberal wing, deploring, in the 1930's, America's isolationism. While he was a pioneer in spirit, at times even an idealist, there was in most of his dreams the greater glory and profit for Snead and Company, and in this too he was typically American. Thus the modular dream, had it crystallized around his hollow column, might have resulted in a Snead monopoly of library construction. Finally, he was practical enough to modify the dream itself to incorporate compact storage.

There is also in Macdonald a strong reflection of Jeffersonian beliefs. In general, cities were despised as places in which to live and work. The rural countryside was distinctly preferred. In part to avoid the labor troubles of the North, in part to be near the large market of the Washington area, but also as a reflection of this belief in the inherent "good" of the country, he established a branch plant at Orange, Virginia in 1937. The company headquarters were soon removed to Virginia also. Macdonald pictured his workers, in their leisure hours, tending ample gardens surrounding clean, comfortable homes, instead of standing on street corners near their grimy tenements in Jersey City's Horseshoe District. Julian Boyd, an eminent Jeffersonian scholar, recognized this strain. In a letter to Macdonald, Boyd wrote:

> If you were listening to the invitation to Learning program last Sunday, you probably heard me quote--or misquote--you when you remarked about your pleasure in looking out of a factory window to see a rural countryside. We were talking on the program about Thomas Jefferson, and I held you and your factory up as an example of the kind of combination industrialism and ruralism that Jefferson would have found congenial. [8]

Jefferson's tribute to Washington[9] was, apparently, of sufficient interest to Macdonald that he had it duplicated, presumably for distribution to his friends. Like Jefferson, he was suspicious of bankers, and after the loss of Snead and Company undoubtedly felt this suspicion justified.

His religious beliefs were mildly nonconformist. He wrote to Cardinal Tisserant that he "adhered to the Christian philosophy... [but] to no organized church."[10] Nevertheless, probably related to early religious and moral training was his belief in work and the value of self improvement. In "A Library of the Future" he objects to the government's "endless highway programs" which only induce "aimless automobiling" on the part of the citizenry. The implication of his argument is that the average man would be better

Summary and Conclusions

off if he spent his leisure time in libraries improving his skills and character. Macdonald was not the first Protestant American with an interest in libraries to adopt this view. He himself was capable of hard work, putting in long hours year after year, to further the war effort or the cause of Snead and Company. To run the company, to travel as extensively as he did, and still to find time to write and speak for his library audience took a man with considerable energy and devotion to his work.

Macdonald as Library Planner

By virtue of his training as an architect, it is likely that Macdonald held an interest in library planning from the moment he joined Snead and Company in 1905. That he participated in the assembling of Snead's classic volume on <u>Library Planning, Bookstacks and Shelving</u>, published in 1915, seems likely. His name does not appear in the library literature, however, until 1931 with "Library Lighting." His efforts as a writer were largely concentrated in two periods, from 1931-1934 and from 1945-1955. Beginning with "A Library of the Future" in 1933, he began to develop a theory of library planning that stressed flexibility, economy, informal comfort, and a reliance on artificial illumination and ventilation. Being in the business, there can be little doubt that the structural frame of the library of the future, its movable partitions and free-standing bookcases were, in his mind, Snead products.

Always, his imaginary modular libraries included some space more than one story high. At times this was accomplished by omitting floor sections, but later he advocated, for economy's sake, a stack-supported mezzanine floor that incorporated a smaller stack module (e.g. nine feet by nine feet) within the larger structural module. In order to obtain maximum flexibility, he advocated vertical rather than horizontal distribution of air, and from the beginning, in 1933, made a shrewd guess about the future of fluorescent lighting in libraries.

In attempting to assess the magnitude of Macdonald's contribution as a library planner, three points should be kept in mind: (1) By virtue of his training and experience, he possessed great prestige among many of the profession's leaders, including, of course, Ralph Ellsworth. (2) The Convertible Stack began to demonstrate the feasibility of interchanging the storage function with other activities in the stacks, before World War II. (3) His description in 1933 of "A Library of the Future" and the model erected on the grounds of Snead and Company in 1945 preceded any other library or model on the modern modular plan.

Macdonald's Prestige and Influence

Looking at Macdonald's life, one might conclude that on an amazing number of occasions he was in the right spot at the right time. He often was involved in the "right" stack jobs, the big jobs that drew attention to himself and his company, and rarely was this an accident. The later stack installations for the Library of Congress, and for the libraries of Harvard, Yale, Northwestern, Columbia, and Texas universities, were all important by virtue of their size. He was in Rome when the Vatican Library was remodeled and in Chicago when it was decided to build the Midwest Interlibrary Center. The prestige that accrued to Macdonald over the years as a result of one successful installation after another undoubtedly enhanced his influence when he attempted to "sell" the modular plan. He was aware of his prestige and in his later years expressed concern that it might have suffered as a result of the difficulties at the Midwest Interlibrary Center. [11]

From the correspondence that remains, from the articles he wrote and the speeches he made, it is obvious that his prestige extended to Canada and, to a lesser extent, abroad. This personal good will that he enjoyed, and the prestige of the company, can be further documented by the fact that a number of the major texts on library planning involved Macdonald or a member of the Snead staff in their preparation. Gerould expressed his thanks to two individuals for technical assistance in writing The College Library Building: one was the Dean of Princeton's engineering faculty, the other was Macdonald. [12] In 1939, the American Library Association published Edna Ruth Hanley's College and University Library Buildings, in which she acknowledged the assistance of several librarians, archi-

Summary and Conclusions

tects, and Thure H. Lindberg, of Snead and Company. Lindberg received the acknowledgement because he had "supervised the preparation of the drawings, and, because of his expert and intimate knowledge of library buildings and their construction...[which] made him a capable adviser."[13] As noted earlier, Macdonald had written the chapter on bookstacks in <u>The American Public Library Building,</u> by Wheeler and Githens, published in 1941. Finally, the University of Chicago's volume in 1946, edited by Herman Fussler, contains a summary article by William Randall,[14] who was with Snead and Company at the time it was written. Snead had also made arrangements to help underwrite the cost of publication.

This prestige that he enjoyed undoubtedly made his articles and public speaking more effective. Of his articles, "New Possibilities in Library Planning" probably generated the most interest, both at home and abroad. Almost certainly his illustrated address before the Canadian Library Association in June, 1948, also entitled "A Library of the Future," was his most successful public speaking effort. From the records that remain, it is obvious that the librarians in the audience that day were listening and thinking about what he had to say. From 1945 to 1954 Macdonald appears to have kept his left hand in almost perpetual motion, writing, speaking, and corresponding (including circularization of such documents as the Canisius College sketches) about the modular plan, while his right hand ran Snead and Company, fought law suits and flew an airplane.

More important perhaps than the articles or speeches or the model or the Beaux-Arts Design Problem were the buildings that were built in close collaboration with Macdonald. His influence on such library buildings as those at Hardin-Simmons University, North Dakota Agricultural College, and the University of Georgia cannot be questioned. Other buildings such as those at the University of Iowa and the New Mexico Agricultural and Mechanical College have acknowledged their debt to Macdonald through their librarians. Still others, including those at Washington State University, Louisiana State University, West Virginia State College, and the Vancouver

Public Library also were influenced by him more or less directly. Even today, the librarian of the new 300,000 square foot library building at the University of Guelph, Ontario, acknowledges his obligation. Macdonald, he states, inculcated the general principles of modular planning many years ago in the informal meetings in the Snead suite of the Edgewater Beach Hotel during the Midwinter Conferences of the American Library Association. [15]

Beyond the buildings for which documentation exists it is impossible to establish any clear relationship. That these buildings in turn influenced other buildings, such as the one at the University of Wyoming, can also be established, but with ever increasing difficulty, and Macdonald's role becomes less and less clear. The chief burden of this section and, indeed, of the entire paper, is that Macdonald, as a writer and speaker, not only enjoyed considerable prestige with the library profession, but his ideas were translated into bricks and mortar in a sufficiently large number of cases to justify his position as a very positive force in altering the course of library architecture.

Other Forces

To be sure, other forces and individuals deserve recognition. More important than any single individual were the improvements in artificial lighting and ventilation, and in building technology generally. During Macdonald's lifetime the span between supporting columns that he considered practical and economical increased gradually from 9 to 27 feet. The introduction of fluorescent lighting and reasonablly well controlled, forced-air ventilation, after World War II, made occupancy, for study purposes, of large interior spaces of the building practical for the first time. For the first time, too, windows were justified for "psychological" purposes only. They were sealed and forgotten, except for the occasional attention of a janitor.

The work of various individuals and groups such as the Cooperative Committee on Library Building Plans also deserves considerable recognition for effecting a change. While Committee members did not always agree on means, all spread the doctrine of

Summary and Conclusions

flexibility. The articles published by its members, the formal and informal speeches made by them before professional groups, and the book, Planning the University Library Building, undoubtedly had an influence. Certainly the buildings built by the Committee's institutional members bore their influence, too.

Also important were the changing educational patterns that forced many of the older but innovative institutions to seek new solutions to their library problems. The general education movement, honors programs, even the influence of accrediting associations, forced the library to the center of the academic community where the old separation of books and readers became impractical. Related to this change were the efforts of institutions such as Princeton and Iowa to bring faculty or subject specialists into the library to advise the students being taught under the new program.

Changes in Public Library Planning

Public libraries present a somewhat different picture. With the population shifting to the suburbs after World War II, and with generally impoverished municipal treasuries, public libraries were slow to recover from the war and depression.[16] Relatively few large public library buildings were built before 1960, but those that were reflected the public librarian's philosophy of keeping in public view only those materials that were of current interest. The less frequently used materials were usually relegated to a traditional multi-tier stack (usually two levels) in the basement, with restricted access. As part of this merchandizing philosophy, the main floor was usually made as attractive as possible, employing either a uniformly high ceiling or a fixed mezzanine. Only the upper floors resembled the highly flexible, interchangeable space of their academic counterparts. Influential in establishing this pattern were the open plan libraries, especially Enoch Pratt. From the remaining records, from the stack contracts executed by Snead and Company, and from the post-war public libraries we must conclude that Macdonald's influence on the large public library building was much less pronounced than on the academic. In either case, there were other, equally important, forces paralleling Macdonald's efforts.

Attempts to make generalizations about public libraries built between 1930 and 1960 have proved difficult because relatively few large central buildings were erected. On the basis of the limited sample, there seems to be a clear trend toward greater flexibility and modular planning, especially in the upper floors. As the survey in Appendix II demonstrates, this trend becomes especially pronounced after World War II. However, while the old style building with its stack at the rear, complete with deck ventilation slits, disappeared in the 1930's, the multi-tier stack has not been abandoned entirely. Attention should be called to the stack arrangement in the Washoe County, Nevada, Public Library (1967?) and the Beinecke Library (1963) at Yale University, both of which display their tiers of books under a lofty ceiling. Architecturally, the effect is striking, and the "magical effect" of so many books in view is not unlike the old gallery libraries, such as the Cincinnati Public Library of 1874.

Changes in Academic Library Planning

The number of college and university libraries erected was much more extensive, as the survey in Appendix II reveals. Further, the academic picture is generally simpler since there were no open plan libraries to confuse the trend. With the exception of the Snead Convertible stacks at the end of the period, and two "transitional" buildings, all academic libraries featured a conventional multi-tier stack structure prior to World War II. Of the two buildings classified as "transitional," neither can qualify as a true modular library. Babson Institute (1939) combined classrooms, offices and "library" in one building. Because of its highly specialized business program, it cannot qualify as an academic library in the usual sense. [17] The Skidmore College Library (1940) did not have free standing stacks. Reader spaces and book storage were not truly interchangeable, and it was planned as the stack wing of a future "T"-shaped building. Conventional reading and work rooms were to be added later. Since it was small, and readers were placed adjacent to the windows, it could function, in daytime, without resorting to artificial light or ventilation. [18]

Summary and Conclusions

After 1950, however, the survey reveals a trend overwhelmingly in favor of the modular plan. Surprising, perhaps, are the conventional stack buildings that persisted down through the period covered by the survey. Conclusive, too, from the survey, is the general popularity of the particular pattern set by the Washington State College, the University of Iowa, North Dakota Agricultural College, and Princeton stacks. The compromises devised for the Massachusetts Institute of Technology and Rice Institute were generally rejected by institutions that built later. To this degree then, operating through Iowa, Washington and North Dakota, the Macdonald influence is indeed far reaching. Only Princeton, and the firm of O'Connor and Kilham, appears to represent an independent strain shaping the University of Idaho, the Trinity College Library, and more recently, the National Library of Medicine.

Conclusion

Without a doubt, a major change did occur in library architecture after World War II. In examining the various forces that were responsible it is clear that some were necessary. These would include the technological improvements that made new building types possible, the changing tastes that made them acceptable and, in the academic field, the changing curriculum that made them desirable. Other forces, or individuals, such as Macdonald and Snead and Company, the Cooperative Committee and its members, Joseph Wheeler and the open plan, are sufficient conditions. That is, the latter were dependent upon the existence of the former before any change could occur.

It seems clear that Macdonald's role as a catalyst must be shared with the firm of O'Connor and Kilham, designers of Princeton's Firestone Library. As demonstrated, this architectural firm was thinking of a flexible building, much like the Bell Telephone Laboratory, as early as 1944. It is conceivable that Princeton would have built its library without any knowledge of Macdonald's ideas. Yet to Macdonald goes the credit of being the first to picture an interchangeable stack-reader arrangement as early as 1933. As late as 1940 Princeton was still planning a conventional (separate stack and reading room) building.

Macdonald, too, drawing on the convertible stack experience, was the first, in the spring of 1945, to bring the idea into three-dimensional form with the model in Orange, Virginia. He also deserves much of the credit for publicizing the idea, through articles, speeches, demonstration of the model, the Beaux-Arts Design competition, correspondence, and extensive traveling and conferring. The waste, in terms of money and space, of the monumental design, the anachronism of the light/ventilation court, the lack of appeal to the man on the street or the young student, and above all the inability to adapt easily to changing interior conditions, made pre-War libraries an easy target for Macdonald's criticism. Macdonald's concept of a flexible library was far closer to the main stream of buildings built after World War II than some of the compromises that were sought early in this period.

For helping to change all this he deserves a large share of the credit; however, causality in history is generally recognized to be multiple in nature. He must share the credit with other forces and individuals. His role is important, and as a catalyst, probably prime, but it is also probable that the technological changes occurring elsewhere in the building industry would have found their way into library design.

Too, Macdonald's importance should not obscure the fact that he embodied the tradition of a great company in the library equipment field. Already, to most librarians, the name of Snead and Company is unknown. And although many will continue to scurry past miles of open bar shelves and cast-iron shelf supports, and will resent the difficulty in finding parts for aging book conveyors, few will ever encounter the company's once proud name. Nevertheless, the buildings in which they work, whether old or new, are likely to be a good deal different because of the Snead tradition of quality and innovation.

Notes

1. Thomas Lincoln Casey, "Report on Building for the State, War

Summary and Conclusions 231

and Navy Departments," U. S. War Department, Annual Report of the Secretary of War, 1886 (Washington: Government Printing Office, 1886), p. 809.

2. One might argue that the basic idea of the Boston Public Library stack (cheap, wooden shelves and uprights on bare concrete floors) eventually emerged again in the nearby New England Deposit Library (1942).

3. Snead continued to offer cast-iron after this date, and made its last major cast-iron installation at the Library of Congress Annex in 1937.

4. "Mobilwalls" were installed in hundreds of buildings in the U. S. and abroad, including the Bell Telephone Laboratories, Murray Hill, New Jersey; the Chrysler Building, and Rockefeller Center in New York City.

5. Donald Bean to the author, July 13, 1968.

6. Macdonald to Alfred Morton Githens, August 22, 1949.

7. Macdonald to Frank Lloyd Wright, July 2, 1953.

8. Letter of Julian P. Boyd to Macdonald, July 6, 1945. Boyd did not use Macdonald's name on the air.

9. Thomas Jefferson, Works, ed. Paul Leichester Ford, (New York: G. P. Putnam's Sons, 1904-05) IX, pp. 446-51.

10. Macdonald to Tisserant, January 8, 1960.

11. Letter of Macdonald to Lutz Helbig, December 30, 1953, and elsewhere.

12. James Thayer Gerould, op. cit., p. vi.

13. Edna Ruth Hanley, op. cit., p. 10.

14. Herman H. Fussler, ed., op. cit., pp. 182-201, viii.

15. Letter of Lachlan F. MacRae to the author, April 5, 1968.

16. See Howard H. Borthwick, "Trends in Post-War Public Library Architecture," (unpublished master's thesis, Carnegie Library School, Carnegie Institute of Technology, 1952), p. 6; Edna L. Lester, "An Analysis of Post-War Trends in... Public Libraries," (unpublished master's thesis in the School of Library Service, Atlanta University, 1957), p. 5; and Charles M. Mohrhardt, "Buildings and Equipment," Library Trends, I (April, 1953), p. 514. There was considerable activity in smaller buildings and branches, but few large central buildings.

17. G. S. Cam, "Babson Institute Library," Library Journal, LXIV, (December 15, 1939), pp. 961-4.

18. Based on author's visit on June 15, 1967 and Eulin K. Hobbie, "Skidmore College Library," Library Journal, LXV, (December 15, 1940), pp. 1057-60.

APPENDIX I

SUPPLEMENTARY MATERIAL

C O P Y

GILBERT D. FISH
101 PARK AVENUE
NEW YORK

January 30, 1947

Messrs. Kaufmann, Lippincott and Eggers
627 South Carondelet Street
Los Angeles 5, California

Subject: Library - Claremont Colleges

Gentlemen:

Reply to your interesting inquiry of January 22nd has been waiting on a preliminary study of your problem. We can now send you some information.

A library of the size and panel dimensions given in your letter can be designed according to the modular system, with hollow columns and hollow girders for air conditioning, with 13 lbs. of structural steel per square foot of floor and roof area. If the panels were 18 feet square, as in the large library being designed for the University of Georgia, the steel requirements would be about 11 lbs. per sq. ft.

Cost estimates are especially difficult now and we are not in touch with California prices. However, the cost per pound of this steel will not differ much from ordinary steel framing with H-columns instead of hollow square columns and single rolled girders instead of double channel girders. For a given column spacing, the weight of the hollow construction will be about the same as ordinary framing, the double channel girders being somewhat heavier than single girders and the hollow columns and earthquake resistant connections being lighter than H-columns and their connections.

To give you an idea of the framing, we would expect to use 16" hollow square columns varying in wall thickness from about 3/8" in the basement to about .14" in the fourth story. The girders would run in the 27 ft. direction and would consist of two 15" channels 16" back to back, braced to each other at intervals, these channels being of minimum weight down to the third floor and of heavier weights in second and first floors. They would be field welded to opposite walls of the columns in such manner as

COPY

GILBERT D. FISH
101 PARK AVENUE
NEW YORK

-2-

to develop their full bending resistance, producing rigid-frame action. Along lines of columns at right angles to the girders there would be pairs of 10" [' s or I's 16" apart, with their bending resistance fully developed at the ends. 10" rolled-steel joists approximately 26" apart would fill in the panels and would be field bolted to the 15" channel girders. Across these joists and the other members would be stretched self-centering steel lath and the floor slab would consist of 2" of stone concrete with wire mesh for shrinkage reinforcement. Presumably there would be a perforated sheet-steel ceiling connected by spring clips to the bottom flanges of the steel joists and channels. Special soffit panels would be used under the girders forming haunches 5" deep and about 22" wide. Air distribution would be through column ports with adjustable dampers into the girders and through a row of holes in the girder webs into the spaces between the joists.

The above described construction would completely satisfy prevailing structural standards and also the California earthquake requirements. We are not suggesting any fireproofing because we think that libraries of noncombustible materials have no fire hazard. This form of construction can however be made fireproof in accordance with very exacting requirements by using a 1" vermiculite-gypsum ceiling on metal lath in place of the perforated metal, carrying this fireproofing as a lining around the inside perimeter of the girders so as to leave an unobstructed air passage through the girders and bringing the air through ports in a sheet metal soffit. Column fireproofing can be formed with the same vermiculite plaster. The writer witnessed tests of this kind of column fireproofing at the Underwriter's Laboratories in Chicago about a year ago.

This form of construction, which is to be used without fireproofing for the Georgia library, was considered for the Princeton library a year ago with fireproofing included. The general contractors reported that it was the most inexpensive construction of the four types considered but that certain delays to be expected in obtaining steel would prevent immediate construction. To avoid this delay, reinforced concrete was adopted for that job. The economy lay in the complete elimination of air ducts except in the plenum space from which conditioned air was to be distributed. In your case, air would presumably be admitted to the plenum columns (and if necessary drawn from the exhaust columns) near the basement ceiling. We expect that you would wish to fireproof the first floor construction above the furnace room.

C O P Y

GILBERT D. FISH 　　　　　　　　　　-3-
101 PARK AVENUE
NEW YORK

We should of course be pleased to design the structural work for your project, leaving it to your engineers in Los Angeles to deal with the local authorities, exercise supervision, and attend to other matters requiring local action. Without having architectural plans to estimate from, we assume that fully dimensioned steel and foundation drawings and checking of shop drawings would cost between four and five cents per square foot of horizontal framed area and basement area. If desired on account of this being a special form of welded construction, we would be prepared to make shop drawings as well, but such work would ordinarily be done for the steel fabricator rather than as part of the structural engineer' services to the architects.

Hoping this preliminary report will be of some use to you and that you will find it feasible to utilize this highly efficient means of incorporating air ducts in modular construction,

          Yours very truly,

          J.D.F.

GDF:hp
CC: Mr. Angus S. Macdonald

Proposed Modular Library (1934). Sketch by Alfred Morton Githens.

Proposed Modular Library (1934). Lobby Area, First Floor.

Proposed Modular Library (1934). Popular Reading Area, First Floor.

Proposed Modular Library (1934). Children's Room, First Floor.

Proposed Modular Library (1934). Reserve Reading Room, First Floor.

Proposed Modular Library (1934). Reference Room, Second Floor.

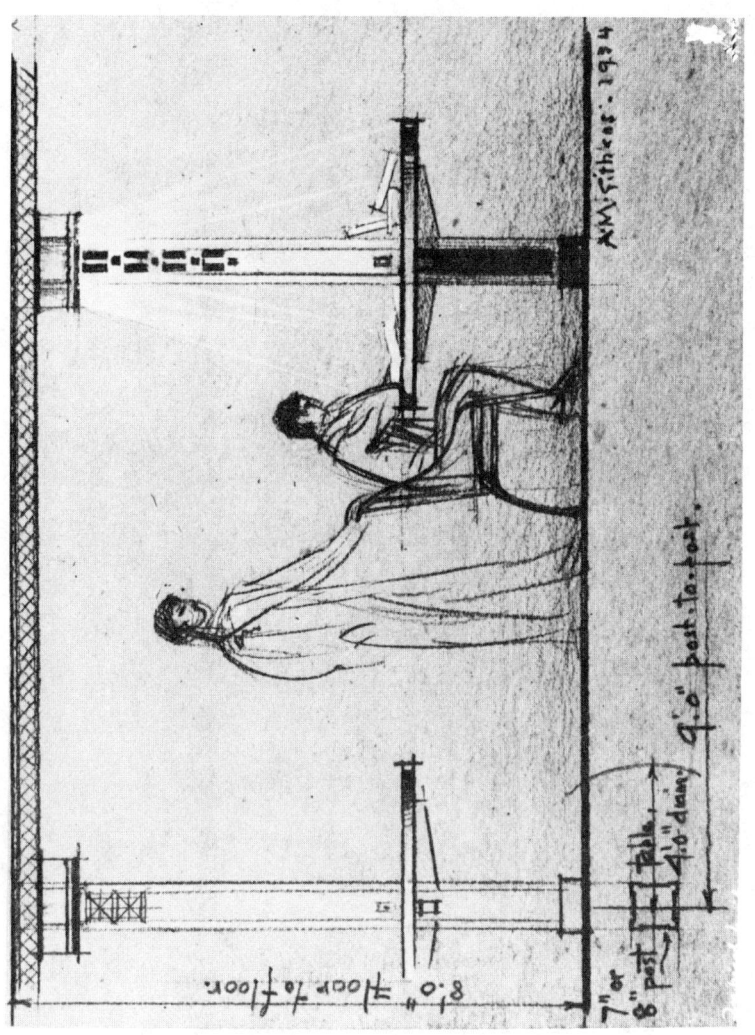

Proposed Modular Library (1934). Study Table Detail.

Proposed Modular Library (1934).

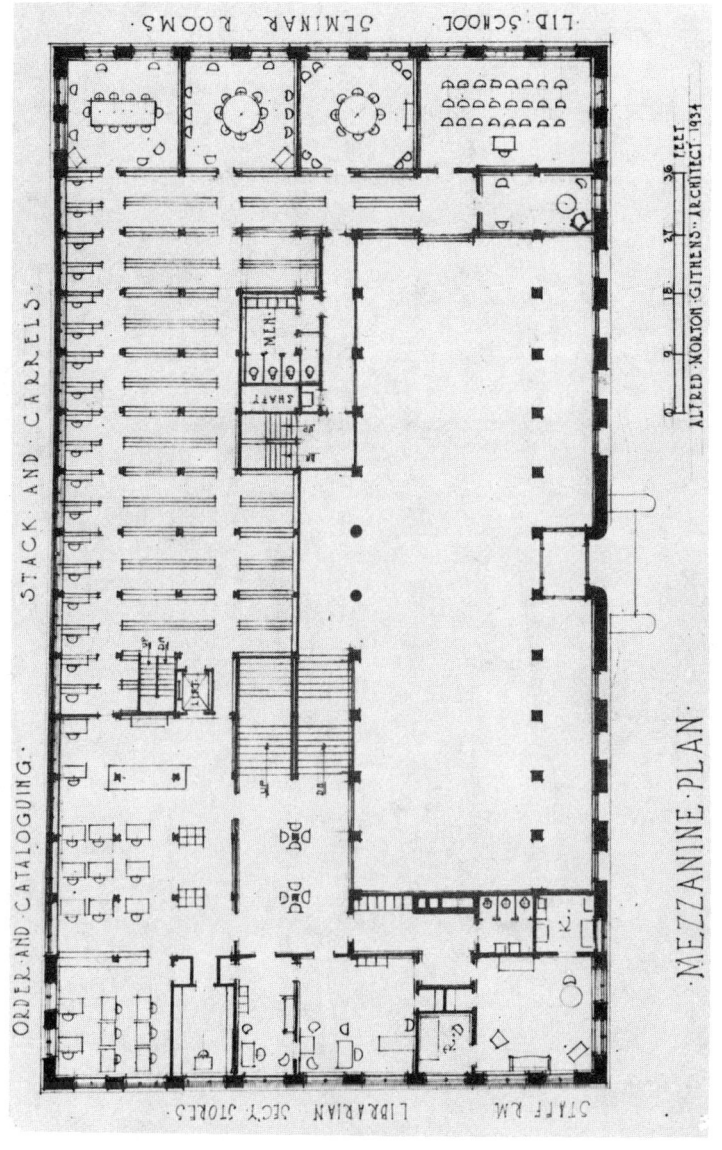

Proposed Modular Library (1934).

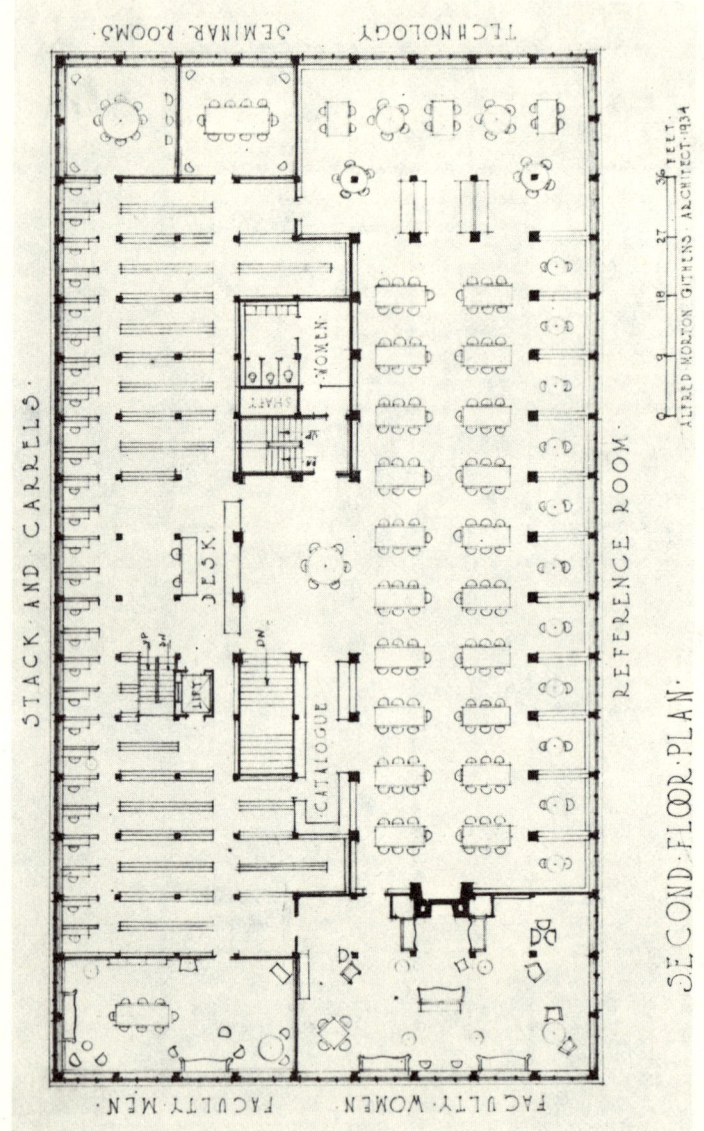

Proposed Modular Library (1934).

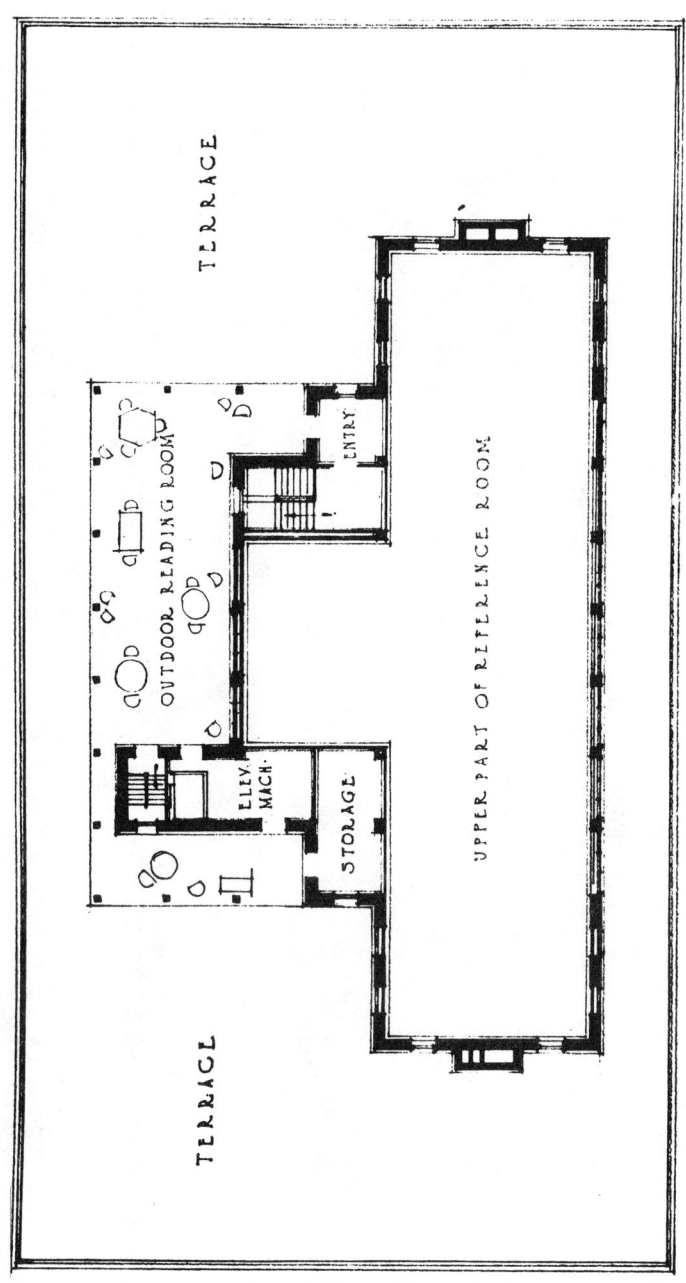

Proposed Modular Library (1934).

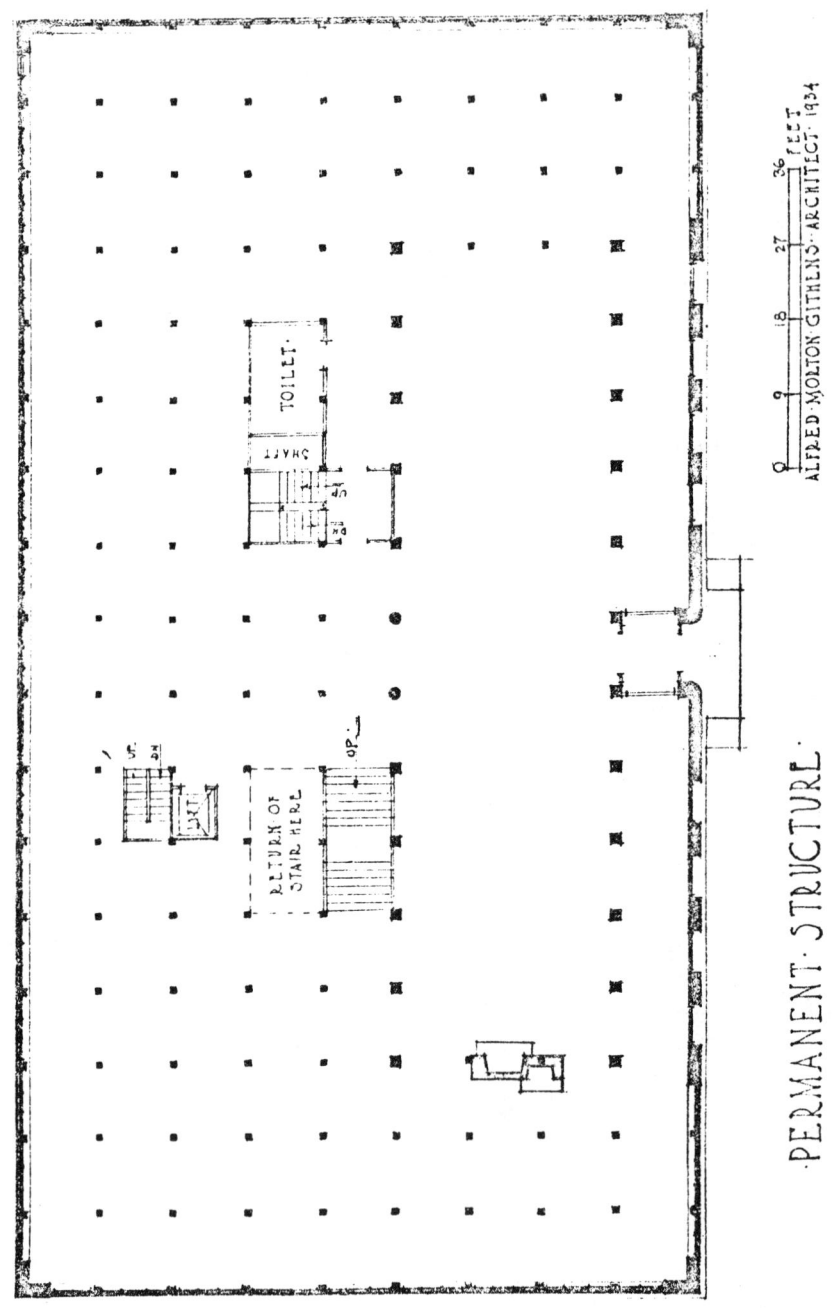

Proposed Modular Library (1934).

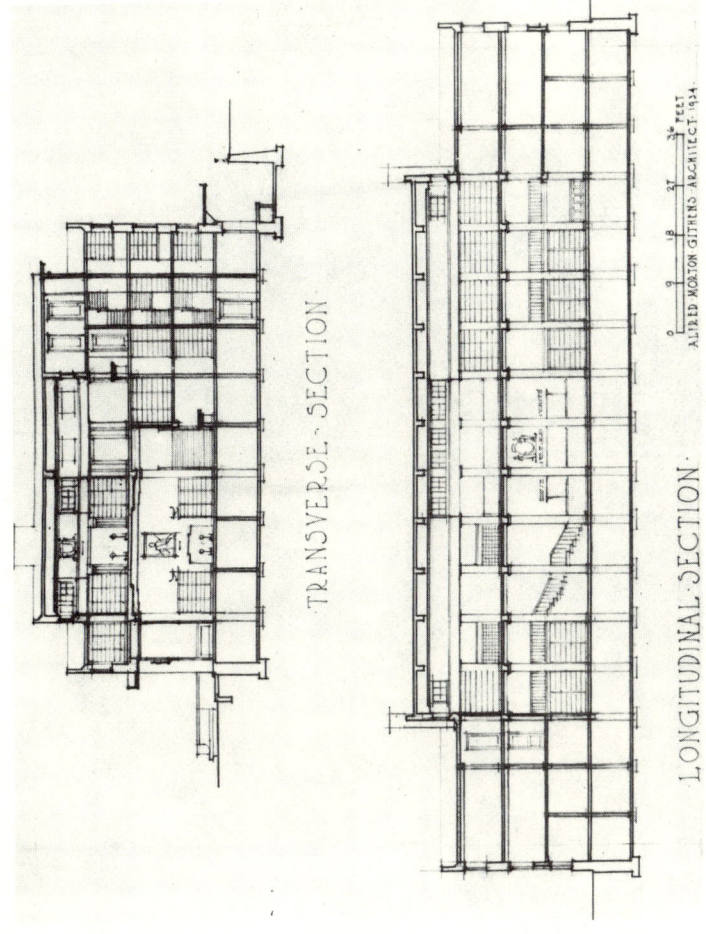

Proposed Modular Library (1934).

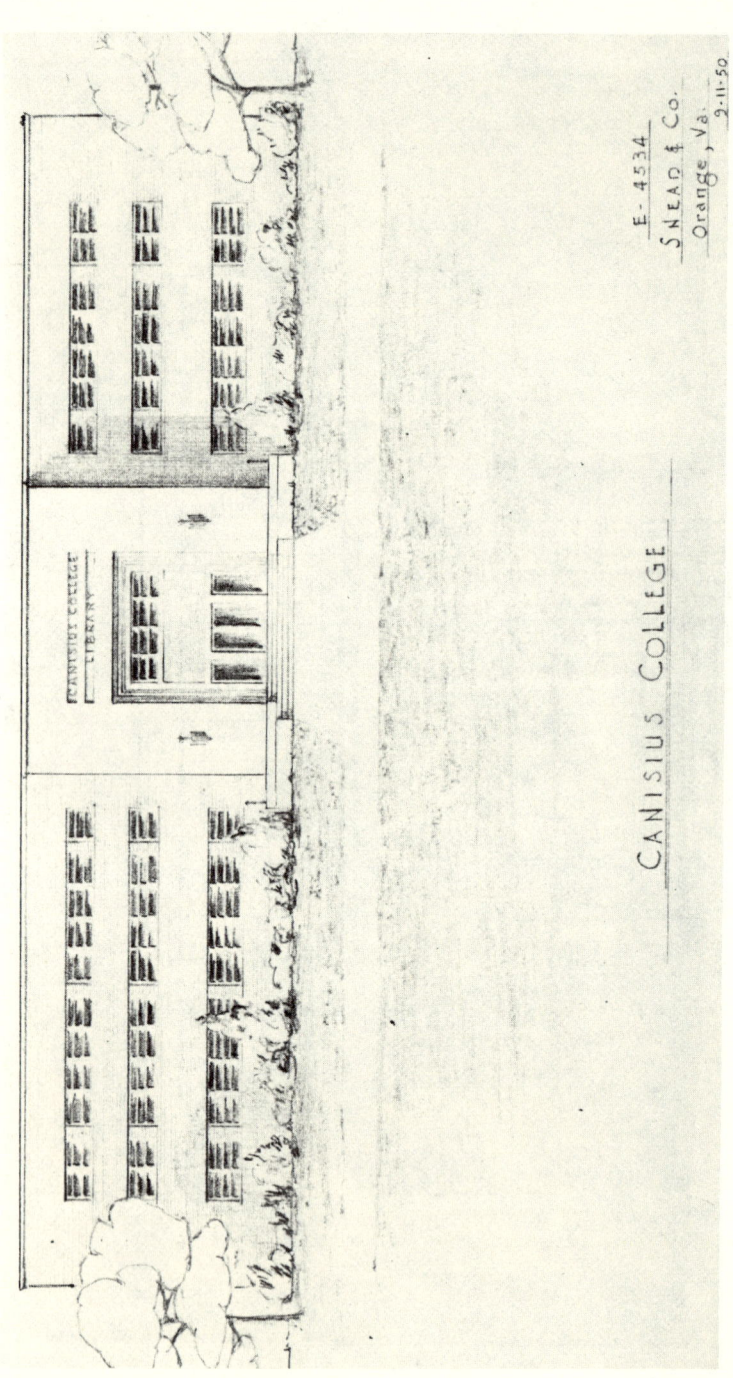

Proposed Modular Library (1950).

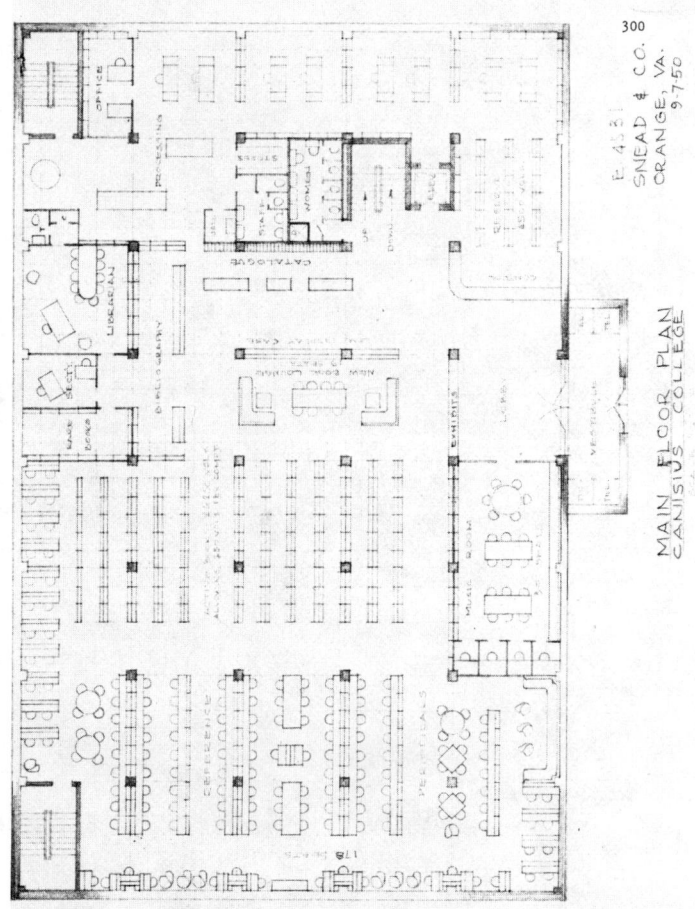

Proposed Modular Library (1950).

Proposed Modular Library (1950).

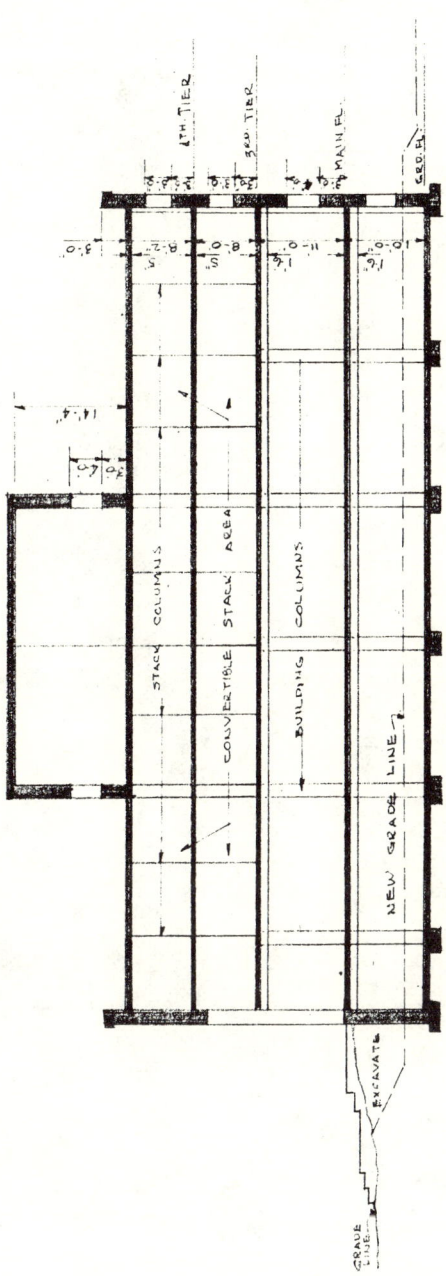

Proposed Modular Library (1950).

CANISIUS COLLEGE
BUFFALO, NEW YORK

FLOOR	GROSS AREA	READER SEATS	READER AREA	⌗ PER READER	NO. VOLUMES	STACK AREA	VOLS. PER AREA	SERVICE AREA
GROUND FL.	14,124 ⌗	385	10794 ⌗	22.8 ⌗	42,625	2660 ⌗	16.02	2670 ⌗
MAIN FL.	14,124 ⌗	208	4586 ⌗	22 ⌗	26,500	3220 ⌗	8.23	6318 ⌗
3RD. TIER	14,124 ⌗	284	6371 ⌗	22.4 ⌗	75,750	5342 ⌗	14.18	2411 ⌗
4TH. TIER	14,124 ⌗	284	6371 ⌗	22.4 ⌗	75,750	5342 ⌗	14.18	2411 ⌗
PENTHOUSE	1,296 ⌗	-	-	-	-	-	-	1296 ⌗
TOTAL	57,792 ⌗	1161**	26,122 ⌗	22.4 ⌗	220,625	16,564 ⌗	13.33	15,106 ⌗

25 SEMINARS AT TABLES: 249
28 STUDIES   AT CARRELS: 434
17 CONF. RM. IN STUDY CHAIR: 72
5 LOUNGES   IN SEMINARS: 272
             IN LOUNGES: 134

* OUTSIDE DIMENSIONS.
** DOES NOT INCLUDE STAFF WORK AREAS.

READERS = 45.2% OF GROSS AREA
STACKS = 28.66% "   "   "
SERVICE AREAS = 26.14% "   "   "

3.81 VOLUMES PER SQ. FT.
49.77 SQ. FT. OF GROSS AREA PER SEAT

SNEAD & CO.
ORANGE, VA.
9-11-50
REV. 9-12-50

Proposed Modular Library (1950). Space Distribution Table.

Appendix II

Library Building Survey, 1930-1960

The chief purpose of this survey is to substantiate the assumption that a change in library architecture, based on the modular plan, did occur in the years immediately following World War II. While this survey was being conducted, it was relatively simple to establish certain other trends that appear to be related.

Before this study could be undertaken, it became necessary to define "modular library" in precise terms. Relying heavily on Macdonald's definition,[1] such a building must have the following attributes: (1) Regularly spaced columns that divide the building into uniform units of space; (2) A flexible interior that permits the easy interchange of stack, reader and staff areas; (3) A reliance on artificial lighting and ventilation. The buildings classified as modular met all three requirements in a major portion of their floor areas.

Three areas caused difficulty in classification. In Macdonald's view a modular library made use of easily moved interior partitions. He was thinking of metal, movable partitions such as those manufactured by Snead and Company, but other types could qualify. For the purpose of the survey, this matter was ignored, although many buildings appeared to have concrete or cinder block interior partitions, and ceiling and floor materials and patterns that greatly inhibited the concept of flexibility.

A second problem arose in regard to classifying the "typical" public library with its basement stack. Although many of these were free-standing stacks, the lighting and spartan finish of these basement levels would be expensive to convert to reader spaces. If the area above ground met the requirements listed above, the building was classified as modular.

The final and most vexing problem in classifying a building concerned its size. Just how small could a library be and still qualify: Macdonald declared that modular construction was "not for a small library of one story" and urged that, in such buildings, the interior be kept free of columns or permanent partitions. Obviously then, the building must have at least two stories, but Macdonald never was specific about a minimum square footage. For the purpose of this paper, the lower limit was set at 10,000 square feet with no floor being less than 3,400 square feet. Assuming a 10-foot ceiling, and applying the "school house" rule of effective daylight reaching inward a distance of twice the height of the windows, it is possible to construct a hypothetical building of four bays or modules, each 20 feet x 20 feet that would not require an artificial environment. In order to employ a normal library column spacing[2] and to accommodate a reasonable number of readers (say eight) in the center of the interior, an additional module, 13 1/2 feet by 13 1/2 feet, would be necessary at the center. This, then, would produce a building having two floors, each of which would be made up of nine modules. Four of these modules would be 22 1/2 feet x 22 1/2 feet, four 13 1/2 feet x 22 1/2 feet, and one 13 1/2 feet x 13 1/2 feet. The total square footage of each floor would be 3,422. Such a building of 6,844 square feet is highly unlikely. For the purpose of the survey, the figure was rounded to 10,000 square feet, and actually only three buildings under 20,000 square feet qualified.

The intent of the survey was not to establish how many buildings were built, but merely to indicate trends and establish that a change in library building design was taking place in the period 1930-1960. The inconsistencies of the reports, or the failure to report at all, make any complete survey difficult, if not impossible, to compile.

The time period, 1930-1960, was judged adequate to establish the trend. It covers a period 15 years in either direction in time from 1945, the year marking the end of World War II and the appearance of Macdonald's article, "New Possibilities in Library Planning."[3]

Most of the literature studied for the survey is not included in the bibliography.

Notes

1. Angus Snead Macdonald, "Modular Construction," Library Journal, LXXX (December 1, 1955), pp. 2728-2730).

2. Library column spacing is usually multiples of four and one-half feet and three feet to accommodate typical stack dimensions.

3. Angus Snead Macdonald, "New Possibilities in Library Planning," Library Journal, LXX (December 15, 1945), pp. 1169-74.

Survey Key

Column Headings:

    I.   Structurally separate stack and reading rooms were (or were not) a feature of these buildings.

    II.   Interior reader spaces required (or did not require) artificial light and ventilation.

    III. Fluorescent lighting was (or was not) employed.

    IV. "Full" air conditioning was (or was not) a part of the building's original equipment.

    V.   The building was (or was not) classified as modular in design.

    VI. The approximate distance in feet between the centers of regularly spaced columns.

Symbols used in the columns:

    A.   Addition of the equipment at a later date was planned.

  AW. Air wash type of ventilation system was employed.

    B.   The basement stack area was unfinished. Although not structurally different from the remainder of the building, it would be expensive to convert to reader spaces.

    M. The building featured a structural mezzanine with free-standing stacks.

  MS. The building had a stack-supported mezzanine.

    N.   No: the feature was not present.

    P.   The equipment was installed in only part of the building.

    Y.   Yes: the feature was present.

         A blank indicates that the necessary information was not reported.

Library Building Survey, 1930-1960

Public Libraries

DATE	LIBRARY	Fixed Stack I	Interior II	Fluorescent III	Air Conditioning IV	Modular V	Column Spacing VI
1931	Berkeley, Calif.	Y	N	N		N	
1933	Baltimore, Md., Enoch Pratt	M	N		Y	N	
1936	Rochester, N.Y., Rundel L.	M	N			N	
1937	Wellsville, N.Y., Howe L.	Y	N		Y	N	
1939	Fort Worth, Texas	Y	N		A	N	
1939	Oreton State Library	Y	N			N	
1940	Concord, N.H.	M		P	P	N	
1940	Mason City, Iowa	Y	N	Y	N	N	
1940	Toledo, O.	M	N	P	Y	N	
1940	Virginia State Library	Y	Y			N	
1941	Brooklyn, N.Y.	M	N	N	A	N	
1941	Glencoe, Ill.	Y	N	P	P	N	
1949	Richmond, Calif.	N	N	Y		Y	
1950	Columbus, Ga., Bradley L.	Y	N	Y	Y	MS	
1951	Hutchinson, Kan.	N	N	Y	Y	Y	18'x21'
1951	Rowan County, N.C.		N			N	
1951	Hawaii County, Hilo, Hawaii	Y	N	Y	N	N	
1951	Stockton, Calif.	N	Y			Y	12' x various
1952	Monterey, Calif.	M	Y	Y	N	Y	
1952	Tacoma, Wash.	N	Y	Y	N	Y	
1953	Oklahoma City, Okla.	N	Y		Y	Y	
1953	Phoenix, Ariz.	M	Y	N		Y	

DATE	LIBRARY	I	II	III	IV	V	VI
1953	Topeka, Kan.	N	Y	Y		Y	
1953	Winston-Salem and Forsyth Co., N. C.	N	Y	Y	Y	Y	
1954	Cincinnati, O.	Y	Y	P	Y	P	21'x27'
1954	El Paso, Texas	N		Y	Y	Y	
1954	Jackson, Miss.	N	Y	Y	Y	Y	
1954	Lancaster, Pa.	N	Y	Y	N	Y	various
1955	Dallas, Texas	M	Y	Y	Y	Y	
1955	Glenview, Ill.		Y	Y	A		
1955	Memphis, Tenn.	Y	Y	N	Y	N	
1955	Midland, Mich., Dow L.	Y	Y	P	Y	N	
1955	Montclair, N. J.	M	Y	P		Y	
1955	San Diego, Calif.	B	Y	Y	Y	Y	
1956	Denver, Colo.	B	Y	Y		Y	20'x20'
1956	Hartford, Conn.	M	Y		N	Y	
1957	Charlotte and Mecklenberg Co., N. C.	N	Y	P	Y	Y	
1957	Johnson Co., Kan.	N	Y			Y	
1958	Flint, Mich.	N	Y			Y	16'x40'
1959	Eugene, Ore.	N	Y	P	Y	Y	
1959	Fresno Co., Calif.	N	Y	Y	Y	Y	
1959	New Orleans, La.	N	Y	Y	Y	Y	
1959	South Bend, Ind.	N	Y	P	Y	Y	22 1/2'x27'
1959	Wenatchee, Wash.	N	Y	Y	Y	Y	
1959	Whittier, Calif.	N	Y	P	Y	Y	varies
1960	Kansas City, Mo.	M	Y	Y	Y	Y	
1960	Louisiana State L.	Y	Y	Y		N	
1960	Minneapolis, Minn.	N	Y	Y		Y	
1960	Seattle, Wash.	B	Y	Y	Y	Y	22 1/2'x22 1/2'

Academic Libraries

1930	Michigan St. Normal Col.	Y	N			N	
1930	Scripps Col., Denison L.	Y	N			N	
1931	Coe Col., Stewart Mem. L.	Y	N			N	
1931	Ohio U. (Athens), Chubb L.	Y	N			N	

DATE	LIBRARY	I	II	III	IV	V	VI
1931	Ripon Col., Lane L.	Y	N			N	
1932	Atlanta U.	Y	N			N	
1932	Northwestern U., Deering L.	Y	N			N	
1932	U. of So. California, Doheny Mem. L.	Y	N			N	
1934	Columbia U., Butler	Y	Y		P	N	
1935	Massachusetts St. Col.	Y	Y			N	
1935	U. of Arkansas	Y	N			N	
1936	Agnes Scott Col.	Y	N			N	
1936	Temple U., Sullivan Mem. L.	Y	N			N	
1936	U. of Pittsburgh	Y	N			N	
1936	U. of Utah	Y	N			N	
1937	Brooklyn Col.	Y	N		P	N	
1937	Denison U., Doane L.	Y				N	
1937	Los Angeles Jr. Col.	Y	N			N	
1937	Rhode Island St. Col.	Y	N			N	
1937	U. of Oregon	Y	N			N	
1937	Vassar Col., Van Ingen Hall	Y	N			N	
1938	Albion Col., Stockwell L.	Y	N			N	
1938	Drake U., Cowles L.	Y	N		P	N	
1938	Franklin and Marshall Fackenthal L.	Y				N	
1938	Howard U.	Y	N			N	
1938	Milwaukee-Downer Col., Chapman L.	Y	N			N	
1938	St. Bonaventure Col., Friedsam L.	Y	N	N		N	
1938	U. of New Mexico	Y	N			N	
1938	Westminster Col. (Pa.) McGill Mem. L.	Y	N			N	
1938	Willamette U.	Y	N			N	
1939	Babson Institute	N	Y	N		Transitional	
1939	Bennett Col.	Y	N			N	
1939	Col. of New Rochelle, N.Y.	Y	N	N		N	
1939	Drew U., Rose Mem. L.	Y	N			N	
1939	Geo. Washington U.	Y	N			N	

DATE	LIBRARY	I	II	III	IV	V	VI
1939	Penn. State Col.	Y	N			N	
1939	South Georgia Col.	Y	N			N	
1939	Southeast Missouri T. Col.	Y	N			N	
1939	Northwest Missouri T. Col.	Y				N	
1939	Talladega Col., Savery L.	Y	N			N	
1939	U. of Wichita	Y	N		A	N	
1939	Western Colo. State Col.	Y	N		AW	N	
1940	Eastern Wash. Col. of Ed.	Y			Y	N	
1940	Illinois St. Normal U., Milner L.	Y	N			N	
1940	Rockford Col., Sherratt L.	Y	N			N	
1940	Skidmore Col.	Y	N	Y		Transitional	
1940	So. Methodist U., Fondren L.	Y	N	N	Y	N	
1940	U. of Alabama, Gorgas L.	Y	N		P	N	
1940	U. of Chattanooga	Y	N			N	
1941	Joint U., Nashville	Y	Y	Y	Y	N	
1941	New Mexico Military Inst.	Y		Y	Y	N	
1941	Tulane U., Tilton L.	Y	N	P	Y	N	
1941	U. of So. Carolina	Y	N	P		N	
1942	Harvard U., Houghton L.	Y	N	Y	Y	N	
1942	St. Mary's Col., Notre Dame, Ind.	Y	N	P	N	N	
1948	Princeton U., Firestone L.	Y	Y	N	A	P	18'x24'
1949	Harvard U., Lamont L.	Y	Y	Y	Y	Transitional	
1949	Mt. San Antonio Col., Pamona, Calif.	Y	Y	N	N	N	
1949	Pasadena City Col.	Y		P	A	Transitional	
1949	Rice Inst., Fondren L.	Y		Y	Y	Transitional	
1949	Villanova Col.	Y				N	
1950	College of the Bible	Y	N	Y	N	N	
1950	E. Illinois St. Col.	Y		Y		N	
1950	Gustavus Adolphus Col.	Y	N	Y	N	N	
1950	Lincoln U.	Y	Y	Y		N	
1950	M. I. T., Hayden Mem. L.	Y	N	N	Y	Transitional	
1950	Montana St. Col.	N	N	Y	N	Y	

DATE	LIBRARY	I	II	III	IV	V	VI
1950	N. Dakota Ag. Col.	N	Y	Y	N	Y	22 1/2'x22 1/2'
1950	U. of N. C. Women's Col.	N	Y	Y	N	Y	18'x18'
1951	E. Oregon Col. of Ed.	Y	N			N	
1951	Fairmont St. Col., W. Va.	N	Y	Y	A	Y	
1951	Mississippi St. Col.	Y		Y	Y	N	
1951	S. Oregon Col. of Ed.	N	Y	N		Y	
1951	U. of Houston	N	Y	N	Y	Y	18'x22'
1951	U. of Minn. Ag. L.	N	Y	Y		Y	22 1/2'x22 1/2'
1951	U. of Oregon (addition)	N	N	Y	Y	Y	18'x22 1/2'
1952	Associated Cols., Claremont, Calif.	N	Y		P	Y	18'x18'
1952	E. New Mexico U.	Y	Y	N	Y	Y	18 1/2'x24 1/2'
1952	Goucher Col.	Y	Y	Y	Y	Y	various
1952	Kansas St. T. Col.	Y	Y	Y	P	N	
1952	Northeastern U., Boston	Y	Y	N	Y	N	
1952	Trinity Col., Hartford, Conn.	N	Y	P	Y	Y	
1952	Youngstown Col., Ohio	N		Y		Y	
1953	Georgia Inst. of Tech. Price L.	Y	Y	Y	Y	Y	
1953	Idaho St. Col.	N		Y	Y	Y	22 1/2'x22 1/2'
1953	Marquette U.	Y	Y	Y		compromise	
1953	New Mexico A. &M. Col.	N	Y			Y	18'x22 1/2'
1953	Oklahoma A. &M. Col.	N	Y	Y	Y	Y	
1953	Oklahoma City U.	N		Y	Y		
1953	U. of Calif., Riverside	N	Y	Y	N	Y	18'x22 1/2'
1953	U. of Georgia	N	Y	Y	Y	Y	18'x18'
1953	U. of Toledo	N	Y	Y	N	Y	
1953	U. of Wisconsin	Y	N	P		N	
1953	Wake Forest Col.	Y	N		Y	N	
1953	Wayne U., Detroit	N	Y	Y	Y	Y	
1954	Bradley U.	N	Y	Y	Y	Y	18'x22 1/2'
1954	Carleton Col.	N				Y	
1954	N. Central Col. and Evangelical Theol. Sem., Naperville, Ill.	Y	Y	Y	N	N	

DATE	LIBRARY	I	II	III	IV	V	VI
1955	Queens Col., Flushing, N.Y.	Y	N	P		N	
1955	S. W. Missouri St. Col.	Y		Y	P	N	
1955	U. of Louisville	N	Y	Y	Y	Y	
1955	Va. Polytechnic Inst.	N	Y	Y	Y	Y	27'x27'
1956	Central Michigan Col.	N			Y	Y	
1956	Michigan St. U.	N	Y	Y	Y	Y	22 1/2'x22 1/2'
1956	N.Y. State U. T. Col., Geneseo	N	Y	Y		compromise	
1956	Rutgers U.	Y	Y	Y	Y	Y	varies
1956	St. Louis U.	M	Y	Y	Y	Y	25'x25'
1956	Seton Hall U.	N	Y	Y		Y	
1956	S. Illinois U.	N	Y	Y		Y	
1956	Washburn U.	N	N	Y	Y		
1956	Western Reserve U.	N	Y	Y		Y	20'x21'
1957	City Col., N.Y.	N	Y			Y	18'x18'
1957	U. of Idaho	N	Y	Y	Y	Y	22 1/2'x22 1/2'
1957	U. of Maryland, Col. Park	Y	Y		N	N	
1958	Colgate U.	N	Y	Y	N	Y	22 1/2'x24 1/2'
1958	Louisiana St. U.	N	Y	Y	Y	Y	24'x27'
1958	Texas Southern U.	Y		Y	Y	N	
1958	U. of Michigan, Undergrad.	N	Y	Y	Y	Y	24'x30'
1958	U. of Wyoming, Coe L.	N	Y	Y	N	Y	22 1/2'x22 1/2'
1958	Washington U., St. Louis, Olin L.	N	Y	Y	Y	Y	21 1/2'x21 1/2'
1958	Wayland Baptist Col.	N	Y	Y	Y	Y	
1958	Western Michigan U., Waldo L.	N	N	Y		Y	
1959	Carleton U., Ottawa, Can.	N	Y	Y		Y	
1959	Drexel Inst. of Technology	N		Y		Y	
1959	Grinnell Col.	N	Y	Y		Y	
1959	Kent St. U. (Ohio) addition	N	Y	Y	Y	Y	
1959	U. of New Hampshire	N	Y	Y	N	Y	18 1/2'x24 1/2'
1960	Barnard Col.	N	Y	Y	A	Y	
1960	Bennington Col.	N	Y	Y		Y	
1960	Case Inst. of Technology	N	Y	Y	Y	Y	26'x27'

DATE	LIBRARY	I	II	III	IV	V	VI
1960	Colorado Col., Colo. Springs	N	Y	Y		Y	
1960	Cornell U., Olin L.	N	Y	Y	Y	Y	
1960	East Texas St. Col.	N	Y	Y	Y	Y	
1960	The Church Col. of Hawaii	N		Y		Y	13 1/2'x13 1/2'
1960	U. of So. Carolina	N	Y	Y		Y	

TOTALS

				I	II	III	IV	V
	1930-	12	Yes	12	1	4	5	0
Public Libraries	1945	Bldgs.	No	0	10	2	3	12
	1946-	37	Yes	6	31	28	20	30
	1960	Bldgs.	No	22	5	2	6	5
	1930-	55	Yes	54	20	7	10	0
Academic Libraries	1945	Bldgs.	No	1	30	4	3	54
	1946-	81	Yes	27	56	65	38	56
	1960	Bldgs.	No	54	11	7	18	17

Appendix III

Snead and Company Bookstack Installations

1887-1915[1]

Arkansas
    Arkansas State Capitol Law Library, Little Rock

California
    Leland Stanford Jr. University Library, Palo Alto

Colorado
    Denver Public Library

Connecticut
    Blackstone Memorial Library, Branford
    Connecticut Agricultural Experimental Station, New Haven
    Ferguson Memorial Library, Stamford
    Hartford Medical Society Library
    Meriden High School Library
    Ridgefield Memorial Library
    Trinity College, Williams Memorial Library, Hartford

Delaware
    Delaware State Capitol, Dover

District of Columbia
    Public Library
    U. S. Army Engineer's School
    U. S. Army War College
    U. S. Bureau of Crop Estimates
    U. S. Bureau of Education
    U. S. Bureau of Mines
    U. S. Bureau of Plant Industry
    U. S. Department of Agriculture
    U. S. Library of Congress
    U. S. Soldiers Home
    U. S. State, War and Navy Department Building

---

1. Snead and Company Iron Works, Library Planning, Bookstacks and Shelving, (Jersey City, N. J.: Snead and Company, 1915), pp. 121-125.

Florida
> Florida Agricultural Experimental Station, University of Florida, Gainesville

Georgia
> Medical College of Georgia, Augusta

Hawaii
> Library of Hawaii, Honolulu

Idaho
> Academy of Idaho, Pocatello
> Wallace Public Library

Illinois
> Appellate Court Library, Mt. Vernon
> Evanston Public Library
> Peoria Public Library
> U. S. Naval Training Station, North Chicago
> University of Chicago, Harper Memorial Library
> University of Illinois, Urbana
>> Altgeld Hall
>> Lincoln Hall
>> Natural History Building
>> Transportation Building

Indiana
> Gary Public Library
> Indiana State Normal School Library, Terre Haute
> Purdue University Library, Lafayette

Iowa
> Iowa State Teachers College Library, Cedar Falls
> Iowa State University Law Building, Iowa City
> Sioux City Public Library

Kansas
> Kansas State Agricultural College Library, Manhattan

Kentucky
> Louisville Public Library

Louisiana
> Loyola University Library, New Orleans
> University of Louisiana, Hill Memorial Library, Baton Rouge

Maine
> Bangor Public Library
> Caribou Public Library
> Maine Historical Society, Portland
> Portland Public Library

Maryland
> Johns Hopkins University Library, Gilman Hall, Baltimore
> Medical and Chirurgical Faculty of Maryland, Baltimore
> Phipps Psychiatric Institute, Baltimore

Massachusetts
> Andover-Harvard Theological Seminary Library, Cambridge
> Beverly Public Library
> Boston Athenaeum
> Brookline Public Library
> Canton Public Library
> Converse Memorial Library, Malden
> Dalton Public Library
> Dowse Library, Sherborn
> Fall River Public Library
> Fitchburg Historical Society
> Harvard University, Widener Memorial Library, Cambridge
> Hyde Park Public Library
> J. V. Fletcher Library, Westford
> Jacob Edwards Library, Southbridge
> Lynn Public Library
> Mason Library, Great Barrington
> Masonic Library, Boston
> New England Historical and Genealogical Society, Boston
> Perkins Institute for the Blind, Watertown
> Reuben Hoar Library, Littleton
> Schauffler Memorial Library, Mt. Hermon
> Somerville Free Public Library
> Southboro Public Library
> Springfield City Library
> Whitinsville Public Library

Michigan
> Sault Ste. Marie Public Library
> University of Michigan Library, Ann Arbor

Minnesota
> Coleraine Public Library
> St. Paul Public Library

Mississippi
> Greenwood Public Library

Missouri
> Louis George Branch Library, Kansas City
> Mercantile Library, St. Louis
> School of Mines and Metallurgy, Rolla
> University of Missouri, Biology Building, Columbia
> University of Missouri, Library, Columbia
> Washington University Medical School, St. Louis

New Hampshire
    Dunbarton Public Library
    Exeter Public Library
    Howe Library, Hanover
    Manchester Public Library
    New Hampshire Historical Society, Concord
    New Hampshire State Library, Concord
    Phillips-Exeter Academy, Davis Memorial Library, Exeter

New Jersey
    Elizabeth Public Library
    Montclair Free Library, Upper Montclair
    St. Elizabeth's College Library, Convent Station
    Summit Free Public Library

New York
    New York City
        American Geographical Society
        American Museum of Natural History
        American Society of Civil Engineers
        American S. P. C. A.
        Brooklyn Public Library, Carroll Park Branch
        Brooklyn Public Library, Pacific Branch
        Brooklyn Public Library, Williamsburg Branch
        Columbia University Law School, Kent Hall
        Columbia University Lowe Library
        Cooper Union Library
        General Theological Seminary
        G. P. Putnam's Sons Co., 45th St. Book Store
        Hispanic Society of America
        Jewish Theological Seminary
        Lotos Club
        New York County Lawyers Association
        New York Genealogical and Biographical Society
        New York Public Library
        Russell Sage Foundation Library
        The Association of the Bar of the City of New York
        United Engineering Societies
        Y. M. C. A. of N. Y. C.
    Canandaigua Historical Society and Wood Library, Canandaigua
    Coburn Free Library, Owego
    Cornell University Law Library, Ithaca
    Flower Memorial Library, Watertown
    Little Falls Public Library
    New Rochelle Public Library
    Rochester Medical Association
    Rochester Theological Seminary
    Syracuse Public Library
    Thomas Mott Osborne, Private Library, Auburn
    Union College Library, Schenectady
    Wells College, Frances Folsom Cleveland Library, Aurora

North Carolina
   University of North Carolina Library, Chapel Hill

Ohio
   Akron Public Library
   Hebrew Union College Library, Cincinnati
   Ohio Mechanics Institute, Cincinnati
   Ohio State University Library, Columbus
   Western College for Women, Oxford

Oregon
   Multnomah County Public Library, Portland
   Supreme Court and Library Building, Salem
   University of Oregon Library, Eugene

Pennsylvania
   Bradford Public Library
   Haverford College Library, Haverford
   Krauth Memorial Library, Mt. Airy
   Lafayette College, Van Wickle Memorial Library, Easton
   Newtown Public Library
   Academy of Natural Sciences, Philadelphia
   American Philosophical Society, Philadelphia
   College of Physicians, Philadelphia
   Dropsie College, Philadelphia
   Gratz College, Philadelphia
   Jefferson Medical College, Philadelphia
   Pittsburgh North Side Carnegie Free Library
   Reading Public Library
   Theological Seminary of St. Charles Borromeo, Overbrook
   U. S. Naval Home, Philadelphia
   University of Pennsylvania Library, Philadelphia
      Biddle Law Library
      Zoology Laboratory

Rhode Island
   East Greenwich Free Library
   Providence Diocesan Office and Library
   Redwood Library and Athenaeum, Newport
   Rhode Island Medical Society, Providence

South Carolina
   Benedict College Library, Columbia

South Dakota
   South Dakota State College of Agriculture and Mechanics Art
      Library, Brookings

Tennessee
   George Peabody College for Teachers Library, Nashville
   University of Tennessee Library, Knoxville

Texas
 Gainesville Public Library
 Sulphur Springs Public Library
 Texas State Library, Austin

Vermont
 Proctor Public Library
 Vermont Free Public Library, Montpelier

Virginia
 U. S. Army Coast Artillary Training School, Fort Monroe
 Virginia State Library, Richmond

West Virginia
 Wheeling Public Library

Wisconsin
 University of Wisconsin, Agricultural Hall Library, Madison
 Wisconsin State Capitol Law Library, Madison
 Wisconsin State Historical Society, Madison

Australia
 New South Wales
  Sydney Public Library

Canada
 Alberta
  Calgary Court House Law Library, Calgary
  Calgary Public Library
  Edmonton Court House Law Library
  Provincial Library, Edmonton
 British Columbia
  Provincial Library, Victoria
 Ontario
  Fort William Public Library
  Hamilton Public Library
  Knox College Library, Toronto
  Legislative Library, Toronto
  Ottawa Public Library, Ottawa
  Tillsonburg Public Library
  Toronto Public Reference Library
  Victoria College Library, Toronto
 Quebec
  Bibliothèque St.-Sulpice, Montreal
  McGill University Medical Library, Montreal
 Saskatchewan
  Moose Jaw Public Library
  Legislative Library, Regina
  Regina Public Library

China
 Dairen Public Library, Dairen

New Zealand
    Parliamentary Library, Wellington

Philippines
    Bureau of Education, Manila
    Philippines Library, Manilla

1916-1930[2]

Alabama
    Alabama College Library, Montevallo
    Birmingham Public Library, East Lake Branch
    University of Alabama Library, Tuscaloosa

Arizona
    University of Arizona Library, Tucson

Arkansas
    University of Arkansas Library, Fayetteville

California
    California State Library, Sacramento
    Los Angeles Public Library
    Occidental College, Mary Norton Clapp Library, Los Angeles
    Pacific School of Religion, Berkeley
    Sacramento City Library
    San Francisco Public Library
    University of California Library, Berkeley

Connecticut
    Burroughs Library and Reading Room, Bridgeport
    Connecticut College for Women Library, New London
    Ferguson Memorial Library, Stamford
    Hagaman Memorial Library, East Haven
    Norwich Free Academy, Peck Library, Norwich
    Phoebe Griffin Noyes Library, Lyme
    Wesleyan University, Olin Memorial Library, Middletown
    Yale University, New Haven
        Sterling Hall of Medicine
        Sterling Law Library
        Sterling Memorial Library

District of Columbia
    Carnegie Institute of Washington, Geophysical Laboratory
    Catholic University of America, Mullen Library

---

2. Snead and Company, Snead Bookstacks and Stack Room Equipment, (Jersey City, N.J.: Snead and Company, 1931) p. 25-26.

District of Columbia (continued)
    U. S. Department of Commerce Building
    U. S. Department of the Interior Building
    U. S. Department of Labor Building
    U. S. Shipping Board
    U. S. Tariff Commission Building
    U. S. War Department Building

Florida
    Lakeland Public Library

Georgia
    Emory University, Atlanta
    Savannah Public Library
    Wesleyan Female College Library, Macon

Illinois
    American College of Surgeons Library
    Chicago Public Libraries:
        Legler Branch
        Douglas Branch
    Garret Biblical Institute Library, Evanston
    Illinois Wesleyan University, Buck Memorial Library, Bloomington
    Loyola University, Cudahy Memorial Library, Chicago
    Northwestern University Library, Evanston
    University of Chicago Libraries:
        Classic Building
        Theology Building
        Wieboldt Hall
    University of Illinois Library, Urbana

Indiana
    Concordia College Library, Fort Wayne
    University of Notre Dame Library, Notre Dame

Iowa
    Davenport Public Library
    Iowa State College Library, Ames

Kansas
    Kansas State Agricultural College Library, Manhattan

Kentucky
    Jefferson County and University of Louisville, Medical Library, Louisville
    Southern Baptist Theological Seminary Library, Louisville

Louisiana
    Louisiana Polytechnic Institute Library, New Orleans
    Sophie Newcomb College, Dixon Hall, (Tulane University) New Orleans

Maryland
    Baltimore Bar Library, Baltimore
    Johns Hopkins University, Welch Medical Library, Baltimore
    Maryland Historical Society, Baltimore
    University of Maryland Library, Baltimore

Massachusetts
    Amherst College Library, Amherst
    Beverly Farms Library
    Concord Free Public Library
    Harvard University, Chemical Laboratory, Cambridge
    Massachusetts College of Pharmacy Library, Boston
    Massachusetts Institute of Technology Library, Cambridge
    William College Library, Williamstown
    Wheaton College Library, Norton

Michigan
    Marygrove College Library, Detroit
    Michigan Agricultural College Library, East Lansing
    Michigan State Normal College Library, Ypsilanti

Minnesota
    Hill Reference Library, St. Paul
    Minneapolis Public Library
    Minnesota St. Normal School Library, Mankato

Mississippi
    Millsaps College Library, Jackson

Missouri
    Concordia Seminary Library, St. Louis
    Drury College Library, Springfield
    Washington University, Law School Library, Biology Department Library, St. Louis

Montana
    University of Montana Library, Missoula

Nebraska
    Creighton University Library, Omaha

New Hampshire
    Dartmouth College, Hanover
        Amos Tuck School
        Baker Memorial Library

New Jersey
    Cooper Branch Library, Camden
    Essex County Court House, Newark
    Free Public Library, East Orange
    Johnson Public Library, Hackensack
    Princeton Theological Seminary Library, Princeton

New York
  New York City:
    American Institute of Banking
    Biblical Seminary
    College of the City of New York
    Columbia University, Schermerhorn Hall, Officers'
      Law Library
    New York Academy of Medicine
    Pierpont Morgan Library
    Union Theological Seminary Library
  Adriance Memorial Library, Poughkeepsie
  Cornell University, Myron Taylor Hall, Ithaca
  Goodyear Memorial Library, Groton
  Huntington Free Library and Reading Room
  Port Chester Public Library
  Rensselaer Polytechnic Institute Library, Troy
  Sarah Lawrence College Library, Bronxville
  University of Rochester:
    Main Library
    Medical School Library
    Eastman School of Music Library
    Research Laboratory
    Art Museum
  Vassar College Library, Poughkeepsie
  White Plains Public Library

North Carolina
  Duke University Library, Durham
  East Carolina Teachers College Library, Greenville
  Elon College Library, Elon College
  North Carolina College for Women Library, Greensboro
  North Carolina Library Commission Library, Raleigh
  University of North Carolina Library, Chapel Hill
  Wake Forest College Library, Wake Forest

North Dakota
  Liberty Memorial Library, Bismark
  University of North Dakota Library, Grand Forks

Ohio
  Allen Memorial Medical Library, Cleveland
  Mt. St. Mary's Seminary Library, Norwood, Cincinnati
  Ohio St. Archaeological and Historical Society, Columbus
  University of Cincinnati Library, Cincinnati
  University of Dayton, Albert Emmanuel Library, Dayton

Oregon
  Library Association of Portland, Portland
  Oregon Agricultural College Library, Corvallis
  Oregon Historical Society, Portland

Pennsylvania
    Lehigh University Library, Bethlehem
    Meadville Public Library
    Muhlenberg College Library, Allentown
    University of Pennsylvania, Philadelphia:
        Duhring Memorial Wing
        Penniman Library
        Bennett Hall
    Spalding Memorial Library, Athens
    Villanova College Library, Villanova
    Wilson College, John Stewart Memorial Library, Chambersburg

Rhode Island
    Knight Memorial Library, Providence
    William H. Hall Free Library, Edgewood

South Carolina
    Clemson College Library, Clemson
    University of South Carolina Library, Columbia

South Dakota
    South Dakota State College of Agriculture & Mechanic Arts
        Library, Brookings

Texas
    Agricultural and Mechanical College Library, College Station
    Baylor University Library, Waco
    Dallas Public Library
    East Texas St. Teachers College Library, Commerce
    El Paso Public Library
    Houston Public Library
    Rice Institute Library, Houston
    San Antonio Public Library

Utah
    Utah State Agricultural College Library, Logan

Vermont
    Vermont State Library, Montpelier

Virginia
    Randolph Macon College, Page Library, Ashland
    Randolph Macon Women's College Library, Lynchburg
    Richmond Public Library
    Sweet Briar College Library, Sweet Briar

Washington
    Ellensberg State Normal School Library, Ellensberg
    Longview Public Library

West Virginia
    Bethany College Library, Bethany

West Virginia (continued)
   Fairmont St. Normal School Library, Fairmont
   West Virginia Collegiate Institute Library, Institute
   West Virginia University Library, Morgantown

Wyoming
   University of Wyoming Library, Laramie

Canada
   British Columbia
      British Columbia Parliamentary Library, Victoria
      University of British Columbia Library, Point Grey
   Nova Scotia
      Dalhousie University Library, Halifax
   Quebec
      Monastery of Fathers of the Blessed Sacrament, Montreal
      Seminary of St. Hyacinthe, St. Hyacinthe

China
   Mukden Public Library
   Tsing Hua College Library, Peking

France
   University of Lyon Library, Lyon

Greece
   American School of Classifical Studies Library, Athens

Italy
   International Institute of Private Law, Rome
   Pontifical Institute of Oriental Studies, Rome
   Russian College Library, Rome

India
   Central Library, Baroda State, Baroda
   Bankiport High Court, Bankiport

Japan
   Imperial University Library, Tokyo

Philippines
   University of the Philippines Library, Manila

Vatican City
   Vatican Library, Vatican City

1931-1941[3]

Alabama
　　Alabama Supreme Court Library, Montgomery
　　Spring Hill College Library, Spring Hill
　　Talladega College Library, Talladega
　　Tuskegee Institute Library, Tuskegee
　　University of Alabama Library, Tuscaloosa

Arizona
　　Phoenix Junior College Library, Phoenix

Arkansas
　　Arkansas Polytechnic College Library, Russellville
　　Arkansas State Teachers' College Library, Conway
　　Hendrix College Library, Conway

California
　　San Diego State Teachers' College Library, San Diego
　　San Mateo Public Library
　　University of Southern California Library, Los Angeles

Colorado
　　Colorado State College of Education Library, Greeley

Connecticut
　　Booth Memorial Library, Newtown
　　Farmington Public Library
　　Guilford Public Library
　　Yale University, Silliman College Library, New Haven

Delaware
　　Wilmington Institute Free Library

District of Columbia
　　Brookings Institute Library
　　Howard University Library
　　Jefferson Jr. High School Library
　　Library of Congress Annex Building
　　Municipal Court Library
　　U. S. Archives Bldg., Contract No. 2
　　U. S. Dept. of Labor and Interstate Commerce Commission
　　　　Library

Georgia
　　Agnes Scott College Library, Decatur

---

3. Snead and Company, Snead Bookstacks, (Jersey City, N. J.: Snead and Company, 1940), p. 38-41.

Georgia (continued)
    Atlanta University Library, Atlanta
    Mercer University Library, Macon
    University of Georgia Library, Athens

Illinois
    Evanston Public Library
    Rockford College Library, Rockford
    University of Chicago, Goodspeed Hall
    University of Illinois Library, Urbana

Kansas
    St. Benedict Abbey Library, Atchison

Kentucky
    University of Kentucky Library, Lexington

Louisiana
    Louisiana State University Medical Library, New Orleans
    Xavier University Library, New Orleans

Maryland
    Maryland Hall of Records, Annapolis
    Washington College Library, Chestertown

Massachusetts
    Lenox Library
    Worcester Polytechnic Institute Library, Worcester

Michigan
    Albion College Library, Albion

Montana
    Kalispell Public Library

New Hampshire
    Kimball Academy, Barnes Library, Meriden

New Jersey
    Drew University Library, Madison
    Montclair State Teachers' College Library, Upper Montclair
    New Jersey Historical Society, Newark
    New Jersey State Library, Trenton
    Newton Public Library
    Plainfield Public Library
    Teaneck Public Library
    Union City Public Library
    Verona Public Library

New Mexico
    New Mexico Normal University Library, Las Vegas

New York
　　New York City:
　　　　Bellevue Hospital, Clinical Record Library
　　　　Brooklyn Public Library
　　　　Columbia University, Butler Library
　　　　Fordham University Graduate School Library
　　　　Fort Greene Health Center
　　　　Frick Art Reference Library
　　　　Hunter College Library
　　　　Mercantile Library
　　　　New York Historical Society Library
　　　　New York Hospital and Cornell Medical Library
　　　　New York Post Graduate Medical School Library
　　　　New York Society Library
　　　　New York University Libraries
　　　　Pratt Institute Library
　　　　Queens County Supreme Court Library
　　　　Sperry Gryoscope Co.
　　　　Webb Institute of Naval Architecture Library
　　Colgate-Rochester Divinity School Library, Rochester
　　College of New Rochelle Library, New Rochelle
　　Great Neck Public Library, Great Neck
　　Hofstra College Library, Hempstead, L. I.
　　New York State Health Department Library, Albany
　　St. Bernard's Seminary Library, Rochester

North Carolina
　　Duke University Medical College Library, Durham

Ohio
　　Denison University Library, Granville
　　Pontifical College Josephinium, Worthington

Oklahoma
　　University of Oklahoma Library, Norman

Pennsylvania
　　Temple University Library, Philadelphia
　　University of Pittsburgh, Cathedral of Learning Library, Pittsburgh

South Carolina
　　Coker College Library, Hartsville
　　Converse College Library, Spartanburg
　　Medical College of South Carolina Library, Charleston

Tennessee
　　University of the South Library, Sewanee
　　University of Tennessee Library, Knoxville

Texas
　　Galveston Public Library

Texas (continued)
    Southern Methodist University Library, Dallas
    University of Texas Library, Austin

Utah
    University of Utah Library, Salt Lake City

Virginia
    Medical College of Virginia Library, Richmond
    R. E. Lee Junior High School Library, Lynchburg
    Virginia Military Institute Library, Lexington
    Virginia Polytechnic Institute Library, Blacksburg
    Virginia State College for Negroes Library, Petersburg
    Washington and Lee University Library, Lexington

Washington
    U. S. Penitentiary Library, McNeil Island

West Virginia
    West Virginia University Law School Library, Morgantown

Wisconsin
    Milwaukee-Downer College, Chapman Memorial Library

Canada
    Ontario
        Queen's University Library, Kingston

France
    The Catholic Institute of Toulouse Library, Toulouse
    The College of Medicine Library, Nancy
    The College of Science Library, Nancy
    Ethnographic Museum of Trocadero, Paris
    Library of the Catholic Institute, Paris
    The Library for the Israelitic Alliance, Paris
    The National Museum of Natural History, Paris

Great Britain
    The British Museum, London
    The Manchester Central Library, Manchester
    New Educational Library, The London County Hall, London
    The Radcliffe Science Library, Oxford
    Rare Book Library, Guildhall, London
    The Royal Institute of Architects, London
    The University College of Exeter Library, Exeter
    The University College of Swansea Library, Swansea
    The University of Liverpool Library, Liverpool
    The University of Manchester Library, Manchester

Italy
    The Sacred Congregation for the Oriental Collection, Rome

Puerto Rico
  University of Puerto Rico Library, Rio Piedras

Syria
  The French School of Engineering Library, Beirut

1946-1952[4]

California
  University of California Library, Los Angeles

District of Columbia
  George Washington University Library

Illinois
  Midwest Inter-Library Center, Chicago
  Northern Illinois State Teachers College Library, DeKalb

Indiana
  Hanover College Library, Hanover

Iowa
  Iowa State College Atomic Laboratory, Ames

Maryland
  Goucher College Library, Baltimore

Michigan
  Michigan State Normal College Library, Ypsilanti
  University of Detroit Library, Detroit

Minnesota
  Gustavus Adolphus College Library, St. Peter
  Luther Theological Seminary Library, St. Paul
  St. Paul Public Library
  St. Paul Seminary Library, St. Paul

Mississippi
  Mississippi State College Library, State College

Montana
  Montana Veterans and Pioneers Memorial Building, Helena

New Hampshire
  Concord Public Library

---

4. Snead and Company, Snead System for Libraries, (Catalog 52; Orange Va.; Snead and Company, 1952?) p. 3.

New Mexico
University of New Mexico Library, Albuquerque

New York
LeMoyne College Library, Syracuse

North Dakota
North Dakota Agricultural College Library, Fargo
University of North Dakota Law Library, Grand Forks

Oklahoma
University of Oklahoma Library, Norman

South Carolina
Converse College Library, Spartanburg
Richland County Public Library, Columbia

South Dakota
South Dakota State College of Agriculture & Mechanic Arts
Library, Brookings

Tennessee
State Library and Archives Building, Nashville (in cooperation
with Forges de Strasbourg, Strasbourg, France)
Tennessee Agricultural and Industrial Institute, Nashville

Texas
Hardin-Simmons University Library, Abilene
Texas Lutheran College Library, Saguin

Canada
Alberta
University of Alberta Library, Edmonton
British Columbia
Parliamentary Library of Victoria, Victoria
University of British Columbia Library, Vancouver
Victoria Public Library, Victoria, (in cooperation with
Luxfer Ltd., London, England)
Ontario
McMaster University Library, Hamilton (in cooperation
with Luxfer, Ltd., London, England)

Australia
National Library of Sydney, Sydney

Belgium
University of Louvain Library, Louvain

France
Archives of the Marne
Library of the Ministry of Fine Arts, Paris

Great Britain
  National Scottish Library, Edinburgh
  St. Andrews University Library

Peru
  National Library of Peru, Lima

Phillipines
  University of Philippines Library, Manila

Puerto Rico
  University of Puerto Rico Library, Rio Piedras

Selected Bibliography

Published Writings of Angus Snead Macdonald

"Library Lighting," Library Journal, LVI (March 1, 1931), 203-10.

"The University Library at Oslo," Library Journal, LVII (January 15, 1932), 69-72.

"The Disaster in the Vatican Library," Scientific American, CXLVI (April, 1932), 226-227.

"Effective Library Lighting," Architectural Forum, LVI (June, 1932), 631-34.

"A Library of the Future," Overbibliotekar Wilhelm Munthe Pa Femtiårsdagen 20. Oktober 1933. Oslo: Grøndahl & Søns, 1933, 168-184.

"A Library of the Future," Library Journal, LVIII (December 1 & 15, 1933), 971-975, 1023-1025.

["On Library Buildings"] "On Financing Libraries," General Discussion at Publicity Institute, American Library Association, Saturday, October 14, 1933. A. L. A. Bulletin, XXVII (December 15, 1933), 764.

"Some Engineering Developments Affecting Large Libraries," A. L. A. Bulletin, XXVIII, (September, 1934), 628-32.

"A Measuring Stick for Shelf Space," Library Journal, LIX (November 15, 1934), 880-881.

"Bookstacks," in Columbia University Library. South Hall, 1935, 36-47.

"The Library Bookstack," in Wheeler, Joseph L. and Githens, Alfred Morton, The American Public Library. Chicago: American Library Association, 1941, 412-327.

"New Possibilities in Library Planning," Library Journal, LXX (December 15, 1945), 1169-74.

"The Library of the Future" Orange, Va.: Snead & Co., 1945. (Macdonald presumed author).

" 'Modular' Library Planning," American Institute of Architects. Bulletin. (July-September, 1947), 16-18.

"A Library of the Future," Canadian Library Association Bulletin V, (July, 1948), 11-13, 29.

Morrow's Library. Orange, Va.: Privately printed, 1948.

"Planning, Adapting and Equipping the Library Building," American Theological Library Association Conference Proceedings, 1949. Evanston, Ill.: Garrett Biblical Institute, 1949, 40-44.

"Libraries Unchained," Library Journal, LXXVIII (January 15, 1953), 77-84.

"Looking Forward and Backward in Library Planning," Suid-Afrikaanse Biblioteke, XXI (Julie, 1953), 3-7.

"Putting White Elephants to Work," Library Journal, LXXVIII (December 15, 1953), 2142-4.

"Building Design for Library Management," Library Trends, II (January, 1954), 463-9.

"Modular Construction," Library Journal LXXX, (December 1, 1955), 2728-30.

"Some Comments on Modular Libraries," Fifth and Sixth Library Building Plans Institutes, Proceedings. (A. C. R. L. Monograph No. 15). Chicago: Association of College & Reference Libraries, 1956, 155-7.

Books and Pamphlets

Alexander, Carter. Tomorrow's Libraries for Teachers Colleges. Prepared for the Committee on Standards and Surveys of the American Association of Teachers Colleges. (n. p., 1944?)

American Library Association. A Survey of Libraries in the United States. Chicago: American Library Association. 1927. 4 vols.

American Library Directory, 1942. Compiled by Karl Brown, New York: R. R. Bowker, 1942.

Berelson, Bernard. Graduate Education in the United States. New York: McGraw-Hill, 1960.

Branscomb, Bennett Harvie. Teaching with Books. Chicago: Association of American Colleges, American Library Association, 1940.

Bright, Arthur Aaron. The Electric-Lamp Industry: Technological Change and Economic Development from 1800 to 1947. New York: Macmillan, 1949.

Brubacher, John S. A History of the Problems of Education. 2d ed., New York: McGraw-Hill, 1966.

Burchard, John. The Architecture of America; A Social and Cultural History. Boston: Little, Brown, 1961.

Butts, R. Freeman. The College Charts Its Course. 1st ed. New York: McGraw-Hill, 1939.

Casseday, Ben. The History of Louisville from its Earliest Settlement till the Year 1852. Louisville, Ky: Hull and Brother, 1852.

Cheyney, Edward Potts. History of the University of Pennsylvania, 1740-1940. Philadelphia: University of Pennsylvania Press, 1940.

Clark, John Willis. The Care of Books. Cambridge, England: The University Press, 1901.

Columbia University. Catalogue and General Announcement. 1900/01-1905/06. New York: Columbia University, 1900-05.

Columbia University, Architectural Society. Yearbook, 1904. New York: The Society, 1905.

Coon, Horace. Columbia; Colossus on the Hudson. New York: E. P. Dutton, 1947.

Cooperative Committee on Library Building Plans. Planning the University Library Building. ed. by John F. Burchard and others. Princeton, N. J.: Princeton University Press, 1949.

Corroyer, Edouard. L'Architecture Gothique. Paris: Société Française d'Editions d'Art, 1891.

Dana, John Cotton. Libraries: Addresses and Essays. New York: H. W. Wilson Co., 1916.

_____. A Library Primer, 2nd ed. Chicago: Library Bureau, 1900.

Ditzion, Sidney. Arsenals of a Democratic Culture. Chicago: American Library Association, 1947.

Ellsworth, Ralph E. Planning the College and University Library, Boulder, Colo.: The author, 1960.

Evenden, E. S., Strayer, G. D., and Engelhardt, N. L. Standards for College Buildings. New York: Columbia University Teachers College, 1938.

Faulkner, Harold Underwood. American Economic History. 7th ed. New York: Harper & Brothers, 1954.

Furnas, C. C. America's Tomorrow, An Informal Excursion Into the Era of the Two-Hour Working Day. New York: Funk & Wagnalls, 1932.

Fussler, Herman H. (ed.). Library Buildings for Library Service. Chicago: American Library Association. 1947.

Gerould, James Thayer. The College Library Building, Its Planning and Equipment. Chicago: American Library Association, 1932.

Giedion, Sigfried. Space, Time and Architecture; the Growth of a New Tradition. 5th ed. Cambridge, Mass.: Harvard University Press, 1967.

Graf, Don. Convenience for Research. New York: Voorhees, Walker, Foley and Smith, 1944.

Hadley, Chalmers. Library Buildings; Notes and Plans. Chicago: American Library Association, 1924.

Hamlin, A. D. F. A Test-Book of the History of Architecture. New York: Longmans, Green, 1896.

Hamlin, Talbot. (ed.) Forms and Functions of Twentieth-Century Architecture. 4 vols. New York: Columbia University Press, 1952.

Hanley, Edna R. College and University Library Buildings. Chicago: American Library Association, 1939.

Hessel, Alfred. A History of Libraries. Translated by Reuben Peiss. Washington, D. C.: Scarecrow Press, 1950.

Hitchcock, Henry-Russell, Jr. The Architecture of H. H. Richardson and His Times. New York: The Museum of Modern Art, 1936.

Ingels, Margaret. Willis Haviland Carrier; Father of Air Conditioning. Garden City, N.Y.: Country Life Press, 1952.

Jefferson, Thomas. Works. Edited by Paul Leicester Ford. Vol. IX. New York: G. P. Putnam's Sons. 1904-05.

Johnson, Elmer D. A History of Libraries in the Western World. New York: Scarecrow Press, 1965.

Kirby, Richard Shelton, and others. Engineering in History. New York: McGraw-Hill, 1956.

Kraehenbuehl, John O. Electric Illumination. 2d ed. New York: John Wiley & Sons, 1951.

Leyh, Georg. Das Buchermagazin in seiner Entwicklung. Berlin: Elsendruck, 1929.

──── . "Vom Büchersaal zum Magazin." Overbibliothekar Wilhelm Munthe På Femtiårsdagen, 20. Oktober 1933. Oslo: Grøndahl, 1933.

Lowe, John Adams. Small Public Library Buildings. Chicago: American Library Association, 1939.

Lydenberg, Harry Miller. History of the New York Public Library. New York: The Library, 1923.

Lyle, Guy Redvers. The Administration of the College Library. New York: H. W. Wilson Co., 1944.

McComb, Dana Quick. Public Library Buildings. Los Angeles, Calif.: The Author, 1935.

Macdonald, Cornelia. A Diary with Reminiscences of the War and Refugee Life in the Shenandoah Valley, 1860-1865... . Annotated and supplemented by Hunter Macdonald. Nashville, Tenn.: Cullom and Ghertner, 1934.

Massachusetts Institute of Technology. Register of Graduates. Boston: Geo. H. Ellis Co., 1904.

Metcalf, Keyes D. Planning Academic and Research Library Buildings. New York: McGraw-Hill, 1965.

──── , and others. The National Medical Library; Report of a Survey of the Army Medical Library. Chicago: American Library Association, 1944.

Milkau, Fritz. (ed.) Handbuch der Bibliothekswissenschaft. 3v., Index. Leipzig: Otto Harrassowitz, 1931-42.

──── . Handbuch der Bibliothekswissenschaft. 3 vol. in 4. Edited by Georg Leyh. 2d ed. Wiesbaden: Otto Harrassowitz, 1961.

Millett, Fred B. The Rebirth of Liberal Education. New York: Harcourt Brace, 1945.

Minneapolis-Honeywell Regulator Company. This Thing Called Air Conditioning. Minneapolis: The author, 1935.

Morey, C. Rufus. A Laboratory-Library. Princeton, N.J.: Distributed by the Princeton University Store [1932?].

Morison, Samuel Eliot. Three Centuries of Harvard, 1639-1936. Cambridge, Mass.: Harvard University Press, 1963.

Munthe, Wilhelm. American Librarianship from a European Angle. Chicago: American Library Association, 1939.

Palustre, Léon. L'Architecture de la Renaissance. Paris: Société Français d'Edition d'Art, 1892.

Princeton University. Committee on New Library. Laboratory-Workshop Library for Princeton, 1746-1946. Princeton, N. J., 1944.

Randall, William M. The College Library. Chicago: American Library Association, 1932.

———, and Goodrich, F. L. D. Principles of College Library Administration. 2nd ed. Chicago: American Library Association and the University of Chicago Press, 1941.

Ransome, Ernest Leslie, and Saurbrey, Alexis. Reinforced Concrete Buildings. New York: McGraw-Hill, 1912.

Reber, Franz. History of Ancient Art... . Translated and augmented by Joseph Thacker Clarke. New York: Harper and Brothers, 1882.

Rider, Fremont. The Scholar and the Future of the Research Library; A Problem and Its Solution. New York: Hadham Press, 1944.

Roth, Alfred. La Nouvelle Architecture. Zurich: H. Girsberger, 1940.

Salamanca, Lucy. Fortress of Freedom; the Story of the Library of Congress. New York: J. B. Lippincott, 1942.

Santa, Leopoldo Della. Della Costruzione e del Regolamento di una Pubblica Universale Biblioteca. Firenza: Gaspero Ricci, 1816.

Schunk, Russell J. Pointers for Public Library Planners. Chicago: American Library Association, 1945.

Snead and Company Iron Works. Book Stack and Shelving for Libraries. Louisville, Ky. and Chicago: Ill.: Snead and Company, 1895.

———. Bookstacks and Shelving for Libraries. Jersey City, New Jersey: Snead and Company, 1901.

———. Illustrations of Ornamental Iron Work. Louisville, Ky.: Snead and Company, 1890.

_____. Library Planning, Bookstacks and Shelving. Jersey City, N. J.: Snead and Company, 1915.

Snead and Company. Snead Bookstacks. New York, N. Y.: Snead and Company, 1940.

_____. Snead Bookstacks & Stack Room Equipment. New York: Snead and Company, 1931.

Snead, William Scott. An American Saga; the Story of the Snead Family of Accomac County, Virginia and of Kentucky. Edited by William E. Stokes, Jr. [North Garden?, Va., 1952].

Soule, Charles C. How to Plan a Library Building for Library Work. Boston: Boston Book Company, 1912.

State University of Iowa, University Library Planning Committee. The Library as a Teaching Instrument. Iowa City, Ia., 1945.

Steinberg, S. H. Five Hundred Years of Printing. Baltimore: Penguin Books, 1961.

Sullivan, Louis H. The Autobiography of an Idea. New York: American Institute of Architects, 1924.

Thompson, Anthony. Library Buildings of Britain and Europe. London: Butterworths, 1963.

University of Illinois. The Library Building. Urbana, Ill.: The University, 1929.

Van Rensselaer, Mariana. Henry Hobson Richardson and His Works. Boston: Houghton, Mifflin, 1887.

Ware, William R. The American Vignola; Part I, The Five Orders. Boston: American Architect and Building News Co., 1902.

Wheeler, Joseph L. and Githens, Alfred M. The American Public Library Building. New York: Charles Scribner's Sons, 1941.

_____, and Goldhor, Herbert. Practical Administration of Public Libraries. New York: Harper & Row, 1962.

Whitehill, Walter Muir. Boston Public Library, a Centennial History. Cambridge, Mass.: Harvard University Press, 1956.

Williamson, William Landram. William Frederick Poole and the Modern Library Movement. New York: Columbia University Press, 1963.

Wilson, Louis Round, and Tauber, Maurice F. The University Library. 2nd ed. New York: Columbia University Press, 1956.

World Almanac, and Book of Facts for 1942. Edited by E. Eastman Irvine. New York: World-Telegram, 1942.

Articles and Periodicals

"A. S. Macdonald, Authority on Library Architecture, Dies," Library Journal, LXXXVI (April 1, 1961), 1433.

"Angus Macdonald, Library Architect," New York Times, CX (February 22, 1961), 25.

"Angus Snead Macdonald, 1883-1961," Virginia Librarian, VIII (Summer, 1961), 22.

"Angus Snead Macdonald to be Consultant," Library Journal, LXXXVII (October 15, 1952), 1790.

Bailey, Arthur L. "Wilmington's New Library Building," Library Journal, XLVIII (September 15, 1923), 751-2.

Bishop, William Warner. "University Libraries: Some Reflections on the Dedication of the Sterling Memorial Library of Yale University," Library Quarterly, I (July, 1931), 243-254.

Blackwell, H. Richard. "Lighting the Library - Standards for Illumination," Library Equipment Institute, The Library Environment; Proceedings of the Institute, 1964. Chicago: American Library Association, 1965. 23-31.

"Bookstacks as Described by Their Manufacturers," Library Journal, XLI (April, 1916), 252-258.

"The Boston Public Library," Scientific American, LXXIII (November 9, 1895), 297-298 + illus., 289.

Bostwick, Arthur E. "The Librarian's Ideas of Library Design," Architectural Forum, XLVII (December, 1927), 507-512.

Bousfield, H. G. "Brooklyn College Triples Size," Library Journal, LXXXVI (January 1, 1961), 78-79.

Boyd, Julian P. "The Harvey S. Firestone Memorial Library," Princeton Alumni Weekly, XLVII (January 24, 1947), 5-8.

Brett, William Howard. "Freedom in Libraries," International Conference of Librarians, 2nd, London, 1897. Transactions and Proceedings. London: The Conference, 1898, 79-83.

"Brooklyn College Library," Library Building Plans Institute, 2nd, Chicago, 1953 Proceedings. (A. C. R. L. Monograph, no. 10.) Chicago: Association of College and Reference Libraries, 1953, 64-9.

["Budget Cuts"], Library Journal LVII (January 1, 1932), 25.

Burchard, John E. "The Library of Tomorrow," American Institute of Architects. Journal, VI (January, February, 1947), 3-11, 90-95.

_____. "Postwar Library Buildings," College and Research Libraries, VII (April, 1946), 118-126.

_____. "A Signpost in Virginia," American Institute of Architects. Journal, V (January, 1946), 23-27.

Bush, Vannevar. "As We May Think," Atlantic Monthly, CLXXVI (July, 1945), 101-108.

Cam, G. S. "Babson Institute Library," Library Journal, LXIV (December 15, 1939), 961-4.

Carter, E. J. "Library Building, 1933-1934," Year's Work in Librarianship, VII (1934). London: The Library Association, 1935, 94-116.

"Century of Progress Exposition Issue," Architectural Forum, LIX (July, 1933).

"Coming: The Age of Leisure," Literary Digest, CXII (January 16, 1932), 26.

"Contribution of Science and Technology to Building Design: 1891-1941," Architectural Record, XIC (January, 1941), 50-2.

Cooperative Committee on Library Building Plans. The Orange Conference...October 26-28, 1945. Philadelphia: Printed by Stephenson Brothers, 1946.

_____. The Second Princeton Conference [Proceedings]...June 12-14, 1946. Philadelphia: Printed by Stephenson Brothers, 1947.

Dana, John Cotton. "The Public and Its Public Library," Popular Science Monthly, LI (June, 1897), 242-53.

Danton, J. Periam. "The College Library: A New Factor in Education," Journal of Higher Education, VIII (October, 1937), 276-382.

Downs, Robert B. "College Curriculum Changes and the College Library," Library Journal, LIX (December, 1934), 961-62.

Eastman, W. R. "Library Buildings," Library Journal, XXVI, (1901) Conference no., 38-43.

"Editorial," Library Journal. LVIII (November 1, 1933), 878.

"Electric Illumination," Collier's Encyclopedia. Edited by Louis Shores. New York: Crowell-Collier Publishing Co., 1962, 711-726.

Ellsworth, Ralph E. "Buildings and Architecture," College and Research Libraries, VI (June, 1945), 279-81.

———. "Colorado University's Divisional Reading Room Plan: Description and Evaluation," College and Research Libraries, II (March, 1941), 103-109, 192.

———. "Library Architecture and Buildings," Library Quarterly, XXV (January, 1955), 66-75.

———. "A Modular Library for the State University of Iowa," American School and University, 18th ed. (1946), 98-105.

"Fixtures, Furniture and Fittings - Fourth Session, Proceedings, Conference of Libraries, Chicago, July 13-22, 1893," Library Journal, XVIII (1893), Conference no., 30-1.

Fletcher, William I. "Library Buildings," American Architect and Building News, XXIV (December 1, 1888), 198, 252.

French, R. B. D. "The Great Library of Trinity College, Dublin," Library Journal, LXXXIV (November 15, 1959), 3533-3535.

Fussler, Herman. [Review of] Planning the University Library Building. Edited by John E. Burchard and others, Library Quarterly, XX (July, 1950), 211.

Githens, Alfred Morton. "The Complete Development of the Open Plan in the Enoch Pratt Library at Baltimore," Library Journal, LVIII (May 1, 1933), 381-385.

———. "The Evolution of a Library," Library Journal, LXXVIII (December 15, 1953), 2131-7.

———. "Libraries," Forms and Functions of 20th Century Architecture, Vol. III. Edited by T. Hamlin. New York: Columbia University Press, 1952, 675-715.

Gondos, Victor. [Review of] Planning the University Library Building. Edited by John E. Burchard and others, The American Archivist XII (October, 1949), 422-25.

Gray, Louis F. "The New Public Library of the City of Boston," Library Journal, XIX (November, 1894), 365-370.

Green, Bernard R. "A Library Book Stack in the Dark," Snead and Company. Library Planning, Bookstacks and Shelving. Jersey City, N. J.: Snead and Company, 1915, 118-119.

_____. "Library Buildings and Bookstacks," Library Journal, XXXI (1906), Conference no., 52-55.

"Green, Bernard R., " National Cyclopedia of American Biography, XX, New York: James T. White and Company, 1929, 355.

Green's Book-Stack and Shelving for Libraries," Library Journal, XVIII (May, 1893), 154-155.

Griffin, Lloyd W. and Kaplan, Louis. "Wisconsin's New University Library After Two Years," College and Research Libraries, XVII (September, 1956), 390.

Hadley, Chalmers. "Some Recent Features in Library Architecture," A. L. A. Bulletin, IX (July, 1915), 125-8.

Hamlin, Alfred Dwight Foster. "Some Essentials of Library Design," Snead and Company Iron Works, Library Planning, Bookstacks and Shelving. Jersey City, N. J.: Snead and Company, 1915, 103-108.

Hamlin, Talbot Faulkner. "Ware, William Robert," Dictionary of American Biography, XIX, New York: Charles Scribner's Sons, 1936, 452-453.

Hardy, LeGrand H., and Rand, Gertrude. "Elementary Illumination for the Ophthalmologist," Archives of Ophthalmology, XXXIII (January, 1945), 1-8.

"Harry Peake Macdonald," New York Times (August 26, 1921), 13.

Hart, Richard. "Enoch Pratt Building Twenty Years After; Staff Reactions, 1953," Library Journal, LXXVIII (May 15, 1953), 864-8.

Hirshberg, H. S. "Four Library Buildings," A. L. A. Bulletin, XXVII (December 15, 1933), 732-7.

Hobbie, Eulin Klyver. "The Skidmore College Library," Library Journal, LXV (December 15, 1940), 1057-1060.

Hutchins, Robert Maynard. "The Chicago Plan," Educational Record, XII (January, 1931), 24-29.

Jackson, William A. "Rare Books at Harvard," College and Research Libraries, XII (December, 1943), 31-35.

Janeway, Eliot. "Balancing America's Metal Requirements," Harvard Business Review, XXIX (November, 1951), 92-102.

Jast, L. Stanley. "Horizontal vs. Vertical Book Stacks," Library Journal, LII (June 15, 1927), 664, 666.

"Jury Returns Verdict in $100,000 Damage Suit in Favor of Defendent Angus S. Macdonald," Orange Review, (April 8, 1954), 1.

Keally, Francis. "An Architect's View of Library Planning," Library Journal, LXXXVIII (December 1, 1963), 4521-25.

Koch, Theodore Wesley. "The Charles Deering Library at Northwestern University," Library Journal, LVIII (March 1, 1933), 189-196.

Kraehenbuehl, John O. "Lighting the Library," College and Research Libraries, II (June, 1941), 231-236.

Kuhlman, Augustus Frederick. "Some Implications in the New Plan of the University of Chicago for College Libraries," Library Quarterly, III (January, 1933), 21-36.

Lamb, J. P., and Stillman, C. G. "Public Library Buildings of the Future," in Library Association Conference, 1947, Brighton, Papers. London: The Association, 1947, 93-104.

Larned, Josephus Nelson. "Report on Library Architecture," Library Journal, XII (September, October, 1887), 377-395.

Ley, E. B. "Study of Illumination," Illuminating Engineering, XXXIX (September, 1944), 501-5.

"A Library and Office Building--Angus Snead Macdonald Prize," Beaux-Arts Institute of Design, Bulletin, XXVI (May, 1950) 54-61.

Library Building Plans Institute, 1st, Columbus, O., 1952, Proceedings. Chicago: Association of College and Reference Libraries, 1952.

"Library Construction for Interchangeable Use," Architectural Record, C, (November, 1946), 115-117.

"Lighting in Libraries," Architectural Record, C. (November, 1946), 120.

Liebers-Kassal, G. "Der Gedanke Der 'Flexibility' in Neueren Amerikanischen Bibliotheksbau," Nachrichten für Wissenschaftliche Bibliothekan, V (Dezember, 1952), 225-242.

Linscheid, Chester H. "New Mexico A. and M. to Move into New Library Building Next Fall," New Mexico Library Bulletin, XXI (January, 1952), 12.

Lorimer, A. Gordan. "Modern Design in Library Building," Iowa Library Quarterly, XV (July, 1945), 26-7.

Lydenberg, Harry Miller. "Unanswered Questions," A. L. A. Bulletin, XXVII (December 15, 1933), 557-568.

Maitre, Henri Le. "Swiss National Library at Berne," Library Association Record, Series 3, III (March, 1933), 73-83.

Maloney, John W. "Modular Library Construction...," Architectural Record, CIV (July, 1948), 102-109.

Martin, Lowell A. "Library Service to Adults," Library Quarterly, XXV (January, 1955), 1-14.

Metcalf, Keyes D. "Spatial Problems in University Libraries," Library Trends, II, (April, 1954), 554-61.

"Midwest Inter-Library Center Considers its Shelving Program," Library Journal, LXXV (April 15, 1950) 726-7.

Miller, Ernest I. "The Library Building Institute," A. L. A. Bulletin, XLI (August, 1947), 252.

Mohrhardt, Charles M. "Buildings and Equipment," Library Trends, I (April, 1953), 514-521.

Montgomery, Helen G. "Blueprints and Books: American Library Architecture, 1860-1960," Library Journal, LXXXVI (December 1, 1961), 4077-80.

Muller, Robert H. "College and University Library Buildings, 1929-1949," College and Research Libraries, XII (July, 1951), 261-265.

Myres, J. N. L., "Oxford Libraries in the Seventeenth and Eighteenth Centuries," The English Library Before 1700. Edited by Francis Wormald, and C. E. Wright. London: Athlone Press, 1958, 236-255.

"A New Fangled Word for an Old Fashioned Principle: Modular," Library Building Plans Institute, 2nd, Chicago, 1953, Proceedings. Edited by Donald C. Davidson. Chicago: Association of College and Reference Libraries, 1953, 6-7.

"New Library Opened," Library Journal, LXXIV (February 1, 1949), 166-168.

"New Sodium Lamp is 70 Percent Efficient," Scientific American, CXLVI (April, 1932), 233.

"Notes on the Construction of the Charles Deering Library," Charles Deering Library, Northwestern University Bulletin, No. 2 (June, 1932), 4.

"Notes on the Erection of Library Buildings," Library Journal, XL (April, 1915), 243-247.

Oates, J. C. T. "The Libraries of Cambridge," The English

Library Before 1700. Edited by Francis Wormald, and C. E. Wright. London: Athlone Press, 1958, 213-235.

O'Connor, R. B., and Kilham, W. H. "Full Size Mock-Up for Library Planning," Architectural Record, CI (January, 1947), 99-101.

Osbourne, Frederick S. "New Library 'Humanistic Laboratory'," Library Journal, LXXIII (December 15, 1948), 1763-70.

Paine, Paul M. "Survey of Borrowers by Occupation," Library Journal, LVI (September 15, 1931), 755.

Patterson, Edwin F. "Library Buildings," in Year's Work in Librarianship, XIII (1946). Edited by J. H. P. Pafford. London: Library Association, 1949, 120-137.

"Planning the New Library," The Harvey S. Firestone Memorial Library. Reprinted from Princeton Alumni Weekly; Princeton, N. J. : 1948?, 18-22.

"Plans for the New Library," New York Times (May 24, 1897), 10.

Poole, William F. "The Construction of Library Buildings," Library Journal, XI (April, 1881), 69-77.

──────. ["Speech on Library Architecture"], Library Journal XVI (Conference no., 1891), 97-102.

──────. "Why Wood Shelving is Better Than Iron," Library Notes, (U. S.) II (September, 1887), 95.

"Printing Press," Encyclopaedia Britannica, 1966, XVIII, 543, 548.

Ranck, Samuel H. "Ventilating and Lighting Library Buildings," Architectural Forum, XLVII (December, 1927), 529-536.

Randall, William M. "Some Principles for Library Planning," College and Research Libraries, VII (October, 1946), 317-325.

Rankin, Rebecca B. "Unemployment Among Librarians," A. L. A. Bulletin, XXIX (March, 1935), 146-149.

Reece, Ernest J. [Review of] Planning the University Library Building. Edited by John E. Burchard, and others, College and Research Libraries, X (October, 1949), 483-5.

Reeves, Floyd W., and Russell, John Dale. "The Relation of the College Library to Recent Movements in Higher Education," Library Quarterly, I (January, 1931), 57-66.

Remond, Paul. "Les Magasins de Livres et les Rayonnages Métalliques dans les Bibliothèques" in World Congress of Universal Documentation, Paris, 1937. Communications. Paris, 1937?, 286-89.

"A Research Laboratories Building," Engineering News-Record, (February 26, 1942), 344-47.

Rider, Fremont. "Warehouse or Microcard?" Library Journal, LXXV (April 15, 1950), 927-31.

Robinson, Edgar S. "Canadian Landmark," Library Journal, LXXXII (December 1, 1957), 3021-3024.

Roden, Carl B. "The Library in Hard Times," Library Journal, LVI (December 1, 1931), 981-987.

Rugg, Earle. "A Library Centered Program of Teacher Education," College and Research Libraries, II (December, 1940), 42-47.

_____. "Planning a College Library," American School and University, 21st ed., 1949-50, 172-9.

Ruml, Beardsley. "The Chicago Plan," Educational Record, XII (July, 1931), 359-68.

Scribner, B. W. "The Preservation of Records in Libraries," Library Quarterly, IV (July, 1934), 371-383.

_____. "Report of Bureau of Standards Research on Preservation of Records," Library Quarterly, I (October, 1931), 409-420.

Sharpe, Jean MacNeill. "Rockford College Library," Library Journal, LXV (December 15, 1940), 1064-1065.

Smith, Sidney B. "New L. S. U. Library in Action," College and Research Libraries, XX (May, 1959), 194-196.

Snead, William S. "The Bookstack Tower [of the Sterling Memorial Library]," Yale University Library Gazette, V (July, 1931), 77-80.

"Snead, Udolpho" [Obituary notice] New York Times (April 21, 1921), p. 13, col. 7.

Social Frontier, III (December, 1936), (January, February, and March, 1937) and V (February, 1939).

Stallings, H. Dean. "Beauty-Efficiency-Economy," Library Journal, LXXV (December 15, 1950), 2109-2112.

_____. "A New Pattern for Economy, Utility and Beauty: The North Dakota Agricultural College Library," College and Research Libraries, XI, (April, 1950), 135-136.

Stanford, Edward B. "Honors Work and the College Library," Library Quarterly, XII (April, 1942), 221-245.

Sweet's Catalogue File (Architectural) 1931-1938.

"Texas Architects will Judge Design Institute Competition," Dallas Daily Times Herald (May 19, 1950), Sec. 4, p. 5, col. 1-3.

Tilton, Edward L. "Library Planning," Architectural Forum, XLVII (December, 1927), 497-506.

_____. "Scientific Library Planning," Library Journal, XXXVII (September, 1912), 497-501.

Toffler, Alvin. "Libraries," Educational Facilities Laboratories, Inc., Bricks and Mortarboards, a Report on College Planning and Building. New York: Educational Facilities Laboratories, 1964.

"Unemployment in the Profession," A. L. A. Bulletin, XXVI (February, 1932), 87-90.

Usher, Robert J. "The Howard-Tilton Memorial Library," Library Journal, LXVI (June 15, 1941), 538-40.

Van Brunt, Henry. ["Speech on Library Architecture,"] Library Journal, IV (July-August, 1879), 295-296.

Van Name, Addison. "Report on Library Architecture," Library Journal, XIV (May-June, 1889), 162-174.

Vitz, Carl. "Pleasantly Functional," Library Journal, LXXIX (December 15, 1954), 2360-64.

Walling, Ruth. "Book Requirements of Survey Courses," Library Quarterly, XII (January, 1942), 75-93.

Walter, Frank K. "Random Notes on Metal Book Stacks," Library Journal, LIII (April 1, 1928), 297-300.

Warren, Dean M. "Library Lighting-A Scientific Problem," Library Journal, LIX (March 15, 1934), 247-250.

"The Way out of the Debauch," Literary Digest, CXII (January 23, 1932), 17.

"What is a Module?", Modular Grid Lines, I (September, 1947), 7.

Williamson, C. C. "Some Unusual Features of South Hall; Abridged," A. L. A. Bulletin, XXXI (October 15, 1937), 798-9.

"Worms Imperil Vatican Treasures," Literary Digest, CXII (January 16, 1932), 17-19.

Yust, William F. "Recent Tendencies in the Planning and Architecture of Central Library Buildings," Library Journal, LV (November 15, 1930), 903-907.

Zimmerman, Lee. "Idaho's Ideal," Library Journal, LXXXI (December 15, 1956), 2757-2761.

_____. "An Invitation and an Opportunity," Moscow, Idaho: University of Idaho Library, 1956. (Reprinted from the University of Idaho Bookmark), 34-44.

Government Publications

Casey, Thomas Lincoln. "Report on Building for State, War and Navy Departments," U. S. War Department, Annual Report of the Secretary of War, 1885-7.

_____. Report Upon the Construction of the Building for the Library of Congress, During the Year Ending December 1, 1891. 52nd Congress, 1st Session, Senate Miscellaneous Document no. 15.

Green, Bernard R. "The Building of the Library of Congress," Annual Report of the Board of Regents of the Smithsonian Institution, to July, 1897, 627-32.

_____. "Report of the Construction of the Building for the Year Ending December 1, 1896," 54th Congress, 2nd Session, House Document no. 20.

Kimberly, Arthur E. A Survey of Storage Conditions in Libraries Relative to the Preservation of Records, U. S. Bureau of Standards Miscellaneous Publications, no. 128.

_____, and Emley, Adelaide L. A Study of the Deterioration of Book Papers in Libraries. U. S. Bureau of Standards, Miscellaneous Publication no. 140.

_____, and Scribner, B. W. Summary Report of the National Bureau of Standards Research on Preservation of Records, U. S. National Bureau of Standards Miscellaneous Publication no. 154.

"[Review of] The Year's Work in Librarianship, 1939-1945, 1946." Library of Congress Information Bulletin, IX (March 20, 1950).

Roberts, Martin A. The Annex of the Library of Congress, n. p., n. d. ("Reprinted from the Report of the Librarian of Congress for fiscal year ending June 30, 1937, 354-359").

U. S. Bureau of the Census. Historical Statistics of the United States, Colonial Times to 1957. 789 p.

U. S. Commissioner of Education, Annual Report, 1870, 41st Congress, 3rd Session, House Ex. Doc. 1, pt. 4.

U. S. Commissioner of Education, Annual Report, 1900-1901, 57th Congress, 1st Session, House Document no. 5.

U. S. Office of Education. Biennial Survey of Education, 1928-1930. Bulletin, 1931, no. 20, v. 11.

U. S. Patent Office. Official Gazette. LII-DCCLXXI, 1890-1960.

Wellman, Hiller C. "Report of the Librarian," Fifty-Third Annual Report of the City Library Association of Springfield, Massachusetts for the Year Ending April Thirtieth, 1910, p. 21-33.

Winsor, Justin. "Library Buildings," in U. S. Bureau of Education, Public Libraries in the United States of America... Special Report, Part 1. (1876) p. 465-475.

Theses and Unpublished Documents

American Arbitration Association, Administrator. "Commercial Arbitration Tribunal in the Matter of the Arbitration between Angus Snead Macdonald Corp. d/b/a Snead and Company and the Midwest Inter-Library Corp., Award of Arbitrators," February 9, 1954.

Andrews, Thelma. "Trends in College Library Buildings." Unpublished Master's dissertation, Graduate Library School, University of Chicago, 1945.

Baber, Carroll Preston. "A Study of Four University Library Buildings." Unpublished Master's dissertation, Graduate School of Library Science, University of Illinois, 1927.

Boll, John Jorg. "Library Architecture, 1800-1875." Unpublished Ph. D. dissertation, Graduate School of Library Science, University of Illinois, 1961.

Borthwick, Howard H. "Trends in Post-War Public Library Architecture." Unpublished Master's dissertation, Carnegie Library School, Carnegie Institute of Technology, 1952.

Burchard, John Ely. "A Program for a New Library Building at the Massachusetts Institute of Technology," Miscellaneous Publications on Microfilm No. 1. Cambridge, Mass.: The Technology Press, 1945.

Columbia University. Registrar. [Transcript of Academic Record of Angus Snead Macdonald.], April 18, 1967.

Cooperative Committee on Library Building Plans. "Final Report on Grant Number 46037 made March 15, 1946 by the Rockefeller Foundation in the Amount of $8,500," April, 1948. (Typewritten, in Princeton University Library.)

Cooperative Committee on Library Buildings. "[Minutes of the] Meeting Held at Princeton University, December 15-16, 1944" Princeton, N. J. : 1945.

Emley, W. E. "Ventilation of Book Stacks and its Effect on Books," unpublished report, February, 1929.

Fish, Gilbert D. "Report to Snead and Company on Tests of Bookstack Columns," May 28, 1945.

Lester, Edna Laverne. "An Analysis of Post-War Trends in the Planning and Design of Public Library Buildings, 1945-1955." Unpublished Master's dissertation in School of Library Service, Atlanta University, 1957.

Macdonald, Angus Snead. "Angus Snead Macdonald," autobiographical notes. April 19, 1955.

_____. "Papers." Four four-drawer filing cases of unpublished letters, reports, and other material.

O'Connor, R. B. and Kilham, W. H., Jr., Architects. "A Survey of Requirements for the Princeton University Library," 1945. (Unpublished, photo copy of typewritten copy, in Princeton University Library.)

Orr, Robert S. "Financing and Philanthropy in the Building of Academic Libraries Constructed Between 1919-1958." Unpublished Master's dissertation in library science, Western Reserve University, 1959.

Reynolds, Helen Margaret. "University Library Buildings in the United States, 1890-1939." Unpublished Master's dissertation, Graduate School of Library Science, University of Illinois, 1946.

University of Georgia. News Bureau. ["William M. Randall"] Press release, May 20, 1947.

Weatherhead, Arthur Clason. The History of Collegiate Education in Architecture in the United States. Ph. D. dissertation, Columbia University. Los Angeles: The author, 1941.

Other Sources

Andrews, Thelma. Telephone interview, January 15, 1967.

Bean, Donald. Interview, July 20, 1967.

Green, Julia M. Scrapbooks Owned by Dr. Julia M. Green. Washington, 1911. Microfilm copy. Original in the Library of Congress.

Kaplan, Louis. Letter to the author, May 20, 1968.

Little, Evelyn Steele. Letter to the author, January 15, 1967.

MacRae, Lachlan F. Letter to the author, April 5, 1968.

Metcalf, Keyes D. Interview, June 16, 1967.

O'Connor, Robert. Letter to the author, April 16, 1968 with memorandum from Walter H. Kilham, Jr.

Wheeler, Joseph. Letter to the author, July 30, 1966.

Willoughby, Mabel E. Letter to the author, January 18, 1967.

INDEX

Academic libraries:
  divisional plan, 199
  growth, 47-50
Alcove shelving, 25
Andrews, Thelma, 166-167

Bailey, J. Russell, 156-157
Bean, Donald, 104
Beaux-Arts Institute, 162
Bibliothèque St. Geneviève,
  31-2, 185
Bookstacks (General):
  early, defects, 64, 81
  manufacturers, early, 81
  origins, 63-65
  public access, 46
  stack below (open plan),
    38-44
  stack in the center, 45-46
  stack at the rear, 33
  see also under individual libraries
Boston Public Library:
  Boylston Street building,
    25, 27-8
  Copley Square building, 31-33
  Roxbury Branch, 28
Boyd, Julian, 158, 190, 222
Branscomb, Bennett Harvie,
  198-199
Brett, William Howard, 46
Burchard, John, 202, 204
Bush, Vannevar, 204
Business depression, 1930,
  118-120

Canisius College Library,
  153-154:
  sketches, 250-254
Carnegie Corporation, 34, 37
  guidelines, 38
Chained books, 19, 23
Chicago World's Fair, 1893, 37
Cincinnati Public Library, 1874:

fig., 22
Cleveland Public Library
  stack, 46
Colorado State College of Education, 107-111
Columbia University:
  Butler Library, 90
  School of Architecture, 58-61
Compact storage:
  rolling type, 92, fig., 94
  swinging type, 163-165, fig.,
    164
"Convertible" Stack, 107-112,
  figs., 108, 109
Cooperative Committee on Library Building Plans, 206-207
Curricular changes, 196-203

Ellsworth, Ralph, 130-131, 160
Enoch Pratt Free Library:
  open plan, 41-44
  ventilation, 192-193
Evanston, Illinois, Public Library, fig., 35

Fish, Gilbert, 148, 154, 168,
  234-236
Flexibility in libraries, 203-204

Georgia, University, Library,
  171
Gerould, James Thayer, 197,
  199
Githens, Alfred Morton, 37, 149,
  167, 207-208, sketches, 237-249
Great hall libraries, 19
Green, Bernard Richardson:
  bookstack designs, 65-75
  engineer in Washington, D. C.,
    65
  influence, 33
  Snead and Company association, 68, 70

Superintendent, Library of Congress, 68

Hamlin, A. D. F., 29, 58
Hardin-Simmons University Library, 166-167
Harvard University:
  Lamont Library, 202
  Widener Library, 89-90, 95

Iowa, University, Library, 169-171, 200-201, fig., 170

Kaplan, Louis, 202
Kuhlman, A. F., 9

Larned, J. N., 28
Library lighting, development, 188-191
Library of Congress, 33-34, 101, figs., 71-73
"Library of the Future," 121-126
Library ventilation, development, 191-194
Little, Evelyn Steele, 151
Louisiana State University Library, 173-174

Macdonald, Angus Snead:
  as architect, 61-62
  bookstack designs, 89-102, figs., 91, 94, 97, 98
  childhood, 56
  children, 89
  education, 57-61
  flying, 155-156
  joins Snead and Company, 62
  marriage, 89, 112 (note 4)
  parents, 56-57
  personality, 221-223
  President, Snead and Company, 89
Macdonald, Harry Peake, 62-63, 76, 89
McKim, Charles Follen:
  Boston Public Library, 31-33
  Snead and Company, 82
Massachusetts Institute of Technology Library, 201-202
Mediceo-Laurenziana, fig., 20
Metcalf, Keyes D., 75, 95
Modular Construction:
  figs., 145, 146

hollow column system, 143-150
Macdonald's theories, 123-137
model, Orange, Virginia, 158-161
publicizing, 151-163
survey, 155-165
"Morrow's Library," 161-162
Munthe, Wilhelm, 118

"New Possibilities in Library Planning," 132-135
New York Public Library:
  bookstack, 77-78
North Dakota Agricultural College Library, 167-169

O'Connor & Kilham, 149, 207, 229
Open plan:
  early development, 38-42
  libraries, figs., 42-43
Open stacks, 197-199
Oxford University, Bodleian Library, fig., 21

Poulson, Niels, 86 (note 49)
Princeton University, Firestone Library, 199-200
Public libraries:
  divisional plan, 195
  early, United States, 26

Randall, William, 157-158, 197
Richardson, H. H., 29-31
Rogers, James Gambles, 83
Rugg, Earle, 110, 111

Santa, Leopoldo della, 28
Snead and Company:
  acquires Green's patents, 70
  architects, 82-83
  bookstacks, figs., 66-67, 71-73, 79, 80, 91, 93, 94, 108, 109, 164
  depression of 1930's, 102-103
  early period, 62-63
  installations, 266-284
  Jersey City plant, 76-77
  Louisville plant, 76
  "Mobile Walls," 104
  Orange plant, loss, 148

306

World War II, 133
Snead, Charles Scott, 63, 76
Snead, Udolpho, 62-63, 76
Springfield, Massachusetts, Public Library, 38-41, figs., 39-40
Stallings, Dean, 168, 203
Stewart, A. T., store, fig., 187
Structural steel and concrete, development, 185-186

"T" Plan, 34
Tilton, Edward L., 38-41, 82

Vancouver, British Columbia, Public Library, 174-175

Wall shelving, early libraries, 23
Ware, William Robert, 57-58
Washington, D. C., Public Library, fig., 36
Wellman, Hiller C., 38, 44
Wheeler, Joseph, 207-208
Winn Memorial Library, 29, fig., 30
Winsor, Justin, 28

Zig-zag ventilation, 100-101

Z
679
B3
1972